MW00985920

WRITTEN
ON THE
HEART

THE CASE FOR NATURAL LAW

J. BUDZISZEWSKI

InterVarsity Press
Downers Grove, Illinois

InterVarsity Press® is the book-publishing division of InterVarsity Christian Fellowship®, a student movement active on campus at hundreds of universities, colleges and schools of nursing in the United States of America, and a member movement of the International Fellowship of Evangelical Students. For information about local and regional activities, write Public Relations Dept., InterVarsity Christian Fellowship, 6400 Schroeder Rd., P.O. Box 7895, Madison, WI 53707-7895.

Scripture quotations, unless otherwise noted, are from the Revised Standard Version of the Bible, copyright 1946, 1952, 1971 by the Division of Christian Education of the National Council of the Churches of Christ in the USA. Used by permission.

Cover photograph: Tony Stone Images

ISBN 0-8308-1891-X

Printed in the United States of America

Library of Congress Cataloging-in-Publication Data

Budziszewski, J., 1952-
    Written on the heart: the case for natural law/J. Budziszewski.
        p.   cm.
    Includes bibliographical references (p.   ).
    ISBN 0-8308-1891-X (alk. paper)
    1. Natural law.   2. Law and politics.   3. Religion and law.
    I. Title.
    K460.B83   1997
    340'.112—dc21   96-29818
                                                                                        CIP

21   20   19   18   17   16   15   14   13   12   11   10   9   8   7   6   5   4   3

14   13   12   11   10   09   08   07   06   05   04   03   02   01   00   99

To the glory of God
in thanksgiving for my daughters
Anastasia and Alexandra

Acknowledgments

I thank Yitzchok Adlerstein, Clarke E. Cochran, Darrell Dobbs, Stanley Hauerwas, Robert Koons, Vukan Kuic and William Stevenson for informative and encouraging comments and conversations; my editor, Rodney Clapp, for good suggestions and for saving me from the sin of sloth; my students for dozens of unexpected questions; the members of my neighborhood fellowship for praying me through the final stages of composition; and all those whose benefits I have not remembered or do not yet understand.

Here and there in the book I have borrowed a sentence, a paragraph or even a few pages from work I have published previously in the form of articles. Thanks then are also due, and gladly rendered, to the editors of *First Things* and *Human Life Review* for granting permission. The Extension Instruction and Materials Center of the University of Texas deserves mention for allowing me to test fly an earlier version of units I through IV as a correspondence textbook.

For my wife and helpmate, Sandra, the tribute is already written, for of her the proverb speaks: "Her children rise up and call her blessed; her husband also, and he praises her. Many women have done excellently, but you surpass them all."

Above all others I thank the triune God, Father of Lights, Kindler of Wisdom, without whom all thought is darkness and all knowledge dusk. Now my mind is smoke; on that Day, O Lord, will it be fire.

Preface

Although this book approaches the natural-law tradition mostly by discussing its original sources, it can be read by itself. Those who do wish to follow along with the classics will appreciate the following guide.

For *Aristotle,* the great natural-right philosopher of pagan antiquity, begin with the *Nicomachean Ethics*—named after his son, Nicomachus. Then turn to the *Politics.* This work of Aristotle *foreshadows* the natural-law tradition; he recognizes an objective standard of right and wrong even though he does not fully grasp that it is law.

For *Thomas Aquinas,* the Roman Catholic systematizer of Christian natural-law theory, study the *Treatise on Law,* which makes up a small part of the massive *Summa Theologica.* Afterward, spend some time with the *Treatise on Kingship.*

For *John Locke,* the Protestant natural-law theorist who had the most pervasive influence on the American experiment in government, read the *Second Treatise of Government.* His earlier *Essays on the Law of Nature* are also helpful.

For *John Stuart Mill,* one of the great modern opponents of natural law, study the short but very dense essay entitled *Utilitarianism.*

Aristotle is considered in unit I, Thomas Aquinas in unit II, John Locke in unit III and John Stuart Mill in unit IV. The fifth and final unit of the book focuses on representative contemporary voices in the literature of natural law. First I offer a Christian appraisal of natural-law theory; from this perspective, I then take a second look at the historical figures presented earlier in the book; finally I present a long critical discussion of current thinking about natural law—Catholic, Jewish,

Protestant and secular. My focus is on contributors rather than challengers, and my intention is to illustrate the possibilities rather than survey every thinker in the field. For these last three chapters readings are suggested in the endnotes.

As a Christian I regard the natural-law tradition as the nearest approach to the truth about the "law written on the heart" which ethical and political philosophy have yet, by the grace of God, achieved. I do not mean to be flippant in speaking of God's grace. True, the law written on the heart is utterly inferior to the revealed truth of the gospel, for though it tells us what sin is, it tells us nothing of how to escape it. Yet it too is a real gift of God, for we have to know the bad news before we can grasp the Good News.

Moreover, natural law is especially pertinent to *politics* just because it *is* written on the heart, for that makes it a standard for believers and unbelievers alike; not only is it right for all, but at some level it is known to all. Even the pagans knew it. They caught hints of it in the plays of Euripides, they heard its name in the treatises of the Stoics, they saw it reflected in the commentaries of the Roman lawyers, and all these things made sense to them because, like us, they felt it pressing upon their inwards: prior to art, prior to philosophy, prior to statecraft.

Yet this law can be repressed. Philosophy itself can be a higher mode of ignorance. One of the distinctive features of this primer then is that it is a book with an attitude; it not only explains but vigorously defends the embattled natural-law tradition. I have also tried to be sensitive to the kinds of difficulties, confusions and questions that actually trouble inquirers in our morally disordered culture. Sensitivity, of course, does not mean approving the disorder!

The book is not *only* about the natural law. For context I have included a great many collateral topics, especially concerning the nature and limits of government. Here I must remark that although all natural-law thinkers agree that politics must have an ethical foundation, the line from ethical premises to political conclusions is often curved or crooked, and they do not always agree about its course.

I write for more than one audience. Although original argument is found throughout, general readers and beginning students will be most interested in units I through IV, scholars and advanced students in unit V. For this reason, although unit V is just as argumentative as the preceding units, it is written in a somewhat different style and includes many more references to contemporary scholarship.

My perspective throughout the book is Christian, and in this last unit I explicitly address fellow believers. Yet the book is not intended for Christians alone. On the contrary, I hope it will interest secular readers curious about the natural law, as well as secular teachers who want to expose their students to a view of things they may not often hear.

One last word. Where pronouns are concerned, I follow traditional English usage, according to which *he* is understood as inclusive unless the context clearly indicates the masculine. The same goes for *man* and *men*. However, I also observe the traditional exceptions to this rule: for instance, nature, the soul and Wisdom (poetically personified and understood as an attribute of God) are spoken of as feminine. The reasons for my choices would take us far afield. Readers who choose differently may write differently; I ask only that they extend the same courtesy to me. In the meantime, since my language includes masculine, feminine, neuter and inclusive pronouns, any rational being who feels excluded has only him-, her- or itself to blame.

If in this book I have managed to convey even a tithe of the subtlety, richness and intellectual surprise of the natural-law tradition, I will deem it a success. Happy reading!

UNIT I

ARISTOTLE

ONE

POLITICS &
THE HUMAN
GOOD

POLITICAL THEORY IS ANOTHER NAME FOR POLITICAL PHILOSOPHY.
What then is philosophy? Aristotle held that if you want to know what
something is, you have to know four things about it: its matter, its
form, its power, and its end or purpose. Consider my chair: its matter
is what it is composed of—wood; its form is its pattern—a seat
attached to a back and supported by a base; its power is what brings
it into being—carpentry; its end is what it is for—providing something to sit on.

Whether or not we agree with Aristotle that these four questions are
always the most fundamental,[1] we can use the same method to arrive
at his idea of philosophy. Aristotle would say that its matter is questions
and answers; its form is logical arguments; its power is wonder; and its
end is wisdom.

In this book we are not studying all of philosophy but only political
philosophy. The matter of political philosophy is not all kinds of
questions and answers but only questions and answers about politics.

Introduction to Aristotle

Politics is the characteristic activity of the *polis,* or City. What then, according to Aristotle, is a City? To understand the answer, remember the formula: matter, form, power and end.

☐ The *matter* of the City is a particular group of human beings, separate from others, whom we call its citizens.

☐ Its *form* is partnership in a way of life, under the regulation of laws which are directed toward justice.

☐ Its *power* is need, for people first come together in Cities simply to live in mutual security.

☐ Its *end* is the good, or perfection, of its members.

Aristotle takes political science to be nothing less than the master science of what is good: the comprehensive study of this partnership in a good life which we human beings so oddly require. A few questions and answers will help us expand this definition.

Question one: Why does Aristotle think that the end, or purpose, of the City is the perfection of its members? *Answer:* Because unlike other creatures, we human beings are incomplete outside political community. We need it not just for living but for living excellently—living in the way our nature demands. Partnership in a good life under the regulation of law is necessary for us to come into our own as human beings. That is why Aristotle offered this famous definition: "The City is the perfect community, lacking in nothing, which came into existence for the sake of mere life, but exists for the sake of living well."[2]

Question two: When Aristotle says that the end of the City is the perfection of its members, does he mean that the *government* is supposed to perfect us? *Answer:* No. Such a suspicion is understandable in dark times such as ours, when the citizens seem to evaporate into a gas of colliding atoms so that all they have in common is the thick glass bottle they call the government. But that is not what Aristotle means by partnership in a good life. What he has in mind is not gaseous but crystalline: not an association of unrelated individuals but an association of associations such as families, friendships, firms, neighborhoods and religious organizations.

Another way to put this idea is to say that the City is not a simple partnership; it is a partnership of partnerships, each of which already has a pattern of its own, a pattern that government did not give it. These partnerships best flourish in that larger partnership which is the City, and law merely assures the background conditions—the most important of which is simple justice—they need in order to do so. Thus the proper aim of the state is not to do everything itself but to support a life which was there before it.[3]

Question three: Partnership, goodness, perfection—all of these are ethical ideas. Why can't Aristotle talk about politics without getting into all that moralistic stuff? *Answer:* Aristotle would find the modern notion that the study of politics can be separated from "all that moralistic stuff" simply confused. If partnership in a good life is what the City *is,* how could one understand the City without understanding the nature of the good?

To be sure, people in our day offer many objections to Aristotle's argument. Let's see how he might respond to some of them.

Objector: You say ethics is indispensable for understanding politics; I say ethics gets in the way of understanding politics. Find me an ethical politician. *Aristotle:* I said that politics concerns partnership in a good life; if statesmen are indifferent to the good, it doesn't follow that I have misunderstood statesmanship but that they are poor statesmen.

Objector: That's just an evasion. Politics isn't about the good; it's about power. *Aristotle:* The first problem with your definition is that it provides no way to tell the difference between the City and a gang of thieves, for power is exercised in both. The second problem is that your definition provides no way to tell the difference between proper and improper uses of power within the City itself.

Objector: But look here, people can get together in a City for any reason they please; they don't have to get together for partnership in a good life. *Aristotle:* You are ignoring my distinction between what brings a thing into existence and what purpose it serves. Just as a chair is brought into existence by carpentry but its purpose is to provide a place to sit, so a City is brought into existence by the desire for mutual security but its purpose is partnership in a good life.

Objector: That smells fishy to me. You seem to be saying that a thing can have a purpose different than the purpose for which a person actually uses it. *Aristotle:* But isn't that true? You may use your chair to stack books on, but its purpose is still to provide a place to sit. You may use your nose to paint with, but its purpose is still to provide a sense of smell. You may use your sexual organs for solitary pleasure, but their purpose is still procreation and delight in the union of husband and wife. You may use the City for personal convenience, but its purpose is still partnership in a good life.

Objector: Okay, so maybe a City does have a purpose connected with a good life. But I don't think the purpose of the City is a *partnership* in a good life; I think its purpose is to provide a place in which people can *individually* seek a good life. *Aristotle:* If you could seek a good life individually, you would be either a beast or a god; for human beings it is impossible. We are supported by a web of mutuality, supporting and supported by parents, children, wives, husbands, friends, teachers, fellow worshipers, business partners and innumerable others. Perhaps what you mean by "individuality" is selfishness.

Objector: If what you say is true, then I am involved in partnership in a good life already: in family, friendship, firm, church and so on. Why do I need yet one more? *Aristotle:* You need yet one more because unless these partnerships participate in a broader partnership under law, there will be no justice.

Now you know why, in order to understand Artistotle's *Politics,* we begin with his *Ethics.*

The Highest Human Good

Have you ever heard the nursery rhyme "For the Want of a Nail"? *For the want of a nail, the shoe was lost; for the want of the shoe, the horse was lost; for the want of the horse, the rider was lost; for the want of the rider, the message was lost; for the want of the message, the battle was lost; for the want of the battle, the kingdom was lost; all for the want of a little nail.* This simple rhyme tells us that things are not disconnected but related in a hierarchical order: little things for the sake of middle things, middle things for the sake of great things, right on up to the greatest things.

Aristotle does not make any such claim about "things" in general, but he does make such a claim about human action. Everything I do, I do for the sake of some good. I button my coat, for instance, for the good of protection from the rain. But almost every good I seek, I seek for the sake of some yet greater good. I seek protection from the rain for the sake of comfort or health, and so on up to higher and higher goods.

Does this chain ever come to an end? Is there some *highest* human good? If there is no highest human good—if we seek literally every good for the sake of some other—we might as well give up trying to give rational order to our lives, for we are like hamsters that run and run in their little wheels but never get anywhere. If there is a highest human good, however, we would do well to discover it, so let's go looking.

Remember that the highest human good would have two qualities. First, other goods would be sought for its sake; second, it would be sought only for its own sake. What do we know that's like that? Aristotle points out that almost everyone, in all times and places, gives the same answer to that question: *happiness.* As he sees no objections to this answer, he accepts it.

Do you see what Aristotle just did? He took as his starting point the universal, or nearly universal, opinion of mankind. In fact, in ethics he always starts with either common opinion or the opinion of men whom common opinion holds wise. You may ask, What's so philosophical about that? After all, the world is still round even if everyone thinks it flat. Isn't Aristotle merely committing the logical fallacy of *argumentum ad populum*—illegitimate appeal to popular prejudices? No, and here is why:

1. Every argument must start somewhere. There has to be data. This is just as true in ethics as in planetary physics.

2. Taking common opinion as data makes better sense with a question such as "Are our actions directed toward some greatest good?" than with a question such as "Is the earth flat?" because, although the latter asks about matters external to our minds, the former asks about matters internal to our minds. We have, so to speak, inside knowledge.

3. True, starting with opinion is likely to cause big mistakes when the only opinions considered are those of one's own time and place. But Aristotle asks about the opinion of mankind in general.

4. And, true, starting with opinion is likely to cause big mistakes if one ends in the same place. But although Aristotle starts with common opinion he does not end there. That which he finds he then refines. His method is not to take common opinion *as* truth but to ascend from common opinion *to* truth. We are about to see an example of Aristotle's attempting just such an ascent.

We've seen that Aristotle accepts the idea that the greatest human good is happiness. But he immediately points out that it needs refinement. The reason is that the common opinion of mankind is not in agreement about what happiness *is*. However, the number of competing views is small:

Definition 1: Happiness is *pleasure.*

Definition 2: Happiness is *honor.*

Definition 3: Happiness is *virtue,* or excellence.

Definition 4: Happiness is *bodily and external goods,* such as health and wealth.

We seem to be in a fix. What are we to do when the common judgment of mankind wavers among several opinions? One possibility is to say, "Well, they're all true. You have your truth, and I have mine." But, although that sort of reasoning may get you by in pop psychology, New Age religion and singles bars, it just doesn't work. If X is true, then not-X is false. They cannot both be true in the same sense at the same time. That is just the way things are. It's a principle for not only this universe but any universe we can imagine. Philosophy and logic call it the principle of noncontradiction. Aristotle knows it well; he learned it from his teacher Plato.[4]

Another possibility is to say, "Okay, let's pick one of the opinions as the whole truth and reject the others as wholly false." But that does not seem to be a good idea either. Remember, human beings have "inside knowledge" about the contents of their own minds. That's why we consulted the opinions of mankind in the first place. But the same principle of respect that directs us to consult them also warns us not to be so dismissive.

Aristotle makes a much more interesting move than either of the two that we have been discussing. He considers whether in each of the four opinions there might be a *grain* of truth mixed with chaff. If he can sift out the chaff, he can grind the grain into flour and bake bread.

Definition 1: Happiness is pleasure. *Grain:* No one would call a man happy who never experienced any pleasure at all. *Chaff:* Still, can we really say pleasure is the *same* as happiness? Unhappiness in the midst of pleasure is a common experience; it seems that, ultimately, mere satisfaction is unsatisfying.[5] Not only that, pleasure comes and goes. By contrast we think of true happiness as something abiding, something that characterizes a whole life. Apparently pleasure is not the essence of happiness but merely its accompaniment or byproduct.

Definition 2: Happiness is honor. *Grain:* No one would call a man happy who never received any honor for his excellences. *Chaff:* But even a seeker of honor admits that to be honored by other people for excellences that he knew he did not possess would be a hollow experience. So he does not want honor for its own sake after all; what he really wants is to *merit* honor. Besides, honor depends on those who confer it, and what is conferred can be taken away. But, as we said above, we think of true happiness as something abiding, something difficult to take away.

Definition 3: Happiness is virtue, or excellence. *Grain:* Unlike pleasure, virtue is abiding, and, unlike honor, it cannot be taken away by others. Not only that, we saw on closer examination that what the honor-seeker really wants is to *merit* honor. But one merits honor by possessing the virtues. *Chaff:* Imagine a man who is perfectly virtuous but who, by some dreadful mistake, is condemned to torture for crimes he did not commit. In the midst of his agony, is he happy? Socrates thought so, but Aristotle thinks that view absurd.

Definition 4: Happiness is bodily and external goods, such as health and wealth. *Grain:* Did we not just admit, in the example of the virtuous man undergoing torture, that happiness depends on outward conditions? *Chaff:* The example of the virtuous man undergoing torture did not prove that virtue is *unnecessary* for happiness; it only proved that virtue is *insufficient* for happiness.

We now have much more data than we did before. How do we put it together? You might be tempted to say, "I get it. We've proven that none of the four things is sufficient for happiness, but we've also proven that some of them are necessary for it. So happiness must be the *combination* of the ones that are necessary for it: virtue, bodily goods and external goods. Pleasure and honor come in not as part of the definition of happiness but as things that tend to accompany happiness."

Close, but not quite there. Aristotle does agree closely with *part* of the previous paragraph. He summarizes the necessary conditions for happiness as first virtue, then its "equipment," and the equipment of virtue, he thinks, does include bodily and external goods. To understand what he means by this terminology, think of the virtue of generosity and the external good of moderate wealth. You can see that the latter is equipment for the former, because without any wealth at all a person hasn't got anything to be generous with. Christianity has called attention to the fact that the more equipment a person has for generosity, the less interested he usually is in using it. However, if Aristotle knows this, he doesn't let on.

The problem from Aristotle's point of view is that the necessary conditions for something are not the same as what that something *is*. Consider fire: Oxygen plus fuel may be what fire needs to exist, but they aren't what fire is. By the same token, virtue plus the equipment of virtue may be what happiness needs to exist, but they may not be the whole story of what happiness is either. So to find out what happiness is we have to reason a little further. Although we hope that our definition will explain the *connection* of happiness with virtue, we won't define happiness *as* virtue or even as virtue plus its equipment.

To launch us on the next leg of our journey, Aristotle once again asks us to consider the way we already think. We have been asking in what we think the good of a human soul[6] lies; maybe we would make better progress by first asking in what we think the good of *anything* lies—the good of a racehorse, the good of a knife, the good of an eye or what have you. The good of a racehorse lies in racing, the good of a knife lies in cutting and the good of an eye lies in seeing; that's easy. But do you see what we've done here? In each case we have defined the good of the thing as an activity: not as any old activity but as its proper work or function.

Now let's take another step. The *good* of a racehorse may be simply racing, but its *highest* good is racing excellently so as to win. In the same way the highest good of a knife is cutting excellently, and the highest good of an eye is seeing excellently. We seem to have uncovered a formula: If X is a thing's function, then the good of the thing lies in the activity of performing X, and its highest good lies in the activity of performing X excellently. Can we apply this formula to the human soul? Sure. If X is the function of the human soul, then the good of the human soul lies in the activity of performing X, and its highest good lies in the activity of performing X excellently. So to find the highest good of the human soul we have to find X. What is its function—its proper work?

You may think that this is just as hard as the question we started out with. Aristotle does not think so. To answer it he borrows again from his old teacher Plato.[7] *Question:* How do you know what a thing's function is? *Answer:* Its function is the activity it performs that nothing else can perform or that nothing else can perform as well. Nothing but an eye can see, so seeing is the eye's function. Nothing can cut as well as a knife, so cutting is the knife's function. We know, then, that the function of a human soul will be whatever a human soul can do that nothing else can do, or at least that nothing else can do as well.

But we do so *many* things! Yes, but we do not have to consider them one by one because we can group them. In the game "Twenty Questions" objects are classified according to whether they are animal, vegetable or mineral. In similar fashion Aristotle classifies the activities of living things according to whether they are vegetable, animal or rational. Vegetative life means all the activities involved in growing and taking nutrition; animate life means all the activities involved in perceiving through the senses and being guided by sense perceptions; rational life means all the activities involved in using reason and following its rules.

Start with vegetative activity then. Do human souls do it? Yes. Are they the only living things that do? No, and the plants and other animals do it just as well, so go on. Next comes animate activity. Do human souls do it? Yes. Are they the only living things that do? No, and the other animals do it just as well, so again go on. Finally comes rational activity. Do human souls do it? Yes. Are they the only living things that do? Yes again. Bingo.

We have our missing X: reason. Plugging it into the formula we came up with earlier, we find that *the good of a human soul lies in the activity of using and following reason, and its highest good lies in the activity of using it and following it excellently.* Doing this, thinks Aristotle, is what it means for a human being to thrive, to flourish, to be happy; doing this is what makes him most truly human, what most truly brings him into his own. We are not speaking here of contemplating frivolous things or of having minds that are so open that they cannot reach decisions. *The human soul is an engine for coming to reasonable conclusions and acting upon them.*[8]

This conclusion can be criticized. For instance, Christianity points out that the human soul seems designed for *at least two* things, not one—at least two activities are unique to it and belong to its proper work. One is to understand, the other is to love; the former employs the reason, the latter employs the will. Both are directed to God and neighbor. To the extent that love and understanding are connected, any defect in one implies a defect in the other, and any defect in the *comprehension* of one also implies a defect in the comprehension of the other. Still, this is no reason for not taking Aristotle as far as he can be taken, and, as we will see in later chapters, many Christian thinkers have done so.

Questions for Reflection

1. Although Aristotle believes in a divine First Cause—something on which everything else is dependent but which is not itself dependent on anything—he does not think of a *personal God* as do Jews and Christians. How might his discussion of happiness have been different had he known of Jewish and Christian claims?

2. Aristotle says that the City is the most comprehensive partnership in a good life. But the apostle Paul says that Christians have their true citizenship in heaven, and their most comprehensive partnership in a good life is not the City but the church (Romans 13:1-7; 1 Corinthians 1:9; Philippians 3:20).[9] Why do Paul and Aristotle disagree? How does their disagreement affect the claim that political science is the master science of the good?

3. The last two questions were warm-ups for this deeper one. Aristotle holds that the end or purpose of philosophy is wisdom. Judaism and Christianity, however, maintain that all wisdom ultimately depends on having the right God. If so, then, if Aristotle does not know the true God, does it follow that *nothing* can be learned from Aristotle? Why or why not?

4. This chapter has claimed both that any defect in love implies a defect in understanding and that any defect in the *comprehension* of love implies a defect in the *comprehension* of understanding. How might these claims be true? (Hint: Think of love not as a feeling—though it may involve the feelings—but as a constant will to the true good of another person.)

5. As we have seen, Aristotle thinks that families and other preexist-

ing partnerships in a good life have their own work and dignity, which the state should not subvert. Yet he also thinks of these partnerships as mere *parts* of the City. Because, in his view, a whole is always a more fundamental reality than its parts, considering them parts seems to make their work and dignity secondary and derivative. Can these two views be reconciled?

TWO

MORAL EXCELLENCE & REGIME DESIGN

LET'S GO BACK TO KNIVES AND EYES AND RACEHORSES. IF I SAID, "THE excellence of a knife is sharpness," you would know what I meant: sharpness is the specific quality that enables a knife not just to cut but to cut excellently. Another word for excellence is virtue. So you would also know what I meant if I said that the virtue of an eye is clearness or that the virtue of a racehorse is swiftness. Clearness is what enables an eye to see excellently, swiftness what enables a racehorse to race excellently. Once again we have a formula. A virtue or excellence of a thing (there may be more than one) is a specific quality that enables it to perform its function or proper work excellently and so to achieve its highest good.

The Virtues
Like our last formula, this one too can be applied to mankind. How do we know whether a particular human quality, such as courage or ruthlessness, is a virtue or not? The proper work of a human soul is using and following reason, so the quality is a virtue only if it helps it

to do so excellently. For instance, one virtue is theoretical wisdom, the discipline of mind which helps us reason our way to truth while avoiding error; another is practical wisdom, the discipline of mind which helps us reason our way to good choices while avoiding evil.

But here we run into a problem. It looks at first as though the only true virtues are the intellectual ones. What about the moral virtues, such as courage, justice, self-control and friendliness? Isn't there a place for them? Yes, for two main reasons. To understand the first one, remember that more than one thing is active in the human soul: not only the power of reasoning itself but also the power of feeling and the power of desiring.[1]

Examples of thoughts: "Bill is a good friend"; "The square of the hypotenuse is equal to the sum of the squares of the other two sides"; "The corner grocer is likely to cheat me."

Examples of feelings: Anger, fear, shame, affection.

Examples of desires: Hunger, thirst, sexual craving—even *sehnsucht.*[2]

Therefore to bring the human soul under the direction of reason it is not enough to order our thoughts; our feelings and desires must be in order too. Just as the intellectual virtues discipline the thoughts, the moral virtues discipline the feelings and desires. An example of a moral virtue that disciplines the feelings is courage, whereas an example of a moral virtue that disciplines the desires is self-control.

To sum up, the first main reason the intellectual virtues are not the only virtues is that different virtues are needed to put each of the different powers of the soul into rational order. The second main reason is that different virtues bring the soul into rational order in different *respects.*

Although the point is Aristotle's, C. S. Lewis has explained it most clearly. We have spoken of *partnership* in a good life, so Lewis asks us to imagine a fleet of ships sailing in formation. For the voyage to be a success, three things are necessary. First, the ships must avoid collision and getting in each other's way. Second, each ship must be seaworthy, with its engines in good order. Third, they must all know the fleet's destination. "Morality, then," says Lewis,

> seems to be concerned with three things. Firstly, with fair play and harmony between individuals. Secondly, with what might be called tidying up or harmonizing the things inside each individual. Thirdly,

with the general purpose of human life as a whole; what man was made for; what course the whole fleet ought to be on; what tune the conductor of the band wants it to play.[3]

Justice, which we have not previously mentioned, is the virtue concerned with fair play and harmony; courage and the other qualities discussed in the last paragraph are the virtues concerned with tidying up or harmonizing things inside each individual; finally theoretical and practical wisdom are the virtues concerned with the general purpose of human life as a whole, the course the whole fleet ought to be on.

Aristotle says that consideration of these two points—the powers of the soul with which the virtues deal and the respects in which they operate—"will also tell us how many virtues there are."[4] However, he does not actually explain how it tells us. This massive task of analysis and classification was not accomplished until Thomas Aquinas came along in the thirteenth century. Instead of undertaking analysis and classification, Aristotle simply offers a list. Books 3 and 4 of his *Ethics* discuss the moral virtues of courage, self-control, generosity, magnificence, high-mindedness, moderate ambition, gentleness, friendliness, truthfulness and wittiness; Book 5 deals with the moral virtue of justice; Book 6 discusses the intellectual virtues, along with the capacities to which they pertain.

The Doctrine of the Mean

To explain virtue further Aristotle introduces the Doctrine of the Mean. Assuming that the function of eyebrows is to keep sweat out of the eyes, the virtue of eyebrows must be their bushiness. That seems clear. But wait a moment. How much bushiness are we speaking of? Unlimited bushiness? The more the merrier? No, of course not. Having no eyebrows at all would be inconvenient, but so would having hairy ones that draped in front of the eyes so that one could not see. It seems then that there are two ways that eyebrows can miss the mark, not one, and these two are opposites.

This is a silly illustration of an important point that many people miss, for human actions can go wrong in opposite ways too: "The more the merrier" is just as false a counsel in morals as it is in eyebrows. The mistake people make is to think that virtues and vices come in pairs:

Cowardice ————————	Courage
Stinginess ————————	Generosity
Grouchiness ————————	Friendliness
Boorishness ————————	Wittiness

This common belief implies that so long as one is extreme in the right direction, being extreme is always commendable. Thus the courageous person is commended for being extreme in fearlessness, the generous individual for being extreme in willingness to part with wealth, the friendly fellow for being extreme in willingness to put up with offenses, and the witty person for being extreme in the effort to be funny.

Actually, virtues and vices tend to come in triples, with *vices* coming in pairs:

Cowardice ————————	Courage ————————	Rashness
Stinginess ————————	Generosity ————————	Extravagance
Grouchiness ————————	Friendliness ————————	Obsequiousness
Boorishness ————————	Wittiness ————————	Buffoonery

In other words, *both* extremes are usually bad—both deficiency and excess miss the mark of virtue. Thus a fireman so fearless that he enters a collapsing building is not courageous but rash; a donor so freehanded that he holds back too little to feed his children is not generous but extravagant; a companion so indulgent as to let himself be struck and abused is not friendly but obsequious; and a joker so eager to amuse that he bares his buttocks on television is not a wit but a buffoon.

You may think the point at issue obvious, but it is usually overlooked. People tend to mistake one of the two ways of missing every mark for the mark itself. Consider for example the contemporary crusade of the Politically Correct to make the public more "tolerant" of various immoral acts. The virtue of tolerance is relatively new to political debate; Aristotle did not discuss it. From the way the debate is usually framed, however, one gets the impression that all one has to do to achieve tolerance is to avoid the vice of narrowminded repressiveness. On the contrary, like other virtues, tolerance is opposed by not one vice but two, with grave dangers in each direction.[5] The diagram should look not like this:

Intolerance ————————	Tolerance

but like this:

Narrowminded Repressiveness — Tolerance — Soft-headed Indulgence
So far we have been talking about an error *opposed* to the Doctrine of the Mean. However, beginners often err in *applying* the Doctrine of the Mean as well. The commonest such mistakes are six in number.

Mistake one: Thinking that because a moral virtue is a mean in *one* respect it must be a mean in *every* respect. *Correction:* A virtue can be a mean in one respect but extreme in another. Thomas Aquinas makes just this claim about the Christian virtue of faith. Faith is believing all the truth and nothing else. It is a mean with respect to *what* one believes because it lies between the opposite errors of doubting the true and believing the false, but it is extreme with respect to *how* one believes because there is no such thing as believing truth too much.

Mistake two: Grasping that one ought to achieve a mean of something but thinking that this something is virtue. *Correction:* Aristotle does not think it possible to have too much courage; but courage lies between too much and too little fearlessness. In the same way, he does not think it possible to have too much generosity; but generosity lies between too much and too little willingness to part with one's wealth.

Mistake three: Thinking that the mean is exactly halfway between deficiency and excess. *Correction:* A mean may be a midpoint in geometry, but that's not what it is in ethics. In calling the point that should be chosen a *mean,* Aristotle is merely communicating the fact that it will always lie somewhere between the two endpoints. The precise location of this somewhere is determined by an exercise of practical wisdom and varies according to both the agent and the circumstances.

Mistake four: Supposing that, because the location of the mean varies according to both the agent and the circumstances, Aristotle must be a relativist. *Correction:* A relativist would say there are *no* objective rules to guide us in finding the mean. Aristotle does not say that. He says that the mean is "defined by a rational principle, such as a man of practical wisdom would use to determine it."[6] He does not become a relativist just for pointing out that in order to apply this rational principle one needs data. Depending on a number of factors—including his personal experience, the plan of campaign and the state of the battlefield—the truly courageous man may either attack or retreat.

Mistake five: Believing that the Doctrine of the Mean is circular. The beginner who makes this mistake usually reasons as follows: (1) Virtue is defined in terms of the mean; (2) the mean is defined in terms of what a man of practical wisdom would do; (3) but practical wisdom is also a virtue, so we go back to step one. *Correction:* Aristotle defines only *moral* virtue in terms of the mean. Practical wisdom is not a moral but an intellectual virtue, so we do not go back to step one after all.[7]

Mistake six: Considering the Doctrine of the Mean too vague to be of any use. *Correction:* Of course the doctrine has a use. Its use is to remind us that moral errors come in pairs so that we are not always escaping frying pans by jumping into fires. By overlooking the use of the doctrine the complainer is guilty not so much of misunderstanding as of harboring unreasonable expectations. What he really wants is for ethics to be more like arithmetic—he doesn't want it to *improve* his moral judgment, he wants it to abolish the *need* for moral judgment.

We do not have to call upon the wisdom of experience to estimate the square root of 30.25; calculation tells us its value precisely. Unfortunately, there is no calculation that can tell a father how to balance praise with criticism, a donor how to balance liberality with discretion or a soldier how to balance daring with caution. That's too bad. But why complain? Blame for the lack of an algorithm does not lie with Aristotle; it lies in the nature of things.

The Unity of the Virtues

Now that we understand the Doctrine of the Mean, only one more important idea of Aristotle's remains to be explored before we turn again to politics. Usually the idea in question is called the Unity of the Virtues. What it means is that all the excellences of character are interdependent: a flaw in one entails a flaw in every other. Aristotle understood but did not explain their interdependence; Thomas Aquinas explained it.[8]

Step one: Every moral virtue depends on practical wisdom. We've seen this already. Courage, for example, requires enough fear to avoid being rash and enough daring to avoid being cowardly. But because the right amount of fear and daring varies from case to case, the discipline of courage depends on practical wisdom.

Step two: Practical wisdom depends in turn on every moral virtue. To achieve practical wisdom, one needs to fear error yet dare to risk it in pursuit of truth. To preserve practical wisdom, one needs to fear its loss yet dare to risk the contempt of others. But to say this is tantamount to saying that just as courage depends on practical wisdom, so practical wisdom depends on courage. In the same way, we could show that practical wisdom depends on friendliness, truthfulness, self-control and each of the other moral virtues.

Conclusion: Every moral virtue depends on every other. If virtue X depends on practical wisdom but practical wisdom depends on virtue Y, then virtue X depends on virtue Y. Think of a bicycle wheel. The moral virtues are to the spokes as practical wisdom is to the hub, but because they are all connected to the same hub, what happens to one affects the others. Thus friendliness is addled in the untruthful man, truthfulness addled in the unjust man, justice addled in the cowardly man and so on. All of the virtues are joined, all are part of the web. A touch on any thread makes the whole web shake.

What does the Unity of the Virtues tell us about the "character issue" in politics? Some people consider moral character irrelevant to politics. An even larger number put different virtues in different boxes, considering those in one box important but not those in the other. For instance, they may say they care about a politician's "public" virtue but not his "private" virtue—the former including such things as upholding justice and resisting the temptation to set private gain ahead of the common good, the latter faithfulness to spouse and loyalty to friends. Presupposed in this distinction is that a bad man can be a good statesman. But if the virtues constitute a unity, the presupposition is false, for whoever cheats his wife will probably cheat the public too.

He may even cheat the public more, for as the English historian David Hume observed, men act less virtuously in their public capacities than in their private. Several explanations can be offered for this: few virtuous men have the stomach to campaign; great temptations bring out hidden faults; and personal responsibility is easier to evade when individuals act in concert. Hume's own explanation is more subtle. What steers most men toward the common good, he claims, is not true virtue but merely the desire for honor, which is not a craving for goodness as such but for the good opinion of others. Unfortunately, whereas in private life a man may crave the good opinion of everyone, in politics he craves it only of his confederates; hence the common good becomes, for him, the good that is common to party. True, some few do keep their hearts pure even in the sewer of faction. But because the policy of a group is determined by its majority, these few count for nothing. Groups are not kind to exceptions.[9]

We have been speaking of the direct relation between character and politics. But there is an indirect relation too, and that is through the very structure of the regime.

The Classification of Regimes

Aristotle classifies the types of regimes[10] according to two criteria: the number of rulers and their motive for rule. Rule may be exercised by the One, the Few or the Many; its motive may be either the common good of the City or the selfish interest of the rulers themselves. In the classroom I am often asked the meaning of the phrase "the common good." The easy answer is that to have something in common is to share it. But there are two different senses in which a number of people can have a good in common. In the weak sense, the common good is whatever is good for each of them irrespective of whether there is any bond between them. You do not have to know that Tom is married to Rosemary to know that having shoes that fit is good for both. But in the strong sense, the common good is what pertains to their *partnership* in a good life. Marital love is a good for Tom and Rosemary in a wholly different way than having shoes that fit; apart from their bond it cannot be understood.

Now remember that according to Aristotle the City too is a partnership in a good life. To be sure it is not a basic partnership like marriage, but still it is a partnership of partnerships. So when Aristotle speaks of the common good he is using the term in a fairly strong sense. He is interested in whether the citizens enjoy a civic friendship, not in whether everyone's shoes fit.

With that bit of definition out of the way, we may now present Aristotle's classification of regimes. For obvious reasons, he calls the regimes in the left-hand column good and the ones in the right-hand column bad or perverted. We are not dealing with the modern type of social scientist, who fancies himself "value-free," but with a philosopher who faced the moral implications of his work.

	Common good	Selfish interest
One	Monarchy	Tyranny
Few	Aristocracy	Oligarchy
Many	Polity, also called Timocracy	Democracy

Aristotle himself admits that this table does not tell the full story. For one thing, the criterion of number is really a criterion of social class. In an aristocracy the Few are not just any numerical minority but gentlemen: those who have land and good breeding. In an oligarchy they are not just any numerical minority but upstarts: those who are filthy rich but otherwise undistinguished. In a polity the Many are not just any numerical majority but those who satisfy a minimum property requirement. In a democracy they are not just any numerical majority but the landless poor. Moreover, social class and motive to rule are correlated. An oligarch's only motive is to exploit the poor, and a democrat's only motive is to soak the rich. Neither can be trusted to act according to justice. That is why oligarchy and democracy are both on the bad side of the table.

The second thing the table does not tell you is that the Few and the Many rule through different institutions. For example, a council at which only the elite are present is oligarchic, whereas an assembly at which everyone is present is democratic. In the same way, to elect the magistrates is oligarchic, whereas to choose them by lot—at random, as in a lottery—is democratic.

A third thing the table does not tell you is that, unlike all the other regimes, which are pure, polity is a *mixed* regime. Aristotle most often describes it as a balanced blend of oligarchy and democracy. His meaning is twofold. First, it blends their *social bases,* for both the rich and a substantial fraction of the poor meet the minimum property requirement. Second, it blends their *institutions,* for it has both a council in which the rich prevail and an assembly in which the poor prevail.

Surprisingly, this blending promotes the common good. One reason is that the selfish rich and the selfish poor keep each other in check. Even though neither wants justice, neither is able to commit injustice. Another reason is that the stalemate between rich and poor gives leverage to two other groups that would normally be powerless: that small minority of persons who are truly wise and virtuous, and the middle class of small property owners, halfway in size between the rich and poor. Although the middle class is no more wise and virtuous than rich or poor, it acts as though it were simply because of its circumstances: it is neither wealthy enough to gain from the injustice of exploiting the poor nor broken enough to gain from the injustice of soaking the rich. Therefore polity is on the good side of the table, even though the regimes from which it is derived are on the bad.

The fourth thing the table does not tell you is that Aristotle does not consider the good regimes equally good or the bad ones equally bad. His ranking is as follows:

> **The best of the good: Monarchy**
> **The next-best of the good: Aristocracy**
> **The worst of the good: Polity**

> **The best of the bad: Democracy**
> **The next-best of the bad: Oligarchy**
> **The worst of the bad: Tyranny**

But this ranking does not tell the whole story either. One wrinkle is that the case for putting aristocracy first is almost as good as the case for putting monarchy first. Imagine a City in which, among a number of very noble men, there is one man of surpassing virtue—a hero of wisdom and justice who overtops the rest. If anyone deserves to rule, he does, so to withhold from him the crown is to commit a great injustice. But what about those others? Haven't they also moral excellence? Don't they also deserve a share in offices and honors? And aren't they deprived of this share under monarchy? Indeed, Aristotle stresses at several places in his *Politics* that in an ideal regime citizens would share in both ruling and being ruled, everyone taking his turn. The first lesson in learning to command is learning how to obey.

Another wrinkle is that virtue is scarce, and whereas polity makes provision for this fact, monarchy and aristocracy make none. We have seen already that polity pits the selfish against the selfish, giving leverage to those who have no motive to be unjust. In monarchy and aristocracy, by contrast, when you run out of virtue the game is over. Worse yet, the better the regime the worse the consequences of its perversion. The perversion of the best is the worst.[11]

For these reasons, although Aristotle holds that monarchy is the best regime when circumstances are ideal, for most times and places he recommends polity. It isn't utopia, but it's safe.

Questions for Reflection

1. Aristotle does not mention humility, but he does mention high-mindedness. Review his description of high-mindedness in Books 3 and 4 of his *Ethics*. Is it possible to regard humility and high-mindedness both as virtues? Why or why not?

2. The Unity of the Virtues implies that a bad man cannot be a good statesman. On the other hand, constant harping on the sins of politicians can itself degrade public life—not only by its tawdriness and lack of charity but also by its hypocrisy. How dare we speak of the sins of others? Yet how dare we *not* speak of them? Can these two fears be balanced?

3. This chapter has presented two different ways in which politics and moral character are related, one having to do with the behavior of government officials, the other with the design of the regime. How about the *policies* of the regime—is moral character related to these too? For example, one writer suggests that widespread divorce and illegitimacy prompt women to support big government social programs to compensate for the moral failings of men.[12] How might this argument be fleshed out—for example, is it necessary to assume that men are more prone to moral failure, or only that women are more likely to be hurt? What other possible connections between moral character and government policy can you suggest?

4. Nazism and communism did not arise until long after Aristotle's time. Still, can the totalitarian type of regime be located anywhere in his classification? (Hint: Is totalitarianism just old-fashioned tyranny, or is it something new?)

5. Aristotle's analysis of the virtue of courage takes for granted that "the most fearful thing of all is death." Does he mean that death is the worst of all evils? If it really were the worst, then wouldn't it make sense to fear it as much as possible? Does his contempt for excessive fear of death imply that something else is even worse than death? What might this something else be? Is it the same as what Jews and Christians regard

as the worst evil, or is it different? If different, then if Aristotle had known and accepted the Judeo-Christian claim as to the worst evil, would his analysis of courage be altered? If so, how? If not, why not?

6. I once brought Aristotle to the twentieth century in a time machine so that he could give a guest lecture to some of my university students. He shocked the class by claiming (1) that democracy is bad, (2) that the American regime is not a democracy, (3) that it does have democratic elements, (4) that some of these democratic elements do our regime good and (5) that others do it harm. Why did he say these things? Why aren't claims (2) and (3) logically inconsistent? Why aren't claims (1) and (4)?

THREE

FRIENDSHIP, JUSTICE & THE MORAL SIGNIFICANCE OF LAW

OPEN ANY GOVERNMENT TEXTBOOK. YOU'LL PROBABLY FIND A LOT OF talk about conflicting interests, a little talk about justice and no talk at all about friendship. The reason for all the talk about conflicting interests will be discussed in the units on Thomas Aquinas and John Locke. It's not hard to see the reason for talking about justice; from Aristotle we get the idea that the common good requires submission either to just men or to just laws—just men would be better if we could find them, but we settle for just laws because usually we can't. On the other hand, the very idea that friendship should be covered in a discussion of politics may seem strange.

Then again, our way of discussing politics would seem narrow to the ancients. It seems probable that they are the ones who are right and we the ones who are wrong in this matter. Political arrangements are no more anonymous than business arrangements; they depend on a great number of personal relationships, sometimes among people on the same rung of the social ladder, sometimes among people on different rungs.

Justice

Aristotle considers three main kinds of justice: (1) justice in the complete sense, which is obedience to law, (2) justice in the partial sense, which is fairness in the allotment of goods and (3) political justice, the civic arrangement that exists among people who are free and equal under law.

Beginners are often confused by the expressions "complete justice" and "partial justice." Aristotle uses "partial justice" for what concerns the sphere of a single virtue, for fairness is a single virtue. That point is clear. He uses "complete justice" for what concerns the spheres of all the virtues, and obedience to law concerns the spheres of all the virtues. That point is not clear. Our question is, How *does* obedience to law concern the spheres of all the virtues? His answer is that obedience to law concerns them all because *law itself* concerns them all.

At first it seems preposterous to say that law concerns them all; surely law does not say anything about, say, wittiness, courage or self-control! But it does. The law of slander touches the sphere of wittiness; military regulations concerning desertion touch the sphere of courage; and the ordinance on public drunkenness touches the sphere of self-control. Indeed, law touches the sphere of every virtue. We are not speaking just of good law; even bad law touches the sphere of every virtue.

On the other hand, good law does not touch *everything* in the sphere of every virtue. It may reach slander, but it does not reach *all* acts of buffoonery. It may reach desertion, but it does not reach *all* acts of cowardice. It may reach public drunkenness, but it does not reach *all* acts of immoderation. Nor does the law reach all acts of the opposite vices—boorishness, rashness and excessive scrupulosity. That is what Aristotle means when he says that obedience to law is complete justice "not in an unqualified sense, but in relation to our fellow men." The way he draws the line may be diagrammed as on page 40.

In short, the law does pay attention to acts in every row, but it does not pay attention to acts in every column. Because its aim is not all good but only the *common* good, it ignores the second column.

	Acts that relate to our fellow men	Acts that do not relate to our fellow men
Acts involving the sphere of wittiness		
Acts involving the sphere of courage		(you may fill in the cells yourself)
Acts involving the sphere of self-control		
Etc.		

Now let us proceed to the other kind of justice. Partial justice, or fairness in the allotment of goods, operates in two different spheres. One is the *distribution* of goods—not money or food stamps but political goods such as honors and offices. The other is the *rectification* of reciprocal exchange between individuals—fixing things when somebody complains that he was cheated. In general, distribution follows a *proportional* norm of equality, while rectification follows an *arithmetic* norm of equality.

This sounds complicated but is really simple. Arithmetic equality means everyone getting equal value: I give you ten dollars cash, so you give me ten dollars' worth of goods. Proportional equality means giving to everyone in proportion to what he deserves: my honors are to my merit as your honors are to your merit.

We also said that political justice is the civic arrangement that prevails among citizens who are free and equal under law. Aristotle further subdivides political justice into natural and conventional justice. Conventional justice is what we agree to call just, whether it really is so or not; natural justice is what is really just, whether we agree to call it so or not.[1]

In every age some people are so blind as to think that there is no such thing as natural justice, no such thing as a standard to which we can be held accountable. In their view, what we choose to call just is the beginning, the middle and the end of the story. This view comes in many varieties and travels under many names: in Aristotle's day it was Sophism, in ours relativism, pragmatism, postmodernism and many others. Usually it is associated with the defense of tyranny, either open or veiled. But it is not Aristotle's view. He admits that ideas of justice vary but insists that there is a standard against which they can be measured.

A good example of variation in ideas of justice is the difference among aristocracies, oligarchies, democracies and polities in the allotment of honors and offices.

☐ Aristocracies apply proportional equality, awarding them on the basis of merit.

☐ Oligarchies apply another version of proportional equality, awarding them on the basis of wealth.

☐ Democracies apply arithmetic equality, giving everyone the same honor and the same chance in the lottery for offices no matter what their merit or wealth.

☐ Polities endure a permanent tug of war among the supporters of all three norms.

Who is right? To put the question another way, which of these norms accords with natural justice? The oligarch's critique of the democrat contains a grain of truth because democracy treats unequals equally. The democrat's critique of the oligarch contains a grain of truth because wealth is no fit basis on which to make awards. If we take both grains without the chaff, we do get a version of proportional equality, but one in which honors and offices are awarded according to merit instead of wealth. Every now and then the polity muddles through to this formula. Aristocracy intends it from the beginning. So says Aristotle.

Friendship

The two kinds of friendship that Aristotle considers are individual friendship and civic friendship, or concord.

Individual friendship may be based on (1) usefulness, (2) pleasure or (3) partnership in a good life between individuals equal in virtue. The first and second kind of individual friendship can exist (though imperfectly) among unequals. The third, which is the highest kind, cannot.

Civic friendship resembles the latter in two respects: in being a partnership in good and in requiring a kind of equality. However, it differs from it in two others: in being greater in scale and in being more watery—just what you would expect in a partnership of partnerships. At any rate, as the civic partnership becomes corrupt, the prospects for individual friendships become dimmer. Thus the degree to which individual friendships flourish has much to do with the kind of regime under which people live.

One of Aristotle's most intriguing claims is that lawgivers seem to devote more attention to friendship (that is, civic friendship) than to justice. One part of his meaning is easy to grasp: lawgivers do not want citizens to break into factions. But to further explain his claim, he makes another claim even more startling than the first: *friends have no need* of justice. What does he mean by this? That he is talking about the highest kind of friendship is clear enough; but is he speaking of justice in the complete sense or justice in the partial sense? He is speaking of both. Let's take them in order.

As we know, complete justice is obedience to law. Its completeness comes in the fact that the law concerns itself with every virtue. But friendship concerns itself with every virtue too; law adds nothing that is not already there. Thus friends have no need for justice in the complete sense.

Have they need for justice in the partial sense? Remember that partial justice means fairness in the allotment of goods. As such it operates in two spheres, one political and one personal. The political sphere in which it operates is the distribution of political honors and offices. Do friends need fairness here? Many people would say yes because buddies give each other unmerited advantages. We even have a term for this pattern: "the good ol' boy network."

Now, Aristotle doesn't think friends unimportant in politics; he thinks they are important everywhere. But being a good ol' boy is not what Aristotle means by being a friend. "The perfect form of friendship," he says, is not that between good ol' boys who are alike in background, but "that between good men who are alike in excellence or virtue." This means that departure from virtue must be reckoned departure from friendship. Therefore, although ideal friends do each other favors, they do not give each other unmerited advantages. The upshot? True friends already practice fairness in political relationships. They do not "need" this kind of partial justice any more than they need complete justice;

they do not need it because they already have it.

What about the other kind of partial justice—fairness in reciprocal exchange? Do friends need that? Here you may be tempted to answer as above: "No, because it adds nothing that was not already there." But this time the answer must be more subtle. As we know, reciprocal exchange is giving each other things. But there are several contexts in which we give each other things. Consider two.

In one, you are my butcher and I am your customer. I give you cash, and you give me lamb chops. If I don't get my chops, I complain; if you don't get your money, you complain. Obviously, both of us are keeping score.

In the other relationship, you and I are friends of the third type, partners in a good life. Two weeks ago you helped me clean out my garage; last week I bought you lunch; this week you loaned me some books. As in the other relationship, the benefits we receive from each other are equal. The difference, though, is that neither of us is keeping score.

If you are in doubt about this difference, consider what would happen if I offered my friend the same payment for helping in my garage that I offered the handyman. The handyman would be insulted if I didn't offer payment; my friend would be insulted if I did. So each relationship is governed by a different set of principles: in the one, fairness, in the other, something like delight in small sacrifices. Thus friends have no need of the second kind of partial justice either. It isn't that they fall below it; they rise above it.

We can now return with greater insight than before to Aristotle's claim that lawgivers, wise ones anyway, devote more attention to friendship than justice. Civic concord means much more than the absence of faction. It means that the citizens are neighbors instead of strangers, supporting each other in a close-woven fabric of crisscrossing bonds. It means that they delight in small sacrifices for the common good and are not so obsessed with keeping score. It means that voluntarily and without direction they teach the young, provide for the old and look out for each other.

You may be thinking, *This is all fine and dandy, but what does it mean for LAWGIVERS to devote attention to friendship? What are they supposed to do? Should they issue decrees that state "Be friends or spend a week in jail"?*

Nothing like that, of course. In fact I suspect that Aristotle does not so much expect lawmakers to *promote* friendship as to *protect* it. Government cannot really promote friendship anyway because friendships form spontaneously. But statesmen can *honor* the customs by which people express their neighborly solidarity and *avoid* actions which might tear this solidarity apart. Like doctors, they can take as their own the rule "First, do no harm."

For example, a graduate student of mine based his master's report on the idea that if modern city planners had taken Aristotle's discussion of friendship seriously, they would never have split old neighborhoods with multilane expressways and relocated their residents in the name of urban renewal.[2] Try out your own imagination. Ask yourself the question, In what ways would Aristotelian statesmen, aware of the importance of friendship, act differently from our own?

Making Men Good
By now you realize what a gulf separates Aristotle's understanding of politics from the way in which most people think of it today. His approach to statecraft gives first place to consideration of excellence of character. We get the kind of government we deserve; where knaves rule a rabble, there can be no concern for the common good.

We have seen how this consideration shapes what Aristotle says about several topics, including friendship, justice and even the design of the regime. In the final stretches of the *Nicomachean Ethics,* we also see how he applies it to the art of making laws. The burden of Book 10, Chapter 9 is to defend what we now call "the legislation of morality." From the horrified way in which modern people usually pronounce the phrase, one would think that all of its vowels were gasps. But let us try to breathe normally.

First we need to understand that it is impossible to legislate without legislating morality. Try to think of a law that is not based on a moral idea; you won't be able to do it. Like me, you may be able to think of some that are based on *false* moral ideas, but that is not the same thing. The law requiring highway taxes is based on the moral idea that people should be made to pay for the benefits they receive. The law requiring graduated income taxes is based on the moral idea that some people ought to be made to pay for the benefits that *others* receive.[3] The law punishing murder is based on the moral ideas that innocent blood should not be shed, that private individuals should not take the law into their own hands, and that individuals should be held responsible for their deeds. The law permitting abortion is based on the moral idea that innocent blood may be shed if the victim is still in the womb.[4] Because laws are based on moral ideas, what could be wrong with making sure that they are based on true ones?

However, Aristotle says more than that laws should be based on true moral ideas. He argues that they should be used to *shape character*—to *make men virtuous*. For good character is not an inborn but an acquired characteristic. We are born with the ability to acquire virtue, he thinks, but we are not born with virtue itself. There is something in us that finds virtue attractive and *wants* to have it, but that is not the same as having it.

The notion that laws should be used to shape character may seem strange to you. The arm of the law reaches only my outward deeds, but virtue is the inward disposition that gives rise to them. How then can law affect character at all? In fact, how can *any* discipline affect character?

Here is one of the most important points to grasp in Aristotle. Having virtue is not the same as doing outward deeds; nevertheless we *acquire* virtue *by* doing outward deeds. Reflect on this everyday story:

Four-year-old Billy, not content with his own cupcake, reaches over and snatches three-year-old Susie's. When Susie begins to cry, Mother notices the crime. "Billy!" she commands. "Put back Susie's cupcake RIGHT NOW! If you don't share, I'll have your father deal with you." Caught, four-year-old Billy puts back Susie's cupcake.

Do we say, "The discipline was useless, because although Billy did perform the virtuous deed he didn't perform it for virtuous motives"? No, because we know that by being made to perform such deeds over and over, Billy will eventually form a habit of sharing. Although this habit is not a full-grown virtue either, nevertheless it is part of the raw material out of which the full-grown virtue of fairness may eventually be developed.

What we see going on with Billy is the first stage of a long process. Parents tame the desires and feelings of the child by inculcating good habits. Provided these good habits are set firmly in place, the child accepts them as normal. Because he accepts them, when he reaches the age of reason his parents can go on to teach him why these habits are good. Still later, when this insight is enriched in him by experience, it ripens into practical wisdom. Finally, when practical wisdom and good habit are working together to shape his choices, we have virtue entire.

So far, so good. But where does law come in? We have spoken only of the parents. Why must law come in at all? There is no reason the parents cannot be completely successful by themselves, is there? Ah, but there is. Compared with the discipline of laws, parental discipline does have two great advantages, but it also comes up against one great limit.

The two great advantages that Aristotle mentions are easy to understand. One is that because of kinship, gratitude, affection and the acquired habit of obedience, parental words are held in greater honor than legal traditions. "My father says" means more to a child than "it's the law." The other is that individual nurture, such as that which parents provide, is more effective than group education. No daycare center can duplicate a mother.

The great limit that parental discipline comes up against is that "a father's command does not have the power to enforce or to compel." To be sure, this limit does not kick in right away. Fathers seem to have no difficulty "enforcing and compelling" so long as their children are small. However, eventually the children become too big for physical punishment, and not long afterward they escape parental discipline altogether. This might be all right if their virtues were fully formed, but they still have a long way to go before they reach that point. Indeed, by this time they have hit puberty, so they require discipline not only to finish taming their old desires and feelings but also to tame their even wilder new ones. A certain amount of coercion is necessary even after they have reached adulthood.

Parental "enforcing and compelling" can lose its effect in another way too, and this one is more subtle; it undermines parental discipline even when the children *are* still small enough to spank. Unless children are cloistered like nuns, they spend a lot of time in other households besides their own. What if different families have different ideas about how children should be reared?

If Susie is just as likely to be scolded for picking on smaller children when she is at Martha's house as she is when she is at home, that supports her mom and dad; but if she can escape their prohibition on watching MTV by watching it over at Lizzie's house where the rules are different, that undermines them. All the parents in the neighborhood must agree about the moral rules, otherwise each household is undermined by the others. In fact they are no longer partners in a good life at all; Aristotle says they are like the lawless Cyclopes.[5]

What is the solution to this problem? If the community *does* neglect the upbringing and pursuits of the young, says Aristotle, then each man ought at least to help his children and friends attain virtue.[6] However, the best solution is to avoid such neglect in the first place. "Upbringing and pursuits"—everything from the education of the young to their music and athletics—should be a concern of the whole community.

Although Aristotle calls this is a matter of "legislation," he does not necessarily mean enacting written laws. To be sure, he says in his *Politics* that there ought to be a uniform system of public schools, establishment of which would certainly seem to require written laws. However, he says in the *Nicomachean Ethics* that "whether the laws are written or unwritten would seem to make no difference," and the study of legislation includes the study of both.

The citizens enact written laws when the assembly is in session, but they enact and enforce unwritten laws at every moment of their lives as they exhort, support and rebuke each other. These unwritten laws are customs. In fact under most circumstances custom has more influence over young people than written law does because they feel it not merely when they happen to brush up against the power of the government but in every social contact. Nor would Aristotle set written law *against* unwritten law; for the most part it would merely recognize good custom and give it teeth.

What would Aristotle think of our own customs concerning the upbringing and pursuits of the young? Here I can only speculate, but the answer, I think, is "Not much." We hardly instruct the young at all and have virtually given up passing judgment on their entertainments. For illustration, not long ago I had the misfortune to attend a music and drama night in the neighborhood public elementary school. The young performers lip-synched to the music of their favorite singers and duplicated all their stage behaviors—right up to simulated masturbation. Viewing this, the crowd of parents, teachers and children merely screamed with laughter and egged them on. We know from his *Politics* that Aristotle considers the "mode" of music by far the most powerful thing about it; in his view, rhythm and melody embody images of states of character, and "to listen to these images is to undergo a real change of the soul" for better or for worse. Even if the words were clean, therefore, our rap and rock would certainly come under his condemnation for the seductive pulse of the former and the brutalizing rhythms of the latter. The increasing violence of some of our contact sports, hockey for example, would remind Aristotle of Spartan athletics, which he thought brought out the ferocity of the beast rather than the courage of the man.[7]

What passes for moral education in our high schools has nothing to do with ethics as Aristotle understands it and undermines parental discipline rather than supplements it. "Values clarification" is based on the premise that it does not matter what you believe so long as you are consistent, and some sex education curricula explicitly instruct high school students to defy and disobey their parents.[8] In the meantime teen pregnancy rates are soaring.

In short, ours is probably the sort of community Aristotle criticized for neglecting the upbringing and pursuits of the young. For us, therefore, his fall-back recommendation seems to apply: until the community is reformed, each person ought at least to help his children and friends attain virtue.

Questions for Reflection

1. Aristotle assumes that friendship between a human being and a god would be impossible—since the god would need nothing, the human being would get all the benefits. This argument presupposes that if the god gets nothing out of the friendship, he has no motive to enter it. Contrast this with the Christian idea of a God who cares for us with self-sacrificial love, even to the point of death on a cross.

2. On the other hand, Aristotle says that a friend of the highest kind is "another self," and he makes clear that even though they mutually benefit from the relationship, friends of the highest kind do not keep score. How does difference of sex affect the prospects for this kind of

friendship? How does marriage? What does Aristotle say? What do you say?

3. The ideal of feudalism was a mutually beneficial friendship between unequals—the lord provided protection and the vassal provided service. What *modern* political arrangements might be described in terms of friendship? How could we distinguish between just and corrupt forms of such arrangements?

4. How was *your* moral formation guided by your family? by the community? by the law? Think in specifics, not generalities. Consider both good and bad guidance.

5. According to Aristotle, as the civic partnership becomes corrupt, the prospects for individual friendship become dim. Why? Is this equally true of friendships based on usefulness, on pleasure and on virtue?

6. How might the arbitrary rule of unjust men be *disguised* as the rule of just laws?

7. Would Aristotle necessarily approve of *all* ways of using law to shape character? Why or why not?

8. In a corrupt community, lawmakers are likely to be as foolish as the rest of the citizens. How then does Aristotle think a corrupt community is to be reformed? How might the view of a Christian, who knows the transforming power of God's grace, be different?

UNIT II

THOMAS AQUINAS

FOUR

THE GRAND DESIGN OF LAW

THOMAS AQUINAS, A THIRTEENTH-CENTURY DOMINICAN MONK AND CHRIS-
tian saint, is generally regarded as the greatest of all medieval philosophers and one of the greatest philosophers of all time. His output
was prodigious. My edition of the *Summa Theologica,* the work from
which his *Treatise on Law* is taken, runs to about three thousand pages,
and the *Summa* is itself only a small part of his life's work. Yet Thomas
can get more onto one page than most writers get into ten. *Summa,* by
the way, means "summary." Written for beginners, the *Summa* was an
attempt to summarize all that could be known about God, about man
and about their relationship.

Introduction to Thomas Aquinas

You may have heard the Middle Ages called "the Dark Ages." Don't
believe it. There were indeed a few "dark" centuries after the collapse
of Roman civilization in Europe. However, a new Christian civilization
rose to take its place, with a powerful intellectual culture of its own

centered in the leading monasteries and universities.

The time during which Thomas wrote was a time of ferment, because previously unavailable works of Aristotle had come to Europe from the Middle East. Thomas, impressed by Aristotle's towering achievement in every field of merely human knowledge, calls Aristotle not just a philosopher, but *the Philosopher.* To do so is to hold him forth as the model for all philosophers.[1]

Yet Thomas recognizes that philosophy is limited in what it can do. Therefore he sets himself the task of *synthesizing* philosophy with the Christian faith. He leaves no doubt which of the two takes the lead: philosophy, he says, is but the handmaid of theology. Some beginners object to the statement. Usually this problem arises from the modern prejudice that faith and reason are somehow *opposites,* so that the more faithful you are, the less rational you are. Thomas would say that this modern prejudice is itself irrational. Both faith and reason come from God, and God does not contradict himself.

Besides, we know that human reason is finite; though it can find its way to some truths without aid, to grasp others it needs assistance. What could be more reasonable than that the infinite God would provide such assistance through his revealed Word? The motto "Reason Alone!" is nonsense anyway. Reason itself presupposes faith. Why? Because a defense of reason *by* reason is circular, therefore worthless. Our only guarantee that human reason works is the God who made it.

The Thomistic synthesis is not a mere cut-and-paste job. Thomas is a profound and original thinker in his own right, and where he considers Aristotle and his other sources mistaken he does not hesitate to go beyond them. Along with the rest of the *Summa Theologica,* the *Treatise on Law* is written in the form of a formal disputation, or debate. This is an efficient way of bringing together what all who have thought about a matter have said about it. You may think of the *Treatise* as though it were the transcript of an eight-day conference. The topic for each day is called a *Question.* The specific issues that topic includes are called *Articles.* Each Article follows the same format. To illustrate, let's use Question 91, Article 2.

1. *Statement of the issue.* The issue is always expressed as a yes-or-no question to which the traditional answer is yes—in this case, "Is there a natural law?"

2. *Objections.* The objections are reasons that philosophers have offered for saying no—in this case, "There is no natural law." These objections are not straw men; in fact, Thomas often expresses the objections more cogently and powerfully than do his sources.

3. *The traditional view.* Preceded by the words "On the contrary," a quotation is offered from a traditional authority expressing the yes answer—in this case, "There is a natural law."

4. *Thomas's own view.* Preceded by the words "I answer that," Thomas gives us his own answer to the question, defending this answer by logical arguments. Usually he defends the traditional view, as he does here. He also sets up the equipment that he will need to answer the objections. For instance, he may mention a distinction which the objectors overlook or discuss the subjects about which the objectors seem to be confused. In this case, he distinguishes between two ways in which a law can be "in" a person, then discusses the definition of natural law and its relation to eternal law.

5. *Replies to the objections.* One by one, Thomas tells where the objections go wrong.

Why should we study the *Treatise on Law* in the first place? The superficial answer is that everyone knows that law is a political topic. However, there is a deeper reason too. Aristotle demonstrated that we cannot understand the politics of either good or perverted regimes unless we first understand what the difference between the good and perverted ones is. To put this idea another way, the proper study of politics begins with the proper study of ethics. Now all ethics concerns two things: rules and virtues. Aristotle's own discussion focused on virtues. Yet even for him, rules were there in the background. One place they peeked out was where he discussed the principles of natural justice. An even more important place was where he said that the mean of virtue is defined by rational principles such as a man of practical wisdom would use—because he understood these principles as universal, brooking no exception. Thomas Aquinas too discusses virtues; in fact, much of his teaching about virtues was blended right into our discussion of Aristotle. The difference is that in Thomas the rules do not stay in the background. He pulls them into the foreground where we can study them for themselves. Rules—from the principles by which God made the universe to the decrees of human legislatures—are the topic of the *Treatise on Law.*

Terminology

Scholars use technical terms for two reasons, one good and one bad. The good reason is that technical terms sometimes simplify the discussion of a complex subject so that it can move more swiftly and with less confusion. The bad reason is that technical terms can sometimes hide bad reasoning or make a writer seem smarter than he is. Thomas always uses technical terms for the good reason, never for the bad one. However, he does use a lot of them, and you need to know what they mean before you begin. *If you can't explain a term or an idea in plain English, you don't really understand it.* For our purposes, some of the most important of Thomas's terms are *creature, substance, nature, type, law, powers, habits, appetite, synderesis, virtues, vices, fomes, speculative reason, speculative wisdom, prudence* and *perfect community.*

A *creature* is a created thing, such as a snowflake, star, angel or human being. Everything but the Creator is a creature. Notice that the theory of creation has in no way been disproven by the Darwinist doctrine of evolution.[2] Even if species did evolve, they could have done so only in accordance with the physical principles of the universe. Where did the universe itself come from? What gave it these principles? As another philosopher once asked, "Why is there something, and not rather nothing?"[3]

A *substance* is something to which God has given its own essence or nature. The *nature* of a thing is "a reason put into a thing by the Divine art that it be moved to a determinate end"; in other words, a rational pattern, put into it by God's workmanship, which causes it to work in the particular way, and for the sake of the particular good, that God has purposed. The preexisting model, or *type*, for this workmanship is found in God's wisdom. That is what Thomas means when he defines the eternal law as "the type of Divine wisdom, as directing all actions and movements."

Everything God made has a nature. However, not everything he made is subject to him in the special way called natural *law.* Natural *law* is a privilege of created *rational* beings—that includes us—because it is a finite reflection of his infinite purposes in their finite minds. This is what Thomas means when he defines it as "the participation of the rational creature in the eternal law."

Our actions have various sources, some of which are within our souls, whereas others are outside them. The two intrinsic principles of the operation of the soul are called *powers* and *habits*.

Powers are permanent abilities. For example, *appetite* is the power by which we apprehend and seek the good. Appetite may be subdivided into *sensitive* appetite and *rational* appetite, according to whether we apprehend the good via our senses or via our minds. Rational appetite is called the *will*. Sensitive appetite may be further subdivided into *irascible* appetite and *concupiscible* appetite; we encountered these terms in the first section of chapter two, although there we called them feelings and desires.

Habits are difficult-to-change dispositions or tendencies to do things in certain ways. They may exist in us either by nature or from other causes. As we see in the next definition, habits shape not only physical actions such as running but also mental actions such as knowing. In contemporary English, the word *habit* is usually reserved for repetitive, compulsive actions such as chewing one's nails. But that is not the sort of thing Thomas has in mind.

The Greek term *synderesis* means roughly "conscience."[4] This is a natural habit of the mind, the one by which people who have reached the age of reason know the first or fundamental precepts of the natural law without having to be taught them. When Thomas says that the principles of the natural law are always "in human reason habitually" but are not always "considered by reason actually," he means the same thing that you might express by saying that they are always in the mind unconsciously but are not always in the mind consciously, or that one always knows them but is not always thinking about them.

Virtues are also habits, but they are acquired rather than natural. The general definition of *virtue* is "that which makes its possessor good, either simply or in some particular respect." For example, sharpness makes a knife good for cutting. Applying this definition to human beings, a virtue is a habit that directs a person's reason toward particular acts: the virtue of courage directs reason toward courageous acts, the virtue of justice directs it toward just acts and so forth. Some virtues—those we call intellectual—have to do with the operation of reason itself. Others—those we call moral—have to do with the obedience of the sensitive powers to reason.

The fact that we speak of virtues as "habits" which direct action according to "precepts" does not mean that virtues operate mechanically. To put this another way, you could know all the rules and yet not know much about how to act because every complete act of virtue requires not only right rules—which concern matters that are universal or nearly universal (respectively, "general" or "common")—but also the right application of these rules to particular facts ("singulars"). Hence the mean in every virtue is found by an exercise of practical wisdom, which no list of rules can exhaust.

Habits opposed to virtue are called *vices;* that which concerns a vice is called *vicious.* This gives the latter term a broader sense than it carries in contemporary English, in which it usually refers only to the vice of cruelty.

The Latin term *fomes*[5] means literally "tinder" or "kindling." Thus the expression "fomes of sin" is a metaphorical expression for the inclination to give way to the sensitive powers instead of using them the way reason commands. Examples are the inclination to give way to anger which is unreasonable because it is unjust and the inclination to give way to sexual desire which is unreasonable because its object is someone other than our spouse. When God made us we were in perfect order; the fomes is a *dis*order which resulted naturally from our rebellion against him, called the Fall.

What most translations of Thomas call *speculative reason* is the same thing that newer translations of Aristotle call "theoretical reason." Speculative reason has nothing to do with wild guessing, often called "speculation" in today's English. On the contrary, it is our capacity to reason about *necessary* truths, truths that remain true no matter how things stand in the world, truths about matters that "cannot be other than they are." An example of a necessary truth is the principle that a whole is greater than a part. You may be talking about a whole adventure novel, a whole apple pie or a whole galaxy: no matter, it will be greater than any part of it. The name for the virtue that perfects speculative reason is *speculative wisdom.*

What most translations of Thomas call *prudence* is the same thing that newer translations of Aristotle call "practical wisdom," because just as speculative wisdom perfects speculative reason, prudence perfects practical reason. Prudence is our capacity to reach choices on the basis of deliberation because practical reason deals with *contingent* truths; it is concerned with things that *can* be other than they are. I may or may not rush into the burning house. If I don't, the people inside may or may not escape without my help. If I do, the roof may or may not fall in on me before I get to them.

Finally, a *perfect community* is a community that satisfies all the prerequisites for partnership in a good life. This includes not only physical prerequisites such as adequate crop land but moral prerequisites such as justice in the laws and good character in the citizens. Aristotle uses this term too, but for him the terms *City* and *perfect community* are synonymous. For Thomas they are not. For instance, a well-ordered kingdom of many cities might yet be a perfect community.

In Thomas Aquinas we see what one writer has called "mind in perfect order." I do not think he is right about everything, but no other philosopher writes more clearly and precisely. Unfortunately, as Thomas himself points out, there is a difference between what is clear in itself and what is actually clear to us. His very clarity and precision make him seem murky to the inexperienced because he puts each point the one right way rather than trying out six or seven ways and because once he makes a point he never repeats it: he expects you to remember it.

Don't despair! If you read the *Treatise on Law* enough times, each time more closely than the time before—for most beginners the requisite number is three or four—then little by little, like a light growing brighter and brighter until everything is illuminated, that which is clear in itself becomes clear to you. The same writer who at first seems hardest to understand eventually appears as lucidity itself.

The Grand Design

To understand the architecture of law we must first understand what is meant by law. Thomas defines law in general as "an ordinance of reason, for the common good, made by him who has care of the community, and promulgated." A few points need explanation. By "reason" Thomas means practical, rather than theoretical, reason— reason directed to choice rather than pure knowledge. "Promulgated" means "made known." Finally, the phrase "*him who has* care of the community" should be understood as meaning "*those who have care of the community,*" because Thomas recognizes not only monarchies (in which authority to make laws belongs to one person) but also aristocracies (in which it belongs to a council) and "free" communities (in which it belongs to the whole people). Therefore we can rephrase the definition of law as "an ordinance of practical reason, for the common good, made by those who have care of the community, and promulgated or made known."

All four elements of the definition are essential. Whatever does not have all four is not a law. Thomas therefore utterly repudiates the common definition of law as merely the command of the sovereign. The judges of the Nuremberg war crimes tribunal were reasoning like Thomas when they rejected the defense of the Nazis that they were only following orders.

The following diagram represents the grand design of law as understood by Thomas Aquinas.

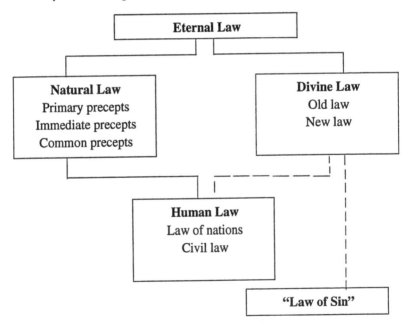

Let's consider each of the five boxes in turn.

1. *Eternal Law: The principles by which God made and governs the universe;*

the pattern of the divine art. Without the eternal law, nothing would be knowable at all; yet only God can know the eternal law as it is in itself, and we created, rational beings can know it only in its "reflections." An analogy might help to make this clear. Think of God as the sun and the eternal law as the sunlight. Without the sunlight, nothing would be visible at all; yet we cannot look at the sun directly because it is too powerful for our created eyes. All law derives its authority from eternal law; whatever does not is not a law.

2. *Natural Law: The reflection of eternal law in the very structure of the created rational mind, directing us to our natural good.* We are speaking here of the "law written on the heart"[6]—the deep structure of all moral knowledge. Thomas classifies its principles, or precepts, into *primary* and *secondary*, then subdivides the secondary precepts, giving us three groups in all.[7]

You may think of the primary precepts, which are also called "first principles of practical reason," as *moral principles that we can't not know,* such as "Good should be pursued and evil avoided" and "Love your neighbor." In one sense these general rules are like axioms in classical geometry, for, although they cannot be proven themselves, they are what every proof depends on. In another sense they are different from axioms, for, rather than beginning with them, we end with them: if we are asked the reasons for our choices, then asked the reasons for those reasons and so on, eventually we come to a standstill; we have reached the deepest reasons of all, and these are the primary precepts of the natural law. Even when we sin, we know and use these precepts—but in a twisted way, for instance by distorting their meaning or deceiving ourselves about the facts to which they apply.

If the primary precepts are like axioms, the secondary precepts, which are more detailed, are like theorems. They are derived from the primary precepts and express moral truth because the primary precepts do. Some are so obvious that almost everyone recognizes their truth in the wink of an eye: these are the *immediate* precepts, such as "Do not murder." Sometimes Thomas even includes them among the primary precepts, the ones we can't not know.[8] But other precepts, still more detailed, are not as obvious and therefore not as well known: these are the *common* precepts, such as "Always return to a person what belongs to him."

The terminology of "general" and "common" requires explanation. To call a principle general is to say that it applies in all cases; there can be no excuse for violating it. But to call a principle common is to say that it applies only in most cases; there are exceptions. For example, ordinarily you should give back an item that a friend has left in your safekeeping, but not if he is drunk and the item is his car key. Therefore having true and objective moral laws does not do away with the need for judgment.

The relationship among the different precepts may be diagrammed as follows.

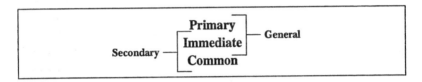

3. *Divine Law: The reflection of eternal law in God's revealed Word, the Bible, directing us to faith in Christ as the only possible means of our reconciliation with God.* Unlike natural law, which aims us only toward our natural good, Divine law aims us toward that unimaginable ultimate joy which is far beyond our merely natural good and consists of the vision of God himself in heaven.

Thomas holds that God gave two different editions of the Divine law: the *old law,* contained in the Old Testament (Hebrew Scripture), and the *new law,* contained in the New Testament. These two laws are not contradictory: the old law points ahead to the new law and is fulfilled (and therefore superseded) in the promised Savior, who offers the way out of sin and guilt, Jesus of Nazareth. Although some parts of Divine law are also contained in natural law and so are discoverable by unaided human reason, other parts go beyond what we could have figured out by ourselves and would not have been known unless God had revealed them.

4. *Human Law: Detailed "determinations" or applications of natural law to the circumstances of particular human societies.* Human law is derived from natural law in two different ways.

Some human laws (as explained later, these are the *law of nations*) are derived by *conclusion from premises,* or, as we would say, deduction.

For instance, poisoning my neighbor would do him harm; so, since natural law says that I should not do harm, I should not poison him. The role of human law is to make this particular act punishable.

Other human laws (as explained later, these are the *civil law*) are derived by *determination of certain generalities,* or, as we would say, filling in the blanks. For instance, we might fulfill the natural-law precept of furthering the safety of the people either by making everyone drive on the right or by making everyone drive on the left. The role of human law is to make and enforce the choice.

Now take another look at the diagram on page 60. A solid line connects natural law with human law, but a dotted line connects Divine law with human law. Why? Is human law derived from Divine law too? No, because government is charged with directing the community to its natural rather than its supernatural good, so God does not intend the enforcement of Divine law upon nonbelievers. But even if human law should not enforce Divine law, it should not *violate* it either—not any more than it may violate natural law. The reason is that any authority human law has comes ultimately from God. The bottom line, holds Thomas, is that if government commands something contrary to either natural or Divine law, its command is not a law but an act of violence.

5. *The "Law of Sin": Not a law in the strict sense but a penalty or consequence resulting from Divine law for man's turning his back on God.* In Romans 7 the apostle Paul comments on the fact that without the help of Christ we often do what we do not want to do and fail to do what we want to do. He concludes from this that there is a "law of sin" in us which battles against the law of God in our minds. Some medieval thinkers found this passage puzzling and asked how sin could be a law. Thomas points out that the term *law* is used in two senses: first, as a command; second, as the penalty or consequence one suffers as a result of breaking a command.

Consider an example from human law: the law in the first sense is that I am to drive on the expressway no faster than fifty-five miles per hour in the city, but the law in the second sense is that if I do, I pay a fine. Consider another example, this one from natural law: the law in the first sense is that I should not do violence to my body, but the law in the second sense is that if I do, I bleed and feel pain.

The "law of sin" is a law in the second sense. Think of a magnet and two iron rings.[9] Anything the magnet touches transmits its power to any iron that touches it, so that if I use the magnet to pick up the first ring, I can then use the first ring to pick up the second. Now think of God as the magnet, the created human mind as the first iron ring, and the created human capacities for feeling and desire as the second iron ring. The penalty or consequence for breaking the magnetic link between the magnet and the first ring is that the magnetic link between the first ring and the second is also destroyed. In the same way, the penalty or consequence of the mind's rebellion against God is that the desires and feelings rebel against the mind; they no longer behave as they ought to. From this consequence others follow, and human life becomes completely disordered.

Questions for Reflection
1. What are some other examples of the primary, immediate and common precepts of natural law?
2. What are some other examples of the old Divine law and the new Divine law?
3. What are some other examples of the civil law and the law of nations?
4. Why can't examples be given of the eternal law? Does this mean we have no knowledge of it? Why not?

FIVE

THE LAW
OF NATURE &
THE LAW OF MAN

THE *FACT* THAT THERE IS A NATURAL LAW IS MORE IMPORTANT THAN ANY *theories* about it. Nevertheless the theories are important because they help us understand the significance of the fact. Another natural-law theory will be presented in the unit on John Locke. Right now we are considering Thomas's.

Common Objections to Natural Law

Some people think that there cannot be a natural law simply because there *is* more than one theory about it. After all, they say, if the natural law is made up of objective moral principles that everyone knows, shouldn't all of us have the same theory about it? This is not a convincing argument because the different theories of natural law *do* agree about its basic content. What they disagree about are *secondary* things, such as where the knowledge of it comes from.

Other people think that there cannot be a natural law just because some people think there isn't. After all, they say, if the natural law is made up of objective moral principles that everyone knows, shouldn't all of us *know* we know them? This is not a convincing argument either, for we know lots of things that we don't know we know.

You know, don't you, that nothing can both *be* and *not be* in the same sense at the same time? Yet before I asked you, you might never have thought about it in these words. And you know, don't you, that good is to be chosen and bad avoided? Yet you might never have consciously formulated the principle to yourself. One of the most famous passages in all of philosophy occurs in Plato's *Meno*, in which Socrates seems to teach a slave boy who has never studied geometry the Pythagorean theorem. The twist is that he *doesn't* teach him. All he does is ask a series of questions that bring out what the boy already knows. When you put the boy's answers together, you have the proof.

Still other people think that there cannot be a natural law because no matter what moral principle we say it includes, someone can be found to deny that principle. After all, if the natural law is made up of objective moral principles that everyone knows, then how could anyone deny one of them? But not only can we not know that we know, we can also *repress* what we know. If you wait long enough the signs of what is going on are bound to emerge because denial takes up so much psychological energy that eventually something has to give.

One form that denied guilt can take is a compulsion to rationalize. For instance, the anthropologist Margaret Mead, herself a sexual libertine, managed to convince herself and the millions who read her books that the Samoan culture she had studied was a paradise of free love. The fact, as proven later, was that the Samoans were ferocious defenders of female chastity and regarded both premarital sex and adultery with horror.[1]

Another form that repressed guilt can take is otherwise unexplainable emotional distress. E. Michael Jones calls this the "Dimmesdale Syndrome" after the Rev. Arthur Dimmesdale, a character in Nathaniel Hawthorne's classic novel *The Scarlet Letter.* In the story, Dimmesdale has committed adultery with Hester Prynne. At first he seems to have escaped the consequences of his deed because, although she is exposed and publicly humiliated, she refuses to name her partner in sin. Yet over the years the burden of awareness becomes intolerable to him; he imagines accusation even in the phenomena of the night sky and sinks into a depression which the community, thinking him a hero, cannot understand.[2]

Compare the symptoms of postabortion stress, as reported by women in literally thousands of recovery groups: they vary from case to case and take different amounts of time to appear, but they commonly include anxiety, compulsive promiscuity, inability to bond even with wanted children, resentment of other women's children, and depression, especially around the anniversary of the abortion or the day on which the baby would have been born.[3]

Finally, some people think that there cannot be a natural law because human beings are always creating new values. After all, they say, if the natural law were made up of objective moral principles that everyone knew, then the creation of new values would be impossible. The problem with this argument is that the creation of new values *is* impossible, impossible in exactly the same way that the creation of new primary colors is impossible.

Suppose someone said to you, "The old primary colors of yellow, red and blue are outdated rubbish. I have chosen new ones to take their place: orange, green and purple."

You would answer, "You have not created new primary colors at all. In fact, the only reason these can even be recognized as colors is that you mixed yellow and red to get the orange, yellow and blue to get the green, and blue and red to get the purple. Besides, I can't get every color by mixing orange, green and purple as I can by mixing yellow, red and blue."

Just so, C. S. Lewis points out that "only by such shreds of the [natural law[4]] as [the Innovator] has inherited is he enabled even to attack it." What purport to be new values always turn out to be "fragments from the [natural law] itself, arbitrarily wrenched from their context in the whole and then swollen to madness in their isolation, yet still owing to the [natural law] and to it alone such validity as they possess."[5] Note well: The language is from Lewis, but the argument is deeply indebted to Thomas. It is *precisely* what Thomas has in mind when he calls the precepts of natural law the "first principles of practical reason," the absolutely inescapable foundations of all possible deliberation about how to live.

To clarify the argument, suppose the Innovator proposes a new

morality in which the fundamental value is the Future of the Human
Race. As Lewis explains,

> he is really deriving our duty to posterity from the [natural law]; our
> duty to do good to all men is an axiom of Practical Reason, and our
> duty to do good to our descendants is a clear deduction from it. But
> then, in every form of the [natural law] which has come down to us,
> side by side with the duty to children and descendants lies the duty
> to parents and ancestors. By which right do we reject one and accept
> the other?

Or suppose the Innovator holds that old-fashioned notions such as
justice and good faith must give way to the fundamental value of Ending
Human Need.

> The [natural law] of course agrees with him about the importance
> of getting the people fed and clothed. Unless the Innovator were
> himself using the [natural law] he could never have learned of such
> a duty. But side by side with it in the [natural law] lie those duties of
> justice and good faith which he is ready to debunk. What is his
> warrant?

Finally, suppose the Innovator is a racist or extreme nationalist who
holds that every other value must yield to the advancement of his own
people.

> But no kind of factual observation and no appeal to instinct will give
> him a ground for this opinion. Once more, he is in fact deriving it
> from the [natural law]: a duty to our own kin, because they are our
> own kin, is a part of traditional morality. But side by side with it in
> the [natural law], and limiting it, lie the inflexible demands of
> justice, and the rule that, in the long run, all men are our brothers.
> Whence comes the Innovator's authority to pick and choose?[6]

Lewis concludes that by whatever name one calls it, the natural law

> is not one among a series of possible systems of value. It is the sole
> source of all value judgments. If it is rejected, all value is rejected. If
> any value is retained, it is retained. The effort to refute it and raise
> a new system of value in its place is self-contradictory. . . . If my duty
> to my parents is a superstition, then so is my duty to posterity. If
> justice is a superstition, then so is my duty to my country or my race.
> If the pursuit of scientific knowledge is a real value, then so is
> conjugal fidelity. The rebellion of new ideologies against the [natu-

ral law] is a rebellion of the branches against the tree: if the rebels could succeed they would find that they had destroyed themselves.[7]

Troublesome Passages Concerning Natural Law

I am often asked questions about each of the following passages from Question 94 of the *Treatise on Law:*

From Article 2: "Now a thing is said to be self-evident in two ways: first in itself; secondly, in relation to us."

What does that mean? Imagine that you are in geometry class, and the teacher remarks, "Of course parallel lines never meet." A student raises his hand and asks, "Why not?" The teacher replies, "Well, it's just obvious." The student retorts, "Maybe, but it isn't obvious to me." What the teacher means by saying that the truth of the statement is obvious is that the concept of never meeting is *contained,* so to speak, in the concept of parallel lines. What the student means by saying that its truth is not obvious *to him* is that he doesn't see how.

This is an example of the phenomenon we mentioned earlier—knowing something (in a sense) without knowing that we know it—and it occurs in every field of knowledge. When it occurs in geometry, of course, no one says, "Aha, geometry must have no objective basis"; instead the student says, "I don't see it yet, but I know it must be true." By contrast, when it arises in ethics people do often say, "Aha, ethics must have no objective basis!"

Why do we indulge in such special pleading? Thomas would reply that it is because of original sin. We do not want God to be God; each of us wants to be his own little god. Ethics threatens us in a way that geometry does not because it reminds us that we are *not* gods, that we are subject to a law we did not make.

From Article 2: "All those things to which man has a natural inclination, are naturally apprehended by reason as being good, and consequently as objects of pursuit, and their contraries as evil, and objects of avoidance."

Is Thomas here saying that natural law commands me to seek whatever I desire? That would be convenient, wouldn't it? I could steal anything that caught my eye and plead in my defense that I was merely doing what came naturally; I could have any woman I wanted and justify my conduct by appealing to natural law; I could sleep with animals or with other men and exonerate myself by saying that it would be immoral to act against the desires that God had given me.

But look again at Thomas's language. He does not speak of all inclinations but only of natural inclinations; and not all inclinations are natural. One reason for this is that some are acquired. That is not the deepest reason, however, because even though an acquired inclination does not arise *in* nature, it may still be in accord *with* nature. The deeper reason is that the condition in which we human beings find ourselves today is not our natural condition; even the feelings and desires with which we are born no longer function in the way that God intended. Had the Fall never taken place, every inclination would be a natural inclination. But the Fall did take place. We rebelled; the iron ring of the mind pulled away from the divine magnet, and in consequence the iron ring of the inclinations fell free.

How, in our disordered state, can reason tell which inclinations are natural and which are not? Some of the Protestant Reformers later said that reason *cannot* tell because it has fallen just as far as the inclinations have. They rejected natural law and relied on the Bible alone. Although Thomas too accepts the authority of the Bible, that is not his answer. He recalls that even in this broken world, high-minded men of every civilization have concurred in what is right. Nor is it merely we who call them high-minded; their own civilizations named them so. Apparently the iron rings do retain some traces of their original magnetism, reminding them of the magnet and calling them back.

The philosophical term for this magnetism is *teleology*, derived from the Greek word *teleios* ("complete, whole"), which itself is derived from the Greek word *telos* ("completion, end, goal, purpose"). Why this term? Because in reflecting on our inclinations, we can still trace something of the purposes they were meant to serve.

In drawing the two sexes together, for instance, sexual desire serves two purposes, one called *procreative* and the other *unitive*. Why not a third: pleasure? Has Thomas got something against having a good time? No, but he follows Aristotle in viewing pleasure as a result of our activities rather than the purpose for which we do them—as a crowning grace, not a goal. The problem is that pleasure can result from doing wrong as well as from doing right. Therefore pleasure cannot be used as a criterion for judging between good and bad inclinations; rather the purposes of the inclinations must be used to judge between good and bad pleasures.

Now the procreative purpose of physical union is to bring children into a secure family in which they can be taught and cared for by a mother and father who love them. Only a man and a woman can procreate a child, and we sever the institution of marriage from the natural purpose of procreation only at our peril. Perhaps that is too obvious to require further discussion. The unitive purpose, however, is not so obvious. What we mean by saying that physical union has a unitive purpose is that it can also further a deeper union between the husband and wife.

To understand the unitive purpose we must recognize that the sexes are not only different but complementary. God could have made just one self-sufficient sex. Instead he made two, each of which feels itself incomplete and longs for the other. The canyon between them is deep, but bridging it is well worth the patience and discipline it requires.

To be sure, there are other ways to use the sexual powers, ways that do not bridge the canyon. For instance, solitary sex sinks a person more deeply in the self; sodomy sinks him into a looking-glass idol of the self; and promiscuity merely uses the other for the purposes of the self. By contrast, marriage holds forth the prospect of altogether forgetting the self in care and sacrifice for the other.[8] We come to ourselves by losing ourselves. This extraordinary intimacy is among the profoundest of natural goods. Of course, Divine law goes even further, describing it as a foretaste of our supernatural good—that still deeper union to which we are invited with the wholly other, who is God—but that is another topic.

Notice how this reflection on the purposes of the sexual inclination has enabled us to distinguish between its natural and unnatural forms. That it can do so is Thomas's point. Of course, when he says that everybody knows the natural law, he does not mean that everybody knows the *theory;* he only means that everyone has some intimation of the *fact.* Hence high-minded men of every civilization have recognized that marriage is sacred, but it does not follow that they knew why.

From Article 3: "If then we speak of acts of virtue, considered as virtuous, thus all virtuous acts belong to the natural law. . . . But if we speak of virtuous acts, considered in themselves, i.e., in their proper

species, thus not all virtuous acts are prescribed by the natural law."
What Thomas means here is that although the natural law commands that I act according to courage, it does not necessarily tell me
whether dashing into this particular burning house would be courageous or merely rash. To know the difference I need practical wisdom,
and to achieve practical wisdom I need to learn not only from my own
experience but from the experience of others: "For many things are
done virtuously, to which nature does not incline at first; but which,
through the inquiry of reason, have been found by men to be conducive to well-living."

From Article 4: "The natural law, as to general principles, is the same
for all, both as to rectitude and as to knowledge." Rectitude is rightness,
so this means that the general precepts of natural law are *always* both
right for all and known to all.[9]

"But as to certain matters of detail . . . [the natural law] is the same
for all in the majority of cases . . . and yet in some few cases it may fail,
both as to rectitude . . . and as to knowledge." In this statement Thomas
is no longer speaking of the general but of the common precepts of
natural law. They are usually both right for all and known to all, but
there may be exceptions—in rightness, in knowledge or in both.[10] A
common precept fails to be right only when it meets an "obstacle,"
defined in Article 5 as a special cause that hinders observance: for
instance, the common precept "goods entrusted to another should be
restored to their owner" would meet an obstacle and so fail as to
rectitude, if the reason for which the owner of a gun demanded its
return was that he wished to commit murder.[11] But even when there is
no obstacle, the common precept may fail to be *known* whenever the
reason is perverted.

There are five ways in which such perversion can occur. Three are
stated here in Article 4: passion, evil habit and evil disposition of nature.
Two are added in Article 6: vicious custom and evil persuasion. The
following are illustrations:

☐ *Corruption of reason by passion:* Momentarily blinded by grief and
rage, I unjustly strike the bearer of the news that my wife is deep in
adultery with another man.

☐ *Corruption of reason by evil habit:* Little by little I get into the habit of
using pornography or cutting corners on my taxes. At first my con-

science bothers me, but eventually I can see nothing wrong with my behavior.

☐ *Corruption of reason by evil disposition of nature:* A defect in one of my chromosomes predisposes me to violence, abuse of alcohol or homosexual acts. Although I am still capable of restraint, it is more difficult for me than it might be for someone else.

☐ *Corruption of reason by vicious custom:* I have grown up among people who do not regard bribery as wrong, and so I take it for granted.

☐ *Corruption of reason by evil persuasion:* I use electronic tricks to make free long-distance telephone calls, justifying my behavior by the theory that I am merely exploiting the exploiters.[12]

From Article 5: "A change in the natural law may be understood in two ways. First, by way of addition. In this sense, nothing hinders the natural law from being changed: since many things for the benefit of human life have been added over and above the natural law, both by the Divine law and by human law." In speaking of Divine and human law as additions to the natural law, does Thomas mean that they become *part of* the natural law? No. The change is simply that the precepts of the natural law are no longer the only precepts that there are.

"Secondly, a change in the natural law may be understood by subtraction, so that what previously was according to the natural law, ceases to be so." In speaking of subtractions from the natural law, does Thomas mean that a precept can permanently drop out of the list? This is no more possible than it would be for the Ten Commandments to become the Nine Commandments. As Thomas explains, he is merely rephrasing the point he made in Article 4—that there may exist unusual cases to which some common principle does not apply because of "obstacles."

We see that the language of "addition" and "subtraction" is somewhat misleading. Actually, the set of natural-law precepts is fixed. However, precepts of Divine and human law may be added *alongside* them, and, in rare cases, the *application* of a common precept of natural law is blocked by an "obstacle."

From Article 6: "As to those general principles, the natural law, in the abstract, can nowise be blotted out from men's hearts. But it is blotted out in the case of a particular action, in so far as reason is hindered from applying the general principle to a particular point of practice, on account of concupiscence or some other passion. . . . But as to the other, i.e., the secondary precepts, the natural law can be blotted out from the human heart."

I take Thomas here to be referring not to all secondary precepts but only to the common ones.[13] What he says about them here is not new to us; we have already discussed the five ways in which knowledge of the common precepts can fail through perversion of the reason. However, Thomas is making a distinction in the passage, one that is both subtle and important. By the perversion of reason, a common precept can be *completely* blotted out of the heart—every now and then one comes across a person, or even a whole society, that does not know it at all. By contrast, the general precepts cannot be forgotten; they can be blotted out only in particular cases, in the special sense of being suppressed.

A few illustrations will make this distinction clear. According to Thomas, "Thou shalt not steal" is a common precept, for I can blot it completely out of my heart. Julius Caesar wrote that the ancient German raiding tribes had no idea that theft was even wrong.[14] By contrast, the rule against the deliberate taking of innocent human life is an immediate precept—a general precept that follows so quickly on the heels of the primary precepts that it can hardly be distinguished from them. I cannot blot it completely out of my heart. But I can rationalize, can't I? "Yes, but the bastard I killed wasn't innocent! He took the job that should have gone to me!" In the same way, I can rationalize that the slave or unborn child whose blood I shed was not human or not alive or that I didn't really have a choice. I find a way to tell myself, "Yes, murder is evil, but this isn't murder"; "Yes, murder is evil, but *this* murder isn't evil"; "Yes, this is murder and wrong, but I have to do it"; or "Yes, this is murder and wrong, but I'll make up for it later."

If someone loses the knowledge of a common precept or suppresses the meaning of a general precept, can he recover? Yes. One way to learn the natural law—or to learn to stop playing dumb about it—is to suffer the consequences of breaking it. Thomas describes law as a kind of discipline that compels through fear of punishment.[15] Although he offers this remark in the context of human law, it holds for natural law too: just as there are civil penalties for breaking the human law, so there are natural penalties for breaking the natural law. What are those penalties?

For breaking a general precept of the natural law, one penalty is guilt, because deep down we cannot help but know the truth. We may repress the guilt, but it is down there anyway, and the effort to hold it down distorts the personality. For breaking both general and common precepts, there are other penalties too. Some show up within the lifetime of the individual; others may not appear until several generations have persisted in the same kinds of wrongdoing. But sooner or later those penalties can no longer be ignored.

We find a good example of natural penalties in the consequences of breaking the precept confining sex to marriage. An immediate consequence of violation is injury to the procreative good: one might get pregnant but have no one to help raise the child. Another immediate consequence is injury to the unitive good: one misses the chance for that heightened personal intimacy which can only develop in a secure and exclusive relationship. Many are the long-term consequences of violation: poverty, because single women must provide for their children by themselves; adolescent violence, because male children grow up without a father's influence; venereal disease, because formerly rare infections spread rapidly through sexual contact; child abuse, because live-in boyfriends tend to resent their girlfriends' babies; and abortion, because children are increasingly regarded as a burden rather than a joy.

The longer people persist in violating the natural law, the heavier the penalties for violation. Eventually, even the dullest among us put the clues together and solve the puzzle. Unfortunately over the course of its history a culture may have to relearn the timeless truths many times over.

The Purposes of Human Law
Earthly rulers are on a leash. They cannot make deeds wrong simply by prohibiting them, nor can they make them right simply by calling them constitutional rights. The reason for this is that there is a higher law from which human law derives its authority and apart from which human law is nil.

One way to see this is to recall the four elements in the definition of law: law is an ordinance of practical reason, for the common good, made by those who have care of the community, and promulgated or made known. The first principles of practical reason are found in the natural law; therefore, to satisfy the first element in the definition human law must be derived from natural law. "If in any point it deflects from the law of nature, it is no longer a law, but a perversion of law."

We saw in the section entitled "The Grand Design" that there are two different ways in which human law can be "derived from," or based on, natural law. One is conclusion from premises, which we would call deduction. That is how we derive the rule that we should not murder from the rule that we should not deliberately harm. The other is determination of certain generalities, which we would call filling in the blanks. That is how we derive the rule that wrongdoers should be punished with prison terms from the rule that wrongdoers should be punished.

Human law derived from natural law in the first way is the same for every country. This unvarying body of human law is called the *law of nations.* By contrast, human law derived from natural law in the second way is different for every country, because the best way to fill in the blanks varies according to local circumstances. This varying body of human law is called the *civil law.* If civil law is filling in the blanks, then how should we fill them in? As the second element in the definition of law tells us, we should fill them in by considering the common good.

Here Thomas raises an interesting question: Does the fact that law must serve the common good mean that it must affect everybody in exactly the same way—that nobody should have any special privileges? In an age such as ours, which makes an idol of equality, most people answer "Of course!" But consider: if nobody may have any special privileges, then if grown-ups are allowed to buy liquor, children must also be allowed; if citizens may vote, so may aliens; if law-abiding people may live in freedom, so may convicted criminals. Obviously we do believe in *some* special privileges. But when are they right, and when are they wrong?

The principle is this: *Special privileges may be given to some, but only when doing so is to the good of all.* What this tells us is that the principle of the common good is deeper than the principle of equality; or perhaps it would be more accurate to say that equality of concern may sometimes require inequality of treatment. There is food in this for thought.

Like Aristotle, Thomas understands the common good as involving partnership in a good life; therefore, like Aristotle he believes that the purpose of the laws is to train the citizens in virtue—to make people good. However, he qualifies this statement in several important ways, which are found in Question 91, Article 4, and Question 96, Articles 2 and 3.

First qualification: All law makes people good, but not all law makes them good in the same way. Human law aims only at the *natural* good. Beyond this there is a supernatural good that cannot be attained by human effort; it can be attained only by the grace of God, through faith in Christ. Therefore, it is the concern of the church, not the government. To be sure, Thomas does say that human law should "foster" religion; but that means being friendly and cooperative toward it, not taking its place.[16]

Second qualification: Human law can be made only about those things that human beings can judge. But human beings can judge only outward acts, which can be seen; they cannot judge the interior movements of the heart, because they are hidden. Therefore, a person can be commanded by human law to do or forbear, to speak or be silent, but a person cannot be commanded by human law to feel or not feel, to believe or disbelieve. To put this another way, human law cannot punish folly, injustice or intemperance as such, but it can and should punish the foolish act of selling liquor to a six-year-old, the unjust act of taking a bribe and the intemperate act of having a drunken orgy in a public place.

Third qualification: For two reasons, human law should not attempt to forbid all evil deeds. The first reason, stated in Question 91, Article 4, is that "while aiming to do away with all evils, it would do away with many good things." For instance, attempting to suppress all greedy profiteering would also do away with many honest efforts to make a living. The second reason, stated in Question 96, Article 2, is that "laws imposed on men should also be in keeping with their condition," leading men to virtue gradually rather than all at once; imperfect men whose favorite vices have been forbidden will "break out into yet greater evils." Therefore human laws should forbid "only the more grievous vices, from which it is possible for the majority to abstain; and chiefly those that are to the hurt of others."[17] Note well: The fact that certain vices should not be suppressed does not mean that the public is not to consider them vices. Indeed people may still express concern about them in other ways, for instance by withholding their votes from immoral candidates. This is reasonable because of the Unity of the Virtues, discussed in the unit on Aristotle: any defect in one virtue brings with it defects in others. One cannot be a bad man and yet be a good senator, governor or president.

Fourth qualification: Human law should not command all acts of virtue any more than it should forbid all acts of vice. Thomas's reasoning here is the same as Aristotle's: there is no such thing as a virtue that cannot become a concern of law; on the other hand, for each virtue there are some acts that clearly pertain to the common good and others that do not, and law may command only the former. It may command a soldier to fight courageously, but it may not command a dilettante to resist musical fads courageously. It may command an airline pilot to be temperate in his consumption of alcohol, but it may not command a diner to be temperate in his consumption of roast beef. It may command a magistrate to be truthful in his public statements, but it may not command a teenager to be truthful in her diary.

Questions for Reflection
1. This chapter has mentioned four common objections to the idea of objective principles of right and wrong, a natural law. Because our age is in rebellion against the natural law, you have probably heard several others. What are they? How might Thomas reply to them?

2. Many psychologists claim that there exist people who literally have no conscience, who are utterly incapable of genuine remorse or concern for others. Terminology varies. Sometimes they are called *psychopaths*, sometimes *sociopaths* and sometimes *narcissistic personalities*. Would the existence of such people disprove Thomas's theory? Why or why not? (Hint: Don't forget the differences between primary, immediate and common precepts.)

3. Thomas's warning that law should prohibit "only the more grievous vices" lest imperfect men "break out into yet greater evils" conjures up Hollywood images of Prohibition-era gangsters. According to former U.S. Health and Welfare Secretary Joseph Califano, the reality of

Prohibition was quite different:
Alcohol consumption dropped from 1.96 gallons per person in 1919 to 0.97 gallons per person in 1934, the first full year after Prohibition ended. During Prohibition, admission to mental health institutions for alcohol psychosis dropped 60 percent; arrests for drunk and disorderly conduct went down 50 percent; welfare agencies reported significant declines in cases due to alcohol-related family problems, and the death rate from impure alcohol did not rise. Nor did Prohibition generate a crime wave. Homicide increased at a higher rate between 1900 and 1910 than during Prohibition, and organized crime was well established in the cities before 1920.[18]

It seems then that Prohibition is *not* a good illustration of men "breaking out into yet greater evils." Can you come up with a better one? And does Prohibition illustrate any *other* things Thomas warned about?

SIX

HUMAN LAW & REGIME DESIGN

THIS CHAPTER DEALS WITH HARD QUESTIONS. SOME ARE ABOUT HUMAN law in itself; the others are about how to design a constitutional order in such a way that it upholds justice instead of perverting it. For many reasons these two groups of questions belong together. For instance, Thomas's reasoning concerning what to do about unjust laws is closely related to his reasoning concerning what to do about unjust governments.

Special Problems in Human Law
Four special problems in human law are what to do when the law is unjust, whether exceptions can be made to the law, whether law can be changed, and how law is related to custom.

What should one do when the law is unjust? Thomas has already made clear that unjust laws are not in the fullest sense laws at all but perversions of law. You may be thinking, *Well then, there's our answer to the question. If it isn't a law, we don't have to obey it.* Not so fast. Thomas points out that a law may be unjust in either of two ways, and each case should be handled differently. One way is that it is contrary to human good; the other is that it is contrary to divine good.

This terminology is a bit misleading. Thomas does not mean that the law may be harmful either to human beings or to God; what he means is that it may be harmful to human beings in either of two ways: it may undermine either their natural or their supernatural good— either their temporal or their eternal well-being. We will consider each of these cases in turn.

Case one: Laws that are unjust because they are contrary to our temporal well-being. This kind of injustice can arise in three ways: defect in their *end,* meaning that they do not promote the common good; defect in their *author,* meaning that they exceed the authority of the lawgiver; and defect in their *form,* meaning that they violate the norm of proportional equality discussed in the unit on Aristotle. To illustrate, a law imposing excessive and burdensome taxes is defective in its end, a law instructing parents how to space their children is defective in its author, and a law giving the best civil service jobs to the least qualified candidates is defective in its form. All three kinds of injustice, says Thomas, are acts of violence rather than laws.

How should one respond to such so-called laws? The rule is this: *You do not have to obey, except perhaps if disobedience would cause either scandal or disturbance.* Why is there any exception at all—even a "perhaps" exception? Thomas is pointing out that the fact that the law is bogus does not emancipate you from concern for the good of your fellow citizens. "Disturbance" is violence, disorder, danger or confusion. A "scandal" is a moral snare or pitfall. If your deed, even though otherwise innocent, gives rise to misunderstanding so that others are led into sin, you have caused scandal. Both of these factors must be weighed before disobeying.

Suppose the city council passed an ordinance cutting the speed limit in my neighborhood from thirty miles per hour to three to punish us for our votes in the last election. Clearly the law would be unjust. Yet if all my neighbors obeyed it, then by violating it I would probably endanger their lives. It could hardly be safe for one car to zip along at thirty miles per hour while all the others were creeping at three.

Case two: Laws that are unjust because they are contrary to our eternal well-being. This kind of injustice can arise in only one way: through contradiction of Divine law. Examples here might be an ancient decree requiring citizens to burn incense before the idol of Caesar or a modern decree forbidding citizens to speak of their faith in public. Any law commanding violation of any one of the Ten Commandments would also be an example, such as a law commanding murder, theft or dishonor to parents. Because nothing can possibly be more important than whether we set our faces toward God or away from him,[1] such cases are easy to deal with. The rule is this: *You MUST disobey. There are no exceptions.*

Modern practitioners of nonviolent civil disobedience are deeply in debt to Thomas Aquinas. Martin Luther King explicitly acknowledges his debt to Thomas in the *Letter from Birmingham Jail,* and even where King differs from Thomas he is building on his teacher's foundation. Consider King's insistence that those who disobey an unjust law should do so publicly, explain the reasons publicly and accept the legal consequences of their disobedience. Although these points are not insisted upon by Thomas, they clearly grow out of Thomas's concern that those who disobey an unjust law avoid leading onlookers into sin. King's precautions make clear to all that in disobeying a particular law the protesters are not acting out of contempt for legal justice but out of the desire to uphold it.

Can exceptions be made to the law? Thomas answers this question in the affirmative. The reason is interesting: Laws are made to fit the *majority* of cases but are expressed as *universal* rules. Under condition A, doing X may serve the common good only 99.9 percent of the time, yet the law must say "Under condition A, do X." What are we do about the other 0.1 percent? One might, of course, try to anticipate special circumstances and deal with them by tacking other conditions onto the law: "Under condition A, do X, except when conditions B, C, D or E are met, in which cases do V, W, Y or Z, respectively." But two objections may be made to this.

One objection is that this makes the law more and more complicated, and beyond a certain point nobody but the experts can understand it. A law that the people cannot understand is like a law that has never been promulgated, making it really no law at all. The other objection is that no lawgiver can anticipate *all* special circumstances anyway. Thus all one will really accomplish by tacking on extra conditions is to reduce the percentage of the time that the law misses its mark from 0.1 percent of the time to, say, 0.05 percent of the time.

Perhaps for these reasons Thomas gives us a different answer to the question of what do about that 0.1 percent. Consult the lawgivers, he says, and ask them to authorize an exception on the spot. His term for authorizing an exception is *dispensing from* the law. But what if an emergency arises so that there is no time for the lawgivers to be consulted? In such cases and in such cases only, ordinary citizens may dispense from the law themselves. For example, a gatekeeper may dispense from the law requiring the closing of the city gate at nightfall if he sees that the retreating army will be trapped outside and destroyed by the enemy.

The special branch of justice concerned with making exceptions to general rules for the sake of the common good is called *equity*. Thomas defines equity as the correction of that wherein the law, by reason of its universality, is deficient.

Can law be changed? Perhaps you are thinking that because human law is derived from unchanging natural law, Thomas should not allow changes in human law at all. However, don't forget that there are two different kinds of derivation. True, the law of nations cannot change because it is derived by conclusion from premises, just as geometrical theorems are derived from axioms. But civil law can change because it is derived by filling in the blanks, and there may be good reasons to change the way that we fill them in. Thomas mentions two such reasons.

Reason one: Our wisdom has become more perfect, so we see that the law we made before is less wise than we thought. For instance, the lawgivers of a certain commonwealth may at first think that the institution of "no-fault" procedures for divorce will reduce hardship among unhappily married women, but later see that they were mistaken.

Reason two: Conditions have changed, so, although the law we made was good formerly, it is not good now. For instance, a law letting people of a certain commonwealth choose their own magistrates by voting may once have been good because the people had moderation and a sense of responsibility, but now it is bad because they have become corrupt and sell their votes to scoundrels and criminals. (Do you notice the secondary point here—that the right form of government is one of the things that depends on circumstances?)

Just as vices come in pairs, so do errors. People who escape the error of thinking that human laws should never be changed at all sometimes think that they should be changed whenever we think of an improvement. "But, but, but—*shouldn't* they be, professor?" Not according to Thomas.

When I began my doctoral work, right turns on red were prohibited throughout my state, and few drivers dared violate the law. One year, to the general delight of the citizens, the legislature amended it; henceforth right turns on red would be permitted provided that the way was clear. Drivers immediately began to make use of their new liberty, usually with due caution but sometimes without. City police quite naturally feared an increase in accidents. However, the new law allowed them to make regulations of their own, prohibiting right turns on red at intersections they considered dangerous. Quickly they set up signs announcing "No Right Turn on Red" at nearly every intersection in town. This angered drivers, most of whom responded by making right turns on red wherever they pleased, whether they were prohibited or not. As the streets became more and more confusing, police recognized their blunder and took just a few of the "No Right Turn on Red" signs back down again. But rather than being mollified, drivers became angrier still. Many seemed to lose their respect for traffic regulations altogether, and some even began making *left* turns on red.

What had gone wrong here? The law had been changed too many times, unsettling people's expectations, weakening their respect for authority and undermining their habits of obedience. Thomas puts his finger on the problem: "To a certain extent, the mere change of law is of itself prejudicial to the common good; because custom avails much for the observance of laws." His conclusion? A human law may be changed, but only if the improvement in the law outweighs the harm done by change itself.

What is the relation between law and custom?[2] Notice that in discussing the question of whether human law can be changed, Thomas argues as though law and custom, though having effects on one another, are entirely different in kind. Now he makes the remarkable observation that they are really two different forms of the same thing. This is easiest to see in the case of *free communities,* or republics, where its implications are most striking.

His model of a free community is probably the ancient Roman republic, in which he sees two conditions as having been satisfied—one moral, one constitutional. The moral condition was that the common people had the moderation and sense of responsibility necessary to make their own laws. The constitutional condition was that through their Assemblies they had the legal power to do so[3]—and, along with this, the power to set aside laws made on their behalf by the Senate.

Now as we saw in its definition, law proceeds from the reason and will of the lawgiver, and in it he makes known what subserves the common good. But custom proceeds from the reason and will of the people he is to serve, and in it they too make known what subserves the common good. Likewise, whereas in law reason and will are announced, changed and expounded through speech, so in custom reason and will are announced, changed and expounded through repeated deeds: "For when a thing is done again and again, it seems to proceed from a deliberate judgment." Finally, because the people are free, custom not only resembles law but enters into dialogue with law; it "has the force of law, abolishes law, and is the interpreter of law." This may be taken as either a description or a defense of the relationship between law and custom. Thomas intends it in both senses.

To illustrate how custom has the force of law and interprets law, consider the Fourteenth Amendment to the Constitution of the United States. What it says is that "no State shall deprive any person of life, liberty, or property, without due process of law." But just what sorts of privileges come under "liberty," what sorts of personal enjoyments come under "property," and what sorts of legal processes are "due"? In a free community, the most obvious way to settle this question would be by appeal to custom and usage: to ask what meanings these words carried in common speech or in the common law. Even in our own community—where we seem more often to settle them by appeal to the arbitrary fertility of the judicial imagination—the dialogue of law and custom is sometimes recognized. For example, the Supreme Court says that community standards must be consulted in determining what counts as obscene.

To illustrate how custom abolishes law, consider the American jury system. In theory, the judge interprets the law and the jury interprets the facts, but what happens in practice is another story altogether. Jurors refuse to bring convictions under laws of which they disapprove, and policemen refuse to make arrests to enforce laws under which they know convictions are impossible. In such cases law is indeed set aside by custom. Naturally prosecutors consider that a miscarriage of justice. It *can* lead to miscarriage of justice, especially when the community is divided along lines of race or faction so that jurors consider the interests of their group rather than the common good. But is it wrong in itself? Many early Americans held the view that a jury that set aside a law which it considered unjust was merely exercising one of the prerogatives of a free people.

Against Thomas's high view of custom, an objection may be offered on grounds that customs are not always just. Of course they are not. That all customs subserve the common good is no more true than that all laws subserve the common good. Not many decades ago the United States was rife with Jim Crow laws—racist code and racist custom in mutual support of each other. But one must remember Thomas's definitions. A law is an ordinance of practical reason, for the common good, made by those who have care of the community, and promulgated or made known. It follows that unjust laws are not laws at all; rather they are acts of violence, perversions of law. Then shouldn't we say the same thing about unjust customs? Thomas's description of the relation between law and custom holds true whether customs are just or not. His defense of the relation applies only when they are just.

Regime Design

The following discussion is based not on the *Treatise on Law* but on the *Treatise on Kingship*. Beginners often wonder why we still read a work like this. After all, we don't have kings anymore, do we? Don't be too sure. As we will see later, Thomas's ideal monarchy is a mixed regime something like Aristotle's polity. The king is merely a chief magistrate who shares power with many other officials. He is not necessarily hereditary and may even be chosen by the people. But our own republic is also a mixed regime something like Aristotle's polity, and we too have a chief magistrate who shares power with many other officials. Clearly Thomas is speaking of *us!* But even if he were not, *On*

Kingship considers problems of enduring importance for any regime: corruption, dissension and how to keep rulers focused on the common good.

Regime design falls mostly in the domain of civil law, not the law of nations. It is derived from natural law primarily by filling in the blanks rather than by deduction, and great allowances must be made for differences in local circumstances. In what follows, Thomas is giving us his best prudential judgment for most times and places.

What is meant by the word "king." Without thinking much about it, most contemporary political scientists assume that the essence of politics is quarreling over "who gets what, when, and how"[4] and that the purpose of government is settling such quarrels. Thomas takes another view altogether. If the community is a partnership in a good life, then quarrels over "who gets what, when, and how" must mark the degeneration of politics rather than its essence. In turn, the purpose of government must be coordination, not conflict resolution.

"In all things which are ordered toward an end wherein this or that course may be adopted, some directive principle is needed through which the due end may be reached by the most direct route." Does man need a directive principle? Yes, because (1) he is an intelligent agent and therefore acts for an end, but (2) men clearly adopt different courses toward that end.

Could the natural reason of each man supply this directive principle? It could if man were intended to live alone, but not if he is a social and political animal. Where there are many men together, with each one looking after his own interest, the multitude would be broken up and scattered. A possible objection to Thomas's argument is that, as economists have shown, independent action can organize some things—such as production and exchange—far more efficiently than central coordination. However, even a self-organizing competitive market has need of a minimal directive principle, for someone must decide what kinds of things can be someone's property in the first place, and someone must also have authority to make and enforce rules against force and fraud.[5]

Is man a social and political animal? Yes, because (1) no man can procure all the necessities of life by his own unaided labor, and (2) no man can arrive at a knowledge of all things necessary for life by his own unaided reason. Further evidence is that (3) man communicates with his kind more completely, through language, than any other social animal.

What then can supply to society its directive principle? A single man ruling for the common good. He should consider the common good because (1) he rules over free men, not slaves, and (2) free men exist for their own sakes, not for the sake of another. Such a man is called a king.

Over what sort of society does he ideally rule? Over one which is "sufficient to itself to procure the necessities of life." Such a community is called "perfect." Is only one kind of society perfect? No; the city is self-sufficient, but the province is even more so because the cities within it can provide mutual security against enemies.

Does this mean that there is only one just form of government? No, there are three: (1) monarchy, (2) aristocracy and (3) polity. The corresponding unjust forms are (1) tyranny, (2) oligarchy and (3) democracy. But the fact that more than one form of government can be just raises the question to which we turn next: Which one is best?

Whether it is more expedient for a city or province to be ruled by one man or by many. Argument from the purpose of government: "Now the welfare and safety of a multitude formed into a society lies in its unity, which is called peace. . . . The chief concern of the ruler of a multitude, therefore, is to procure the unity of peace." But the rule of one man is more conducive to unity. We know this because (1) "what is itself one can more efficaciously bring about unity than several—just as the most efficacious cause of heat is that which is by its nature hot," and (2) "several persons could by no means preserve the stability of the community if they totally disagreed."

Argument from nature: Now "artificial things are an imitation of natural things and a work of art is better according as it attains a closer likeness to what is in nature." But every natural governance is governance by one. We know this by (1) the abstract principle that "every multitude is derived from unity," and (2) many examples.

Argument from experience: Provinces and cities which are ruled by many are "torn with dissensions and tossed above without peace," whereas those which are ruled by one king "enjoy peace, flourish in justice, and delight in prosperity." The goodness of monarchy raises the question of the goodness or badness of tyranny.

That the dominion of a tyrant is the worst. Argument from contraries: Judging by the criterion of the number who rule, tyranny is the contrary of monarchy, oligarchy the contrary of aristocracy and democracy the contrary of polity. We have already seen that monarchy is the best form of government. But "it is the contrary of the best that is worst." Therefore tyranny is the worst.

Argument from effectiveness: "Just as it is more useful for a force operating for a good to be more united, in order that it may work good more effectively, so a force operating for evil is more harmful when it is one than when it is divided." But the most united of the unjust governments is tyranny. Therefore tyranny is worst.

Argument from the number who benefit: The further a ruler departs from the common good, the more unjust his government will be. The fewer the number whose advantage is sought, the greater the departure from the common good. But the number whose advantage is sought is fewest under tyranny. Therefore tyranny is worst.

Argument from the order of divine providence: "If the government should turn away from justice, it is more expedient that it be a government by many, so that it may be weaker and the many may mutually hinder one another." This argument has the same form as the argument from effectiveness but is prompted by a different consideration: the order of divine providence, in which "good ensues from one perfect cause . . . while evil results from any partial defect."

Argument from resultant evils: Many evils come from tyrants, including (1) seizure of goods, (2) shedding of blood, (3) sowing of discords, (4) deliberate hindrance of virtue because of suspicion and (5) incidental discouragement of virtue because of fear. The evil of tyranny raises the next question Thomas considers: Why monarchy, its contrary, is hateful to so many people.

Why the royal dignity is rendered hateful to the subjects. (1) Recognition of risk: "Both the best and the worst government are latent in . . . the rule of one man," and people recognize this. (2) Suspicion of fraud: Tyranny is sometimes exercised "under the cloak of royal dignity." (3) Alienation: When men live under a king, they sometimes attend to the common good "as if it belonged to another," but when they are ruled by many, "each man attends to the common good as if it were his own."

The next two parts of Thomas's discussion can be read as a critique of
this popular attitude.

*That it is a lesser evil when a monarchy turns into tyranny than when an
aristocracy becomes corrupt.* Many readers are puzzled when they reach
this part of Thomas's discussion, for in it he seems to repudiate his
previous claim that tyranny is the worst form of government. Actually
he does no such thing; he continues to stress that a greater depth of
evil can be reached by tyranny than by any other form of government.

However, in this part of Thomas's discussion we are considering not
what *can* happen but what *usually* happens following the corruption of
particular regimes. Those tyrannies that succeed monarchies usually
do not reach their limit of depravity. Those oligarchies and democracies that succeed aristocracies and polities usually do reach theirs.
Polyarchy is group government—any form of government, whether
aristocracy, polity, oligarchy or democracy in which rule is by more than
one.

Argument from loss of unity: Polyarchy breeds dissension, which is
contrary to the principal social good—peace. "A tyrant, on the other
hand, does not destroy this good; rather he obstructs one or the other
individual interest of his subjects." However, this does not apply to
extreme tyrants, who, in their "rage against the whole community,"
inflict the five evils previously mentioned: "sow[ing] discords among
the people, foster[ing] any that have arisen, and forbid[ding] anything
which furthers society and co-operation among men."

Argument from probability of corruption: Polyarchy is more likely
to degenerate than monarchy, because (1) under polyarchy there are
more rulers, and (2) only one of them has to defect from the common
good for the evil of dissension to result. Moreover, even when a king
does turn away from the common good, "it does not immediately follow
that he also proceeds to the total oppression of his subjects."

Argument from path of corruption: When polyarchies *do* degenerate, they tend to go all the way to tyranny because dissensions often
culminate in the seizure of power by one. In fact, this is the most typical
way for tyrannies to arise.

It is ironic that the strongest reason the people find monarchy
disagreeable is fear that it may degenerate into tyranny. As we now see,
tyranny is more likely to arise from the degeneration of a polyarchy

than from the degeneration of a monarchy. But the possibility of tyranny raises the question of how it might be prevented or remedied. *How provision might be made that the king may not fall into tyranny.* Careful selection: The man who is chosen to be king should be of such virtue that he is unlikely to become a tyrant.

Constitutional precautions: The government should be arranged in such a way that (1) the king is less likely to defect from the common good and (2) he is less able to tyrannize if he does.

In *On Kingship* Thomas does not spell out, and may not have worked out, just what sort of arrangements might achieve these goals. By *Summa Theologica* I-II, Question 105, Article 1, he has reasoned his way to a *mixed* monarchy, which is in fact a kind of polity: "being partly kingdom, since there is one at the head of all; partly aristocracy, in so far as a number of persons are set in authority; partly democracy, i.e., government by the people, in so far as the rulers can be chosen from the people and the people have the right to choose their rulers."

Notice that such a government balances not only different social classes but also different *principles* that are all necessary for good government: in the king, unity; in the council of subordinate dignitaries, wisdom; in both of them together, virtue; and in the assembly of the people, consent, which is the privilege of liberty. Something like this was the goal not only of Roman thinkers such as Polybius and Cicero, but also of American thinkers such as Hamilton and Madison.

	Thomist Ideal	Roman Republic	American Republic
Monarchical element	King	Consuls	President
Aristocratic element	Subordinate dignitaries	Senate	Senate
Democratic element	Assemblies of the people	Assemblies of the people	House of Representatives

The way in which *Treatise on Law,* Question 105, uses the term *democracy* in this discussion may also be puzzling because it seems to present democracy as one of the good rather than the bad forms of government. That is precisely correct. *On Kingship* uses the term in the Aristotelian sense, which was discussed before and which is diagrammed as follows:

	Common good	Selfish interest
One	Monarchy	Tyranny
Few	Aristocracy	Oligarchy
Many	Polity, also called Timocracy	Democracy

But *Summa Theologica* I-II, Question 105, uses it in the Roman sense, which is better diagrammed as follows:

	Common good	Selfish interest
One	Monarchy	Tyranny
Few	Aristocracy	Oligarchy
Many	Democracy	Oligocracy, the rule of the mob
Mixed	Polity	——

Remedies: What should be done if the government degenerates into tyranny despite the precautions that Thomas recommends? There are several cases.

Mild tyranny: It is more expedient to tolerate than to oppose a mild tyranny, for evils are likely whether the revolt is successful or unsuccessful. If it is unsuccessful, it may provoke the tyrant to rage yet more. If it is successful, then (1) the people may be deprived of unity by the rise of factions, and (2) their leader may seize the tyranny for himself. In the latter case, the new tyranny is likely to be even harsher than the old because the new tyrant fears to suffer its fate.

Extreme tyranny—first opinion: Some propose tyrannicide, and it seems at first that there is biblical precedent in Aioth's slaying of the Moabite king Eglon. But this opinion must be rejected because (1) it is not in accord with apostolic teaching, (2) Aioth should be regarded as having slain a foe rather than assassinated a ruler and

(3) if assassination were regarded as an option, it would more often be exercised by wicked men to slay good kings than by good men to slay tyrants.

Extreme tyranny—Thomas's opinion: "It seems that to proceed against the cruelty of tyrants is an action to be undertaken, not through the private presumption of a few, but rather by public authority." Therefore those who have the authority to provide a king have also the authority to remove him. In some regimes this will be the whole body of the people; in others it will be a higher authority, for example, the emperor. Should no human aid be forthcoming, the people must turn to God; but "to deserve to secure this benefit from God, the people must desist from sin, for it is by divine permission that wicked men receive power to rule as a punishment for sin."

Notice how respect for the *principle* of legitimate authority unites Thomas's response to illegitimate reign in *On Kingship* and his response to unjust law in the *Treatise*.

Just as the last two parts provided a critique of the popular attitude toward monarchy, the following provides a critique of the tyrant's attitude toward it.

What advantages which are rendered to kings are lost by the tyrant. Ironically "the very temporary advantages for which tyrants abandon justice work to the greater profit of kings when they observe justice." Let's see how Thomas works out this insight.

(1) Friendship is supremely desirable. The most worthy of worldly things is friendship. (Compare Thomas's discussion of politics and friendship with Aristotle's.) (2) Tyrants too desire it. Not even the cruelest tyrant can fail to long for this pleasure. (3) Yet tyrants cannot obtain it. All friends are united by something they have in common. But when tyrants pursue their own interest instead of the common good, they have nothing in common with their subjects. (4) Kings can obtain it. Because good kings diligently love their subjects, they are in turn loved by many of them. (5) By obtaining it, kings obtain another good as well. "The government of good kings is stable, because their subjects do not refuse to expose themselves to any danger whatsoever on behalf of such kings." (6) But this good too is forfeited by tyrants. The basis of their rule is fear, not love. But fear is a weak support, because the more it is employed, (a) the more it provokes the subjects

to revolt and (b) the more desperate the rebels will be.

Questions for Reflection

1. Thomas says that if a law is not promulgated it is not really a law at all. But as this chapter has argued, a law that the people cannot understand is like a law that has never been promulgated. What might this fact suggest about the legitimacy of our own bureaucratic state—in which the Federal Register is tens of thousands of pages long and even the regulators are uncertain as to the meaning of the rules they enforce?

2. In his *Reflections on the Revolution in France,* Edmund Burke approves of those learned men who, "instead of exploding general prejudices, employ their sagacity to discover the latent wisdom which prevails in them. If they find what they seek, and they seldom fail, they think it more wise to continue the prejudice, with the reason involved, than to cast away the coat of prejudice and to leave nothing but the naked reason." He adds elsewhere in the book that the political arrangement of the English people "appears to me to be the result of profound reflection, or rather the happy effect of following nature, which is wisdom without reflection, or above it."[6] In these thoughts about custom, does Burke agree with Thomas, disagree with Thomas, or agree in part and disagree in part?

3. Thomas argues in *On Kingship* that the reason for having a king is that "in all things which are ordered toward an end wherein this or that course may be adopted, some directive principle is needed through which the due end may be reached by the most direct route." Does he mean that the government should run (or regulate) everything? Why or why not?

4. Many Americans believe that "representative democracy" is the only just form of government and ought to be "exported" to other lands. How would Thomas respond? (This question is *not* about whether democracy is superior to monarchy, for as explained earlier, Thomas would probably say that our government *is* a form of monarchy.)

UNIT III

JOHN LOCKE

SEVEN

THE STATE OF NATURE & THE SOCIAL CONTRACT

I HAVE IN FRONT OF ME A NINTH-GRADE CIVICS TEXTBOOK THAT WAS POP-
ular in the 1980s. Perhaps it will remind you of yours when you were
fourteen years of age. In one chapter the question is posed, "Why Is
Government Necessary?" By way of answer, the book tells the story of
an imaginary town called "Whiz Bang":

> Following the discovery of oil, the town came into being almost
> overnight. The great majority of the people were willing to obey the
> law, but because the town was so new, everybody was busy taking care
> of his own interests. . . . Criminals came to town. People were killed.
> When an oil driller and his family arrived, the children were sick
> with measles. Instead of keeping them at home, the parents permit-
> ted them to go wherever they pleased. Thus they exposed others to
> their germs. Since there was no public health officer, other people
> in the community had no way of protesting about the spread of the
> disease.

Conditions grew worse—until a committee of citizens called a mass meeting at which the people elected officers. The people agreed to help the officers in keeping law and order. Criminals who did not leave the city of their own accord were arrested and thrown in jail. Persons with contagious diseases were quarantined. Rules were made for the disposal of sewage and garbage. Through community organization, government came to Whiz Bang.[1]

There is a trickle-down effect in the history of ideas, according to which some of the obscure doctrines of one age are taken for granted in a later one. That certainly seems to have happened here. The story of Whiz Bang is nothing less than a watered-down version of *social contract* theory, just like that developed in the seventeenth century by various thinkers, including John Locke. Let's see if we can do better with Locke than the ninth-graders.

Introduction to John Locke

The basic steps in Locke's version of the theory are as follows:

□ To have a government is to have known, authorized, impartial judges over all, whose judgments can be "executed" or enforced.

□ In the beginning, however, there is no government. This is not just our original condition but our *natural* condition—our state of nature.

□ Having no government does not mean moral chaos because the state of nature has a law of nature to govern it.

□ But the fact that people recognize the law of nature does not mean that they always obey it, so it must be enforced.

□ Enforcement of the natural law means especially enforcement of natural *rights,* probably because individuals are responsible only to God in points of natural law that do not affect others.

□ Enforcement also entails imposing *punishments,* provided they do not exceed the natural-law limits of reparation and restraint—that is, provided that they do not go beyond what is necessary for compensation of damages and prevention of further wrongdoing.

□ But because there is no government, each person is himself an "executioner" or enforcer of the law of nature.

□ Now, even when a person knows the principles that ought to be enforced, he finds it difficult to apply them with coolness and impartiality when his own interests are concerned.

☐ For this reason, self-enforcement does not work very well; natural rights are persistently violated, and in punishment the limits of reparation and restraint are persistently transgressed.

☐ The remedy for this inconvenience is for all the people in a particular area to appoint certain persons to serve as impartial judges—to be a government.

☐ But this does not work unless the judges can enforce their judgments, and they cannot enforce their judgments unless people first agree to transfer their "executive," or enforcement, power to the community as a whole.

☐ The mutual promise or agreement that transfers the enforcement power to the community as a whole is called the social covenant, or social contract. Once this agreement is made, people are said to have left the state of nature and entered the state of civil society.

☐ Entering civil society is not the same thing as setting up a government. There is no going back on the agreement to enter civil society; however, the people can change their minds about the proper form of government.

These thirteen points are the reservoir from which the Whiz Bang story trickled down. But Locke takes the story much further, because he uses it as a foundation for an extended analysis of property, political obligation, despotism, tyranny and revolution. We will be covering these topics little by little in the following sections. For now we will concentrate on what he says about regime design.

How is the form of government to be decided? By the vote of the majority. Why? Because by agreeing *explicitly* to enter civil society, the people agreed *implicitly* to whatever was necessary to make it a going concern.[2] Majority rule is one of the necessary things, for if unanimity were required, no decision could be reached at all. Someone will always disagree.

If the form of government is chosen by the majority, does that mean all of the government's officers must also be chosen by the majority? No. For instance, the majority of the people may consent to have a hereditary king. However, they cannot consent to allowing the government to violate their natural rights. Therefore, no matter what the form of government, it cannot be given arbitrary power over the lives and fortunes of the people.

Once the form of government is chosen, does the role of the people end? No. The prohibition on the arbitrary exercise of power entails that every act of legislation require the fresh consent of the majority of the people. Consider for instance the decision to levy a tax. People have a natural right to dispose of their property as they see fit; but taxes take their property away. Therefore, the government may not tax them without their fresh consent, expressed either directly or through those whom they agree to regard as their representatives. No taxation without representation! Does that sound familiar?

Could the majority make a law which violates the law of nature? No. For instance, a poor majority could not simply seize the property of a rich minority. Because there is a natural right to keep property that has been justly acquired, redistributive taxation is not an act of compassion but an act of simple theft.

How might the majority be *prevented* from tyrannizing the minority? Although Locke does not discuss the problem, we can guess his preferred solution because he gives a particular form of government a privileged place whenever he resorts to examples. This form is precisely the one which emerged from the Glorious Revolution in his home country, England: a form in which legislative power is *shared* among the Crown, the Lords and the Commons. In the view of English writers of the day, the Settlement provided a mixed and balanced regime in the tradition of Aristotle, Polybius and Cicero. As we saw in the last unit, something of the same idea survives in the American scheme of checks and balances. It is through Locke and the other English writers that we get it.

Here is how the English system was supposed to work: Imagine a playground seesaw with a child at each end. The children have equal weight and ought to be in balance; however, each child is selfish and wants to keep the other stuck up in the air for his own amusement. Consequently each child bounces in his seat, scoots back to the very end of the board, puts rocks in his pockets to make himself heavier and employs other tricks to gain unfair advantage. To prevent this, a third child is also part of the game. His job is to stand on the fulcrum, leaning now one way, now the other to compensate for the pranks of the others and restore them to balance.

The seated children are the Lords and Commons; the child on the fulcrum is the Crown; and the game is dead serious. The theory is that justice can be maintained only where the two opposed social orders are approximately equal in political strength and balanced by a third, with all three armed with legislative checks. Although Locke never expresses this theory, he presupposes it.

Before Going Further: The Use and Abuse of Biography

The next section will present a few facts about Locke's life and times. To do so is to risk misunderstanding what biography is good for, so perhaps I had better explain. One of the commonest fallacies in teaching is to present a thinker's beliefs as though they were merely the product of his life and times—his region, race, era, sex, social class and supposed personality traits. C. S. Lewis called this "the Biographical Fallacy," and it is closely related to the *ad hominem* fallacy discussed in the appendix.

You've seen how it works: John Calhoun is supposed to have developed his theory of concurrent majorities *because* he was a Southerner; Thomas Aquinas is supposed to have believed in monarchy *because* he lived in medieval times; Frederick Douglass is supposed to have opposed slavery *because* he was black; Augustine is supposed to have taken fornication seriously *because* he had hang-ups about sex; and so on. I have even seen an argument that Martin Luther championed the doctrine of justification by faith *because* he was chronically constipated. The biographer, who was a Freudian, thought that the need for physical relief must have been expressed as a desire for spiritual relief, and the evidence—if you can call it that—was that Luther sometimes passed the time by praying when he was waiting for his bowels to move.

The problem with such "explanations" is that history is full of Southerners who did not believe in concurrent majorities, medieval folk who did not believe in monarchy, blacks who did not oppose slavery, sexually hung-up people who did not take fornication seriously and constipated people who did not believe in the doctrine of justification by faith. Biography *can* determine thought, but it doesn't necessarily. An unsound thinker goes where his motives and interests invite him; a sound thinker goes where the argument takes him. There is no way to know whether a thinker is sound or unsound until we look at the arguments he proposes. He is a sound thinker if his terms are clear, his premises true and his arguments logical; he is an unsound thinker if they are not. Do these points imply that biography has no use at all? No, three legitimate intellectual purposes remain.

Knowing premises by their fruits. Although biography has no bearing on whether the terms of an argument are clear or whether its reasoning is logical, it *may* sometimes have bearing on whether its premises are true. For instance, if a thinker posits the premise that wealth produces happiness, but we see that he is both wealthy and unhappy, we are entitled to reject the premise. The data of his life refutes it.

Explaining fallacies. Although the conclusions of valid arguments need no further explanation, the conclusions of invalid arguments do. To put this another way, although biography cannot tell us *whether* a thinker has reasoned poorly, it may sometimes tell us *why.* Of course even a good thinker can make a mistake; but if an argument is so obviously fallacious that the thinker himself should have been able to see what was wrong with it, then we may ask what it was that prevented him. His motives or interests are among the possibilities.

Getting the point. Finally biography may increase our appreciation of an argument that we already know to be valid by telling us why it needed to be made. The fact that Augustine once belonged to the sect of the Manichees but later did intellectual battle against them doesn't tell us which side was right. But if we already know on other grounds that the Manichees were wrong, the story of how he broke away may help us understand what was at stake, not only for him but also for us.

In argument, biography is properly used for these three purposes. When deployed for any other, it is abused.[3]

Locke's Target

What does the preceding discussion of the use and abuse of biography have to do with John Locke? Simply this: I am about to speak about his life and times, but in using biography I do not want to give inadvertent encouragement to its abuse. My reason falls under the third purpose—*getting the point.*

Thomas Aquinas recommended a mixed monarchy—really a kind of polity, a balance of monarchical, aristocratic and democratic elements. This is a far cry from absolute monarchy, and medieval monarchs were in no position to claim supremacy anyway because their power depended on the support of their barons. For reasons that do not concern us here, by Locke's century the political situation had changed, and some kings *did* think they might get away with a claim to supremacy.

Indeed, several of England's Stuart kings thought so, but their calculations turned out to be wrong. The absolutist policies of Charles I provoked a civil war, after which the monarchy was first abolished, then restored. Provoked again by his descendent James II, Parliament responded with the Glorious Revolution, in which James was deposed and William and Mary invited to reign in his place. The Revolution culminated in a Settlement in which Crown, Lords and Commons accepted the need to share power in the government of the realm. Although Locke wrote most of his *Two Treatises of Government* before the Revolution, the timing of its publication was probably intended to assist in the justification of the Settlement.

It is easier to grasp Locke's argument if one understands what he is arguing against. His main target is Sir Robert Filmer, a royalist whose own work, *Patriarcha: Or the Natural Power of Kings*, had been composed some decades earlier but published only in 1680. In the *First Treatise* Locke makes mincemeat of his enemy's theory of legitimate government, while in the *Second* he develops his own.

Filmer had maintained in *Patriarcha* that kings have absolute power by both natural and divine right. Their absolute power is *naturally* ordained, he said, in that human beings are born into absolute subjection to their fathers; in turn it is *divinely* ordained in that every king inherits the fatherhood of his people as an heir of Adam, whom God made the first father of the human race.

John Locke had no problem whatsoever with the story of Adam and Eve in Genesis; in fact he defends the Bible in another book, *A Vindication of the Reasonableness of Christianity*. What he objected to is the idea that the Bible somehow justifies Filmer's theory, which he considered not only wrong but a cowardly pretence for enslaving the English people. Thus he sets out to prove four things: (1) that Adam did not have absolute power over his children; (2) that even if he did, his heirs did not; (3) that even if they did, the lines of inheritance could not have been determined; and (4) that even if they could have, by now they have been lost beyond recovery.

In order to prove points 1 and 2, Locke has to show that human beings are naturally free and equal, and in order to do that he has to set Filmer straight about God, fatherhood and the law of nature. *That* is what earns Locke a place in the annals of political philosophy, because it affected so many other things from rights to revolution. As we will see later, the founders of our own republic were probably more profoundly influenced by Locke than by any other thinker.

The skeleton of the argument about God, fatherhood and the law of nature can be found in the *First Treatise,* Sections 53 and 86, and in the *Second Treatise,* Sections 4-6 and 54. Section by section, it unfolds something like this.

1. Remember that Filmer had argued that all human beings are born unfree—subject to absolute fatherly authority, of which royal power is a special case. Locke begins by admitting that fatherhood—provided it be fatherhood of the most ultimate kind—really does provide a moral foundation for absolute authority. If you can create someone, you may decide whether and how he is to live. However, only God himself can satisfy this condition. Earthly fathers cannot; they do not create, they only beget. Earthly kings certainly cannot. Therefore, neither earthly fathers nor earthly kings have absolute authority. But God does (*First Treatise,* Section 53).

2. If God has absolute authority, how are we to know what he expects of us? Our senses, reason and desire for self-preservation do not merely happen to exist; God put them in us as an exercise of his authority. He gave them to us to let us know how he intends us to live. It follows that we may use God's lesser creations in whatever ways our senses and reason show us to be useful to self-preservation[4] (*First Treatise,* Section 86).

3. May we also use *each other* for self-preservation? Does God ordain some human beings the natural superiors of others, as human beings are the natural superiors of animals? Had he so ordained, he would have made this clear to us by giving us different natures—by making different kinds of human beings, giving some kinds different capacities than others. That is how he made the ants and bees, with queens, drones and so forth (*Second Treatise,* Sections 4-6).

4. Well, *has* he made different kinds of human beings, giving some kinds

different capacities than others? Clearly we are not equal in all respects. We are of greater and lesser virtue, greater and lesser abilities and greater and lesser age. Some of us may also owe particular respect to certain others, which other people do not owe, because of our family relations with them, because of the benefits they have conferred on us or because of our alliances with them. Those are important differences, but we can see that none of them is of the sort we are talking about. Clearly God has *not* made fundamentally different kinds of us with fundamentally different kinds of capacities (*Second Treatise*, Section 54).

5. In the sense just explained, God has made us equal. And if we are equal, then we must be free: that is, God must intend us to serve only his purposes, not the purposes of one another. From this it follows that each of us is obligated to preserve not only himself but also, so far as possible, *every other human being*, and that therefore every human being has rights against all the others. Except to deal out justice to aggressors, no one may rightly take away or impair either the life or the means of living of another (Back to *Second Treatise*, Sections 4-6).

The preceding argument prompts several questions. First, you can see that Locke stakes his entire argument for natural law and natural rights on the existence of God. But how do we know that God exists? Locke answers in his other writings that we know him by his works. The universe shows magnificent order and design; however, design presupposes a Designer. Called the Argument from Design, this is but one of about twenty arguments philosophers have advanced for the existence of God.[5] In our own century many theorists of rights try to do without God, or at least (as one of my colleagues once proposed) to shove him offstage. For Locke, however, *no God* means *no rights*, because our dignity is founded solely on our being made by his hand. But if you accept God, you have to accept the whole package: not only rights but law too.

Another question is why Locke doesn't use the Bible to determine God's will, for we have seen that he does believe in it. He does use the Bible for historical examples, but that is not the same thing. The answer is that he is trying to make his arguments stronger by showing that you ought to accept them even if you *don't* believe that the Bible is the Word of God. This does not mean that he considers human reason all-sufficient. Like Thomas Aquinas, he believes that Divine law upholds, completes, perfects and transcends the natural law, pointing the way to salvation through Christ. It's just that he does not use Divine law in the *Two Treatises.*

A third question concerns the Lockean idea that we are not to use others as means to our ends. The philosopher Immanuel Kant said this too, and you can read in many books that this makes the two thinkers very close. Does it really? In my opinion, no. The difference between them is the *reason* they give for not using others as means to our ends. Locke says we are here to serve God's ends; Kant says each of us is an end in himself. Locke says we belong to Another; Kant says we belong to ourselves. In short, while Locke roots our dignity in God, Kant makes us out to be little gods. The two thinkers turn out to be as far apart as two thinkers can be, for they worship different deities.

A final thought. You may be tempted to skim through Locke's careful elaboration of the difference between paternal power and political power, thinking that once Filmer has been demolished it has no further use. Don't. Regarding the family and the state as the same kind of thing is one of the most enduring fallacies in the history of political thought. In the time of Aristotle it was made by the barbarians, who regarded a kingdom as merely a family writ large—with the subjects in the position of slaves. In the time of Locke it was made by the royalists, who also regarded a kingdom as merely a family writ large—but with the subjects in the position of children rather than slaves. In our own time it is made by radical feminists, who reverse the model by regarding a family as a kingdom writ small—the idea behind the phrase "sexual politics."

The fallacy is alluring. After all, the household and the state are both communities, and in both there is a kind of power. Doesn't that make the family political, or the polity familial? Like Aristotle before him, Locke answers in the negative. To be sure, the two thinkers disagree about some points. For instance, Aristotle calls both the family and the state natural. By this he means that both are necessary for human beings to develop as they ought. By contrast, Locke calls only the family natural. He agrees that the state is necessary but thinks it necessary for a lower reason: human beings could develop as they ought even if it didn't exist. (We will learn more about why Locke thinks the state is necessary later, but there is no need to take up the matter just now.)

The important point is that about the main differences between state and family, Aristotle and Locke were in complete agreement:

1. The family is a primary partnership; the state is a partnership of partnerships.[6]

2. Offices in the family correspond to complementarity between the sexes; offices in the state correspond to individual merit.

3. Parents have authority over children by nature; magistrates have authority over citizens by consent.[7]

These differences between political and domestic justice show why attempts to collapse state and family into a single category must fail. Royalists who speak of the fatherhood of the ruler and feminists who speak of sexual politics turn out to be making the same mistake.

Questions for Reflection

1. Was there ever really a time without government? Were there ever really social contracts? What difference would it make to Locke's theory if the answer were no? More about this later.

2. Many objections can be offered to the theory that justice can be maintained by a balance of forces—whether these forces are Crown, Lords and Commons or Executive, Legislative and Judiciary. For example, balanced government is complicated government, and the more complicated the government, the more difficult to know who to blame when something goes wrong. What other objections might be made? Have they merit? Why or why not?

3. No God, no rights. In Locke's view the reality of rights presupposes the reality of God. At what other points in Aristotle, Thomas and Locke have you seen an idea about God presupposing an idea about something else, or an idea about something else presupposing an idea about God?

4. What other differences are there between state and family? Begin with the following:

a. How is domestic friendship different from civic friendship?

b. Does anything in the family correspond to law in the state?

EIGHT

TWO VIEWS
OF NATURAL LAW

previous chapter, did you notice that Locke *deduced* a fundamental
principle of natural law? That is deeply significant because it shows how
Locke differs from Thomas Aquinas. Thomas never *deduced* the fundamental principles for three reasons: (1) they don't *need* to be deduced,
because they are the principles we can't not know; (2) they *can't* be
deduced, because they are what everything else is deduced from; (3)
from these points it follows that any principle that *can* be deduced is
not really fundamental.

Locke rejects point 1 because he does not believe in underived
knowledge; in his view God created the mind a blank slate. In turn he
rejects point 2 because he thinks that moral knowledge, like all knowledge, is learned from experience. I confess I do not see how the mind
could learn, if it didn't already know, that good is to be chosen and bad
avoided, or that nothing can both *be* and *not be* at the same time. Indeed
Locke's theory of knowledge has not worn very well.[1] But let that pass;

the point is that Thomas and Locke are different.

The differences between them should not be exaggerated. Thomas and Locke both adhere to the ancient tradition that philosophers call natural law. First, they agree that there is such a thing as natural law—moral principles that are both right for everybody and knowable to everybody by the ordinary exercise of human reason. Second, they agree about what these principles are—do not murder, do not steal, care for your neighbor and so forth. Finally, they agree that the authority of these principles is rooted ultimately in God.[2]

However, they disagree about certain other matters, and even though these matters are secondary, they are sufficiently important that we speak of the two thinkers as following different branches of the same tradition. Thomas follows classical natural law, whereas Locke follows modern. The most important differences are that they disagree about *how* the precepts of the natural law are known and that they disagree about *how* their authority is rooted in God.

Locke and the New Natural Law

The crisis in natural-law tradition was triggered by the Protestant Reformation. No development in the history of ideas is ever simple, and this one wasn't either. For instance, moderate Reformers, such as Philipp Melanchthon, saw no problem with natural law. Eventually, however, some other Reformers did—let us call them "rejectionists" because of their rejection of natural law—and eventually some of their ideas were accepted even by the moderates.

To explain the problem as the rejectionists saw it, we need first to remember natural law as Thomas saw it. Remember that Thomas viewed nature as a realm of purposes implanted into things by their Creator. Everything is *for* something, as the heart pumps blood for the purpose of physical life, the thumb opposes the fingers for the purpose of grasping, marriage unites man and woman for the purposes of procreation and spiritual union, and society unites citizens for the purpose of a secondary partnership in goodness. The purpose of human reason is to participate in the wisdom by which God made the universe, and one way human reason participates is to grasp the purposes that God has implanted in human nature itself. If this were impossible, natural law would be impossible.

The rejectionists' objection was that it *is* impossible. It might have been possible in Eden, but it isn't possible for us. The reason is the Fall. We are broken people living in a broken world. First, the desires and passions are now so corrupt that even a perfect human mind could no longer trace God's intentions within their disorder. Second, no human mind is perfect any longer anyway. Sin has twisted the faculty of reason at least as much as it has the passions. To be sure, the rejectionists did not deny that God had written his law on the tablets of the heart; this is affirmed in Scripture itself.[3] They merely insisted that rebellion has obscured his handwriting. Enough remains on the tablets to generate a vague consciousness of sin, but not enough remains either to guide or to motivate us.

This bleak interpretation of the Fall left the rejectionists only two plausible responses to natural law. One was to *reject* natural law and rely on Scripture alone, trusting the grace of God to hold the wayward mind steady in the effort to understand it. We see this response among some. of the Puritans—William Ames, for instance:

Object[ion]: But it may be objected that if the Moral [Law] were the same with the law of nature, it had no need to be promulgated either by voice or writing, for it would have been writ in the hearts of all men by nature.

A[nswer]: That to nature upright, *i.e.*, as it was in the state of innocency, there was no need of such a promulgation. But ever since the corruption of our nature, such is the blindness of our understanding and perverseness of our will and disorder of our affections, that there are only some relics of that law remaining in our hearts, like to some dim aged picture, and therefore by the voice and power of God it ought to be renewed as with a fresh pencil. Therefore is there nowhere found any true right practical reason, pure and complete in all parts, but in the written law of God (Psalm 119:66).[4]

The same position may have been taken by William Selden:

I cannot fancy to myself what the law of nature means, but the law of God. How should I know I ought not steal, I ought not to commit adultery, unless somebody had told me, or why are these things against nature? Surely, 'tis because I have been told so. 'Tis not because I think I ought not to do them, nor whether you think I ought not. If so, our minds might change. Whence comes the restraint? From a higher power. Nothing else can bind. I cannot bind myself, for I may untie myself again; nor an equal cannot bind me: we may untie one another. It must be a superior, even God Almighty. If two of us make a bargain, why should either of us stand to it? What need you care what you say, or what need I care what I say? Certainly because there is something above me, tells me *fides est servanda* [contracts are to be kept]. And if we after alter our minds and make a new bargain, there's *fides servanda* there too.[5]

The other response was not to reject but to *reinterpret* natural law, by using the wayward mind a different way. This second response is the origin of modern natural law. Its key is reasoning not backward to the order of creation but forward from the consequences of its ruin. Whereas classical natural lawyers drew attention to the pattern that was broken, the moderns drew attention to the brokenness of the pattern. Whereas classical natural lawyers asked, "What clues to the divine design have *survived* the corruption of human nature?" the moderns queried, "What follows from the bare fact that it *is* corrupt?"

Consider for instance the modern natural lawyer Thomas Hobbes. In his view fallen men are such seething caldrons of chaotic desire that left to themselves they endanger one another's very lives. But each can deduce the rules that all would have to follow if any were to enjoy security. These rules, these "theorems of prudence," turn out to be the precepts of natural law. Although they aren't really "laws" until enforced, that can be arranged; for the sake of sheer survival, people will agree to submit to an authority which is strong enough to enforce them.

Unfortunately, the rejectionists took the idea of the Fall to such an extreme that they shot their own theory in the foot. Here are the problems their theory could not solve. First, if the mind is so fallen that it cannot figure out what clues to the divine design have survived its own corruption, how can it figure out what follows from this corruption? Second, if the desires and passions are so fallen that no order can be detected in them at all, how can *anything* follow from their corruption? For instance, how can Hobbes treat the desire to stay alive as more fundamental than any other desire, such as the desire to die and get it over with?

Locke is a moderate modern; he takes the Fall seriously but not to such an extreme as the rejectionists. As to the first problem, he agrees that the fallen mind is flawed, but he does not think it is too flawed to figure out the obvious. Although it can be carried away by the boundless heats of passion, still, whatever can be learned from experience it can learn; it just has to want to. As to the second problem, he believes that some order *can* still be detected in the desires and passions. If you return to the argument presented in the previous section, you can see these assumptions at work.

Special Problems in Locke

Is politics natural? In calling anarchy our *natural* condition, our state of nature, Locke implicitly takes issue with Aristotle and Thomas.

1. They thought the *political* condition our natural condition. Locke agrees that human nature cannot come into its own except in society, but he rejects the idea that for human nature to come into its own, society must be political. Although prepolitical society is inconvenient, it has everything necessary for people to live truly human lives.

2. They thought government was necessary to coordinate diverse activities toward the common good. Locke agrees about the importance of the common good, but in anticipation of Adam Smith's "invisible hand" he sees far less need for coordination. Therefore he considers government primarily as a device for improving the security of natural rights.

This Lockean view of the purpose of government does reduce its dignity. On the other hand, it increases the dignity of those nongovernmental partnerships in good life that depend on government for their security—be they families, churches, neighborhoods, businesses, trade unions or what have you. To be sure, Aristotle and Thomas also value these nongovernmental partnerships in good life. However, they consider them incomplete in a way that Locke does not.

Is political community based only on contract? This is really just another way to ask the previous question. If human beings do need the political form of community to be themselves, then whether or not they use a social contract to get the political community started is not very important. For in that case political community is not like a business deal; it may come into existence for mere "convenience," but it exists for living well. Its essence is determined not by the fact that people made an agreement but by their natural need for the kind of relationship to which they agreed—a relationship in which the sole concern is the common rather than the private good. This is the view of Aristotle and Thomas. Locke rejects it; in his view people can care for the common good in all sorts of ways that are not political.

The disagreement among these thinkers about the social contract and the state of civil society is much like the contemporary disagreement about the marriage contract and the state of matrimony. According to the traditional view, the marriage contract is the agreement by which the parties *enter* the state of matrimony, but this state is a union which they did not invent and which transcends the contract by which it was entered. According to some modern people, by contrast, the marriage contract *defines* the state of matrimony; consequently there is nothing transcendent about it and the parties may arrange its terms to suit themselves. Lockean politics is like modernist matrimony; Aristotelian politics is like traditional matrimony.

Can natural rights ever be given up? First-time readers sometimes get a strange idea about Locke: that he thinks people give up their natural rights when they leave the state of nature. Nothing could be further from the truth. Certain other social contract theorists did believe that upon entrance into civil society, people gave up their natural rights and got civil rights in their place. Not Locke. According to him, natural rights come with being human; they *can't* be given up. The only way to lose them is by forfeiture—as a penalty for acting as though one were *not* human by violating the natural rights of others.

Then does Locke think that people give up nothing at all to enter civil society? No. What they give up is not their natural rights but the power to enforce them; this power is transferred into the hands of the community. Yet they give it up for the sole purpose of protecting their rights even better than before. Therefore, the protection of natural rights is the one and only purpose for which government comes into being.

This is not quite the same as saying that the protection of natural rights is the one and only purpose government may pursue. However, any purpose that *conflicted* with the protection of natural rights would be illegitimate. Very few of the purposes contemporary governments pursue qualify as legitimate by this test: for instance, income redistribution conflicts with the right of owners to their property, abortion conflicts with the right of unborn children to their lives, and compulsory "value-free" sex education conflicts with the right of parents to arrange the upbringing of their offspring. *But Lockean government can carry out capital punishment. Don't people have a natural right to life?* They do—but they forfeit this right when they intentionally threaten the lives of others. The only way government gets any power is by transfer from individuals, and individuals cannot transfer more power than they have in the first place. Therefore the only reason government may impose capital punishment to enforce the natural law is that individuals in the state of nature may impose capital punishment to enforce the natural law. Really then the fact that government can take away life is not a contradiction of Locke's insistence on the limitation of government but an expression of it.

You may think a government authorized to use capital punishment may do anything it pleases. That would be true if there were no law of nature, because in that case government could define wrongdoing in whatever way it found convenient—for instance, as opposition to its will. But there *is* a law of nature; therefore government is on a leash. It may not so much as set up a toll booth on the highway without your consent. The terrible thing is not a government authorized to use capital punishment but a government that denies the natural law.

But Locke even justifies slavery and despotism! How does that count as limited government? It doesn't, but that's not the point. Locke justifies despotic government (of which slavery is merely a special case) only over unjust aggressors whom one has been able to defeat. Through violating the rights of others, the aggressors have lost their own. Had the victors chosen to inflict the ultimate penalty, death, they could have done so without moral wrong; therefore, should they choose to take the risk of letting the aggressors live, there can be no wrong in the lesser punishment of reducing them to servitude.

Further, Locke stresses that despotic government may be exercised only over the actual perpetrators of wrong. Their children, who are blameless, retain not only their liberty but even their right to inherit their fathers' estates.

Thus despotism is one of the three legitimate kinds of "government": the parental government of parents over children, which arises by nature; the political government of magistrates over free subjects, which arises by voluntary agreement; and the despotic government of conquerors over captives in a just war, which arises by forfeiture of natural rights. Contrast despotism with tyranny. This is the exercise of power *beyond* right; it is what one suffers if the unjust aggressor wins.

Do natural rights justify selfishness? Writers who call Locke the philosopher of "possessive individualism" have not read him carefully. When he says that in the state of nature each man is an enforcer of the law of nature, he does not mean that individuals give no thought to their fellows; nor does he mean when he speaks of self-preservation that no other goal could be higher.

In the first place he teaches that a person is not to throw away his life *except* "where some nobler use than its bare preservation calls for it"—and that implies that life does have nobler uses than bare preservation.[6] In the second place he holds that by the Fundamental Law of Nature, we are obligated to preserve not only ourselves but also other human beings—giving preference, in cases of conflict, to the innocent.[7] Finally he agrees with the sixteenth-century Christian philosopher Richard Hooker that natural equality implies not only the duty of justice but also the duty of "charity"—or, as we would now say, love.[8]

So you and I and the others in the neighborhood might help the Widow Brown beat off the attack of thieving Old Man Wilkins if he tried to seize her horse for himself. In fact we ought to if we can. We would deny our common humanity with her in ignoring her cries for help just as surely as Old Man Wilkins denied it in taking her possession by force.

Do we have a natural right to disregard the natural law? Let's review for a moment. According to Locke, the condition befitting the nature of men is "a state of perfect freedom to order their actions and dispose of[9] their possessions and persons as they think fit, *within the bounds of the law of nature,* without asking leave or depending upon the will of any other man" (emphasis mine). Notice that freedom means not having to take orders from a master; it does *not* mean being able to do whatever I please.

To make the point crystal clear, Locke adds a few paragraphs later that "though this be a state of liberty, yet it is not a state of license," for "the state of nature has a law of nature to govern it." This law of nature is the moral law that is known by reason but has its authority from God. Almost the first thing we learn from it is that "men being all the workmanship of one omnipotent and infinitely wise Maker," no man, "unless it be to do justice to an offender," may "take away or impair the life, or what tends to the preservation of the life, the liberty, health, limb, or goods of another."

What these passages clearly show is that for Locke rights are something we deduce *from* the demands of morality. To many people today, however, rights are something to protect us *against* the demands of morality. A good example may be found in a case settled in 1994 by the Supreme Court of the state of Alaska. On religious grounds, landlord Thomas Swanner declined to rent apartments to several unmarried persons who intended to live in them with persons of the opposite sex. He did not want his property to be used for purposes of sexual sin. However, the rejected applicants filed petitions with the Anchorage Equal Rights Commission, demanding that he be compelled to rent to them anyway. What would Locke say about this?

So long as Mr. Swanner was acting within the bounds of the law of nature, he should not have had to ask leave or depend upon the will of any other man in disposing of his apartments as he thought fit. Was he then acting within the bounds of the law of nature? Yes, for Locke holds that the use of property is a natural right, that the practice of religion is a natural right,[10] and that licentious sexual intercourse is against the natural law. There cannot be a right to fornicate on other people's property, much less the property of those who object on religious grounds. Unfortunately for Mr. Swanner, the Anchorage Equal Rights Commission held in effect that there *is* a right to fornicate on other people's property, and, over the vigorous dissent of the chief justice, the state supreme court agreed.[11] The other justices seemed to view "rights" as shield against the moral law and a license to impose on others.

Locke—a libertarian, not a libertine—would abominate this view of rights. For him liberty is the freedom of a mature and intelligent agent to direct himself to the proper moral ends of a human being. Therefore natural rights without natural law is a contradiction in terms.

Was the social contract a real historical event? Locke thinks so. His historical evidence is provided in Chapter 8 of his *Two Treatises*—along with his critique of the competing theory, that government is an outgrowth of family. Then why don't we read of a state of nature in the history books? His answer is that record-keeping does not begin until long after the establishment of civil society. Before that, people did not have enough food, security or leisure to give thought to such things.

Not all theorists of social contract are "actual" contractarians like John Locke; some are "hypothetical" contractarians like Jean-Jacques Rousseau. This means that they regard the story of the social contract merely as a metaphor, model, parable or thought experiment rather than an actual event. In their view whether or not the story happened is unimportant. Its point is that if you want to understand political obligation, you should study contractual obligation; the relation among citizens is just like the relation among, say, business partners.

Locke's view is that a purely hypothetical contract is useless. Men are by nature free and equal. The only way that free and equal beings can acquire new duties—over and above the ones they already have because of natural law—is to agree to them. A *story* in which they agree to them is not enough, even if the people who tell the story are doctors of philosophy. If the social contract isn't real, political obligation isn't real either.

How can future generations be bound by a promise made by their ancestors? A standard objection to Lockean theory is that if the only way that free and equal beings can acquire new duties is to agree to them, then an actual social contract is just as useless as a hypothetical contract. It may have bound the long-ago people who made it, but it couldn't have bound their descendants.

Locke agrees that people cannot be bound by promises made by their ancestors. But why couldn't they *reenact* these promises—for instance, why couldn't each individual take an oath of allegiance when he reaches the age of meaningful consent? To the credit of the people of Locke's day, they took their promises seriously, and the renewing of loyalty by oath was a common feature of political life.

Even today we administer naturalization oaths to people who desire to become citizens. From Locke's point of view, we ought to administer them to everybody, for nobody is born a citizen. The very term *naturalization* is based on a false premise. Why? If some people have to be natural-*ized*, then the others must be citizens by nature—for instance, by inheritance from their parents. But that's Filmer's theory, not Locke's. From Locke's point of view, political obligation is based not on nature but on consent.

How can resident aliens be obligated to obey the laws in a country which is not their own? Locke regards every adult who has not explicitly consented to the obligations of citizenship in a particular civil society as a resident alien. In our own civil society, for instance, he would include a businessman of Canadian citizenship living in California to manage the U.S. branch of his business as well as a housewife born of American parents in Wisconsin who is old enough to take an oath of citizenship but has never done so. Neither of these people has given explicit consent. If political obligation is founded on consent, how can they be obligated to obey U.S. law? Locke's answer is that although they have not consented explicitly, they have consented tacitly. How do we know this? Because just by living here they are enjoying the benefits of civil society—protection against violence, enforcement of contracts and so forth. So what? So this: by accepting a benefit, a person tacitly consents to the authority that makes these benefits possible.

Because the preceding idea links benefit with obligation, let's call it the *Linkage Principle.* Is it true? Let's consider some examples:

1. After coughing up blood one day, you are taken to the emergency room. Though you never signed a contract, two weeks later you receive a bill for your treatment.

2. You take a job at a company where wages, benefits and grievance procedures are hammered out by collective bargaining between union and management. Though you haven't joined, union dues are automatically deducted from your pay.

3. Several children have been injured playing in an abandoned quarry, so the neighborhood association hires a handyman to surround it with a fence. Though you are not a member of the association and have not been consulted, you are expected to pitch in because you have children.

4. Six weeks later the neighborhood association hires a sound truck to drive through the neighborhood every night at sunset playing elevator music, which you detest. Again you are expected to pitch in.[12]

Judgment is hard to render because the case for applying the Linkage Principle seems strong in example one, weak in example four and debatable in examples two and three. Still, Locke is on fairly solid

ground so long as we agree that making resident aliens obey the laws
is more like example one than like the other three.

*If acceptance of benefits of civil society implies tacit consent to its authority,
doesn't that make every resident a citizen?* According to Locke, no. The
reason is that although both tacit and explicit consent give rise to
obligation, they don't give rise to the same degree of obligation.

In explicit consent you make an unconditional promise, in words,
to yield your personal enforcement power to the community as a whole.
It has to be unconditional because if you could opt out of civil society
at any moment, civil society would be indistinguishable from the state
of nature. Now, the only way to be released from a promise is by the
consent of the people to whom the promise was made—either directly
or through their representatives. Therefore, unless the community you
joined releases you, you are part of it for life.

In tacit consent you also make a promise. Here, though, the promise
is inferred from your action rather than understood from your words:
the only way we know that you have accepted authority is that you
accept the benefits that authority makes possible. But if consent is
inferred merely from your acceptance of benefits, it seems to end when
you stop accepting the benefits. Therefore tacit consent is *conditional,*
not unconditional. You don't have citizen privileges; on the other
hand, you may escape the authority of the community by leaving its
jurisdiction.

*If my promise to the community is unconditional, how can Locke justify
revolution?* Your promise was to the community, not to the government.
The government is merely the community's agent. If it violates its trust,
the people may dissolve it, just as you may fire your lawyer or tax
accountant. Even then the promise to the community itself is still
binding. That's why people who have dissolved the government cannot
go back to the state of nature. Instead they must form a new government as quickly as possible.

What is a just war? At several points in the *Two Treatises* Locke refers
to "just" war. What does he mean? We can make a good guess. The first
attempt to distinguish systematically between just and unjust wars was
made in the fifth century by St. Augustine. The problem was further
studied by Thomas Aquinas and others, and by Locke's time the theory
of just war was well developed. Exactly where in this tradition Locke

stakes his tent we don't know, because he does not discuss the topic at length. Following, though, are principles that all or almost all just-war thinkers would accept.[13]

First come seven criteria for *when* one may go to war *(jus ad bellum)*. When all seven are satisfied, war becomes permissible, but even then it is not mandatory. *Competent Authority:* War may be declared only by a government, not by private parties. *Just Cause:* War may be waged only to protect innocent life, to ensure that people can live decently and to secure natural rights. *Right Intention:* Not only must there *be* just cause to go to war, this just cause must be the *reason* for going to war. *Comparative Justice:* We do not require that one side be *wholly* in the right; that never happens. However, war should not be waged unless the evils to be fought on the other side are sufficiently greater than those on the other to justify killing. *Proportionality:* War should not be waged unless the goods that may be reasonably expected from taking up arms are greater than the evils.[14] *Probability of Success:* There must be a reasonable likelihood that the war will achieve its aims. *Last Resort:* War should not be waged unless all peaceful alternatives have been exhausted.

The next three criteria concern *how* war may be waged *(jus in bello)*. *Right Intention:* Because the aim of those who go to war should be the achievement of a just peace, they should avoid any acts or demands that would hinder ultimate reconciliation. *Proportionality:* No tactic may be employed unless the goods that may be reasonably expected from its employment are greater than the evils. *Discrimination:* Directly intended attacks on noncombatants and nonmilitary targets are impermissible.

These ten principles may be used as a benchmark for all thinking on just war, including Locke's. They were most recently debated in the United States during the War in the Gulf, which is, incidentally, the first war in American history in which military and political leaders explicitly committed themselves to following the principles of just war.

Questions for Reflection

1. How are the *political* implications of saying "Man is a good being gone bad" (the Christian view, which Locke shares) different from the *political* implications of saying "Man is good," "Man is bad," or "Man is

a mixture of good and bad"?

2. According to Locke, although people can dissolve a government in order to establish a new one, they can never go back to the state of nature because the promise each person made to transfer the executive power of the law of nature to the community is still binding. Can you think of any way in which the promise could be canceled?

3. If the main purpose of government, and the one for which it comes into being, is the protection of natural rights, then government is primarily an instrument of *justice*, not an instrument of *compassion* as in some contemporary thought. Yet Locke does believe in the Christian virtue and duty of compassion. If *not* primarily through the state, then how *is* compassion to be exercised?

4. Locke said that the natural law *can* be known by everybody, although one must take the trouble to think about it; Thomas said that the natural law *is* known by everybody, although its secondary precepts can be blotted out of the heart. Would this difference in theory make any difference in practice? Why or why not?

5. According to Locke, only actual promises establish duties; if there never really was a social contract, then political obligation isn't real either. Hypothetical contractarians sometimes reply that we *ought to* act as we *would have* promised to act if we had ever been in a state of nature. Is this a good reply? Why or why not? Can you think of any other area of life in which what you *would have* promised determines what you *ought to* do?

6. This chapter has given four examples of situations in which we might consider applying the Linkage Principle, concluding that Locke's argument about tacit consent is on fairly solid ground so long as we agree that making resident aliens obey the laws is more like example one than like the other three. But *is* it more like example one than like the other three? What do you think? Why?

7. For history buffs: Pick a war and carefully measure it against both the seven just war principles for *whether* war may be waged and the three just war principles for *how* war may be waged. It does not have to be an American war, and it does not have to be a war in which leaders expressed commitment to the principles. Just make sure of your facts.

8. According to Locke, slavery can be justified *only* over people who have forfeited their rights by unjust aggression against others: Think

of murderers serving life terms who are forced to work on road gangs. Was this condition satisfied by the slavery of the Old South?

9. In suggesting that aggressors forfeit all their natural rights, does Locke really mean that we may treat them however we please? Is such an idea reconcilable with the biblical teaching that human beings are made in the image of God?

NINE

PRIVATE PROPERTY & REVOLUTION

JOHN LOCKE DISAGREES WITH THOMAS AQUINAS CONCERNING WHAT TO DO when the government becomes tyrannical. Before we can understand his theory of revolution, however, we have to know more about his theory of rights, in particular the right to acquire and make use of property. It may seem strange that he speaks so much more about this right than about all the others. Perhaps he views it as a sort of model for the other rights. Perhaps he thinks it is more often misunderstood. Perhaps he thinks that if property rights are precarious, then so are all the others. One thing, at least, is clear: Locke views the security of property as crucial to a decent political order.

Property

Locke observes that God has given the earth to man for his use and enjoyment. However, he seems to have given it to all mankind in common, for no one is born owning this piece or that. These two facts produce a paradox, because in order to use and enjoy something I have to withdraw it from the common stock; the apple that I eat is no longer there for everyone else. How then can anything be removed from the common stock—how can it become private property?

One possible answer is voluntary agreement. But how many people would have to agree? *Any* number of men can agree to establish a civil society among themselves, Locke explains, because "it injures not the freedom of the rest; they are left as they were in the state of nature." By contrast, if the earth is owned by the whole human race at once, then the *whole human race* must consent to any removal. But universal consent could never be achieved. A few political theorists have drawn from this fact the conclusion that property must be theft. Such a conclusion is unreasonable, because by the same token using anything in nature at all would be theft, and the only way to avoid using anything at all would be for everyone to starve. Besides, Locke has already said that the earth has been given to us for our use and enjoyment. Therefore the answer to the question "How can anything be removed from the common stock?" cannot be voluntary agreement.

Locke proposes a different answer. The earth, by God's gift, may originally belong to everyone in common, but my labor, under God, is my own. Therefore by *mixing* my labor with something—picking an apple, tilling a field, taking an ax to a tree—I acquire a personal claim to it. True, the rest of the human race has a claim in it as well. But that claim is negligible compared to mine because nearly 100 percent of the value of anything comes from labor. God has given the world to us for our *use and enjoyment*. How useful is the apple before I pick it? How useful is the field before I till it or the tree before I've chopped it down? Not very. Because the bulk of their value comes from my labor, the picked apple, the tilled field and the chopped-down tree are no longer *ours* but *mine* by natural right. They are like joint-stock companies that I get to run because I own almost all the shares.[1]

This idea makes a strong appeal to intuition but is easily misunderstood. Suppose I like the new car my neighbor has just brought home. If I mix my labor with it by washing and waxing it, that makes it mine, right? Wrong. My neighbor's car is *already* private property; it isn't in the common stock. Then how about the city park? That's not private. So if I cut down all the trees and chop up all their wood, *they* become mine, right? Wrong again. The city park is common, but by consent, not by nature. We've all agreed *not* to appropriate the things within it for ourselves. When then can I appropriate things by mixing my labor with them? Only when they belong to the original common stock of nature.

You might think that if people can appropriate whatever they want from nature, then those who get there first will divide the whole earth into private lots. But that isn't necessarily true either, says Locke, because the law of nature sets certain limits on the accumulation of private property.

First natural limit: labor. Obviously, if appropriation takes place by labor, I cannot appropriate more than I can work for.

Second natural limit: enjoyment. I cannot appropriate more than I can use, because in that case the value added by my labor is canceled out, and the property interest of the rest of the human race kicks back in. Therefore anything I waste or allow to spoil can be taken back by others. Depriving them of what they might have used themselves is not merely inefficient but morally wrong.

Third natural limit: leavings. In fairness I must leave enough in the common stock that those who come later can appropriate as much, and as good, as I have. The only possible exception would be if those who came later consented, for some reason, to the unequal division of the earth.

In the early days of the human race, only the first two limits were important. At first each man produced everything he needed himself, barely surviving. Then people discovered the advantages of barter and division of labor, in which one man farms, another hunts, and they trade—say, corn for hides. Even so, the natural limits of labor and enjoyment kicked in so quickly that people did not even come close to reaching the natural limit of leavings. As hard as they worked and as carefully as they stored their produce, they could only accumulate so much; there was always plenty left in nature for others, and just as good.

Barter is terribly inconvenient. Suppose you have some corn to trade, and you need hides. Five miles north in the settlement lives a Mr. Smith who is usually willing to trade for corn, but he offers only molasses. Another two miles beyond the settlement Mr. Whitfield has hides, but he's not willing to trade for corn; he'll take only tin. Three miles from your farm in the other direction is Mr. Black. He does not want corn, and he does not have hides, but he is willing to trade cheese for molasses. Finally, another two miles beyond Mr. Black is Mr. Stone-house. He has a little mine and is willing to trade tin for cheese. So in order to get what you want with what you've got, you have to visit the settlement to trade corn for molasses with Smith, turn around and walk eight miles to trade molasses for cheese with Black, carry the cheese another two miles to trade it for tin with Stonehouse, then turn around again and walk twelve miles to trade the tin for hides with Whitfield.

One way to lessen the inconvenience of barter is to hold a regular market day in the settlement. But that has drawbacks too. In our example, if even a single person fails to show up on market day you cannot complete your chain of transactions to get what you need. To keep that from happening, everybody can keep a little bit of everything on hand just to be ready to trade. But that solution has drawbacks as well. In the first place the corn, molasses, cheese and other tradestuffs take up space in storage sheds that people need for other things. Besides, keeping all sorts of tradestuffs increases spoilage, because you never know how much time will pass before someone wants what you've got.

You can see then that people will be selective. They will prefer to keep as few tradestuffs on hand as they can. Moreover they will converge on the *same* few tradestuffs because they will prefer the kinds that are compact and divisible and that do not spoil. A day will probably come when everybody keeps some of a particular tradestuff on hand just for trade—say, tin—and everybody is willing to take that tradestuff in exchange for what he has to offer because he knows the others will too. By tacit consent, without any meetings or hullabaloo, our barter economy has just graduated to a money economy, with tin in the role of money.

The invention of money has enormous advantages. Trade now takes up far less time and requires far less storage space. All that time and storage space can be put to productive use so that everyone is more prosperous than before. But the invention of money has another consequence: it circumvents two of the three natural limits on the accumulation of private property. It does not abolish them; it merely offers a way around them.

First, the invention of money offers a way around the enjoyment limit. You can eat only so many apples before they spoil. Now, though, you can trade your excess apples for tin, which can be stockpiled without limit because it does not spoil at all. Second, the invention of money offers a way around the labor limit. You can labor on only so many acres of apple trees. Now, though, you can use some of the stockpiled tin to pay others to labor for you.

Before long estates become so large that we exceed the third natural limit on the accumulation of private property: leavings. Those who get there first divide the whole earth into private plots after all, and there is no longer as much, and as good, left in the common stock for those who come later. At first it looks as though we are going to have to carry out land reform, dividing the estates of the rich so that the poor can have land too. But not so fast, says Locke. We said earlier that the third natural limit could be exceeded without wrong provided that those who come later *consented* to the unequal division of the earth. And haven't they done just that? For in the first place, the unequal division of the earth is an inevitable consequence of the use of money. In the second place, they consented to the use of money. Here is the formal argument:

Major premise: By consenting to doing something, I implicitly consent to the inevitable consequences of doing it.

Minor premise: But the unequal division of the earth is an inevitable consequence of using money.

Conclusion: Therefore, in consenting to the use of money, I implicitly consent to the unequal division of the earth.

The sentiment of equality is so strong today that when most first-time readers reach this point in Locke's argument they suspect a trick. There are four common objections.

Objection one: People *don't* consent to using money. They use it because they have to. *Reply:* In the first place, they do consent to using it. If people refused to accept tin or gold or federal reserve notes in exchange for goods, it would cease to be money at all. In the second place, some people *do* opt out of the money economy; after using money to buy a piece of land, they raise what they need for themselves and stop using money altogether. Survivalism is not impossible. It is merely backbreakingly inconvenient.

Objection two: Perhaps people do consent to using money, but surely they don't give *informed* consent. If long-ago people had known that an unequal division of the earth would result, they would not have gone along. *Reply:* Why wouldn't they? Even the poor are better off in a money economy than in a barter economy. If that were not the case, far more people would be survivalists. But that is the choice of only a tiny minority.

Objection three: All right, people do give informed consent to using money. But Locke doesn't have to *gloat* over the resulting inequality; it's still a raw deal for the poor. *Reply:* In the first place, it isn't a raw deal, because, as we said before, even the poor are better off in a money economy than under barter. In the second place, Locke doesn't gloat, for he is interested in what governments can do to make *all* better off, rich and poor alike.

For evidence see Section 42, where, after explaining that labor increases the value of all that is found in nature, he remarks,

> This shows how much numbers of men are to be preferred to largeness of dominions; and that the increase of lands and the right employing of them is the great art of government; and that prince who shall be so wise and godlike as by established laws of liberty to secure protection and encouragement to the honest industry of mankind, against the oppression of power and narrowness of party, will quickly be too hard for his neighbors.

In other words, even princes should be able to figure out that a small country in which everyone enjoys the fruits of honest labor and efficient cultivation is not only more just but also more prosperous and defensible than a large country in which the many are exploited by the few.

Objection four: Even if we concede that inequality in property is not necessarily unjust, aren't there great advantages to reducing it as much as we can? *Reply:* There may not be advantages in reducing inequality per se, but there are certainly advantages to bringing as many people as possible into the benefits of property ownership. A mixed and balanced regime of the sort favored by Aristotle and Thomas—and now Locke—depends for its stability on a large and prosperous middle class. The more people there are with at least a little property, the more people there are with a stake in order and justice; self-interest cooperates with moral restraint.

But how can the government foster widespread ownership of property without violating natural rights—without playing Robin Hood? Although Locke does not discuss any ways to do this, they are easy to figure out. Following are a few of the most obvious; some of them were anticipated in the reply to the last objection. All but the last are as pertinent to our own day as to Locke's.

☐ *Confiscate and redistribute wasted land.* No one has a right to what exceeds the natural limit of enjoyment; waste is an injury to the entire community.

☐ *Enforce justice in contracts for labor and for purchase.* People will never be able to acquire property if they are always being cheated.

☐ *Keep taxes low.* Nor will people be able to accumulate the fruits of their labor if they are burdened by confiscatory taxes.

☐ *Avoid those types of taxes which discourage saving.* Under Lockean principles the income tax is unjust in the first place. Even if it were not unjust, it would be stupid because it treats all income the same, whether it is saved or spent. How much more sensible to tax spending alone.

☐ *Avoid inflation.* Inflation penalizes the hard-working and thrifty by eating away at the value of their savings. Although it may also seem to help the poor by reducing the value of their debts, it robs those who lent to them in good faith and discourages them from lending again.

☐ *Abolish provisions of law which penalize voluntary generosity.* Another way in which the income tax, already unjust, becomes stupid is that it limits that portion of charitable contributions which can be deducted from taxable income.

☐ *Abolish provisions of law which hinder the voluntary division of property.* In Locke's day chief among these were *primogeniture,* which allowed only the oldest child to inherit the family estate, and *entails,* which limited inheritance to a particular and unchangeable line. The purpose of such feudal practices was to keep large estates intact generation after generation.

The trick is to find ways to include more and more people in the benefits of property ownership without taking away the rightful holdings of those who have already attained wealth by honest means. Let us call the policy of doing so *Lockean Equity.* Then the alternatives before us can be roughly illustrated in the following table. Don't take the numbers too seriously; in the real world they change over time and are used here only to show in which states one is better and worse off.

	Solitary Production	Barter Economy	Money Economy	Money Economy with Lockean Equity
Moneybags	2	9	50	200
Barefoot	1	3	10	40

Some of nature remains in the common stock	None of nature remains in the common stock

Inequality cannot reasonably arouse envy under either solitary production or barter, because if Barefoot wants more, he can get more; as much land as he could possibly work or enjoy remains in the common stock. When we graduate to a money economy the situation changes, because all of the earth is now taken. Barefoot could object because he has missed his chance to stake a claim. However, this would require him to withdraw his consent to the use of money, and he is no fool: despite the unequal division of the earth he is better off now than he was under barter. Some cause for envy may still be left if he is hindered from saving his earnings and eventually buying a plot of his own from Moneybags, but this objection can be eliminated by the implementation of Lockean Equity.

Revolution

We have seen that government is limited. But what happens if government exceeds its limits—if it exercises powers that go beyond the enforcement power that each individual had in the state of nature, if it disregards the natural law, if it violates natural rights instead of protecting them? In this case, says Locke, the power that the people gave to the government reverts back to them; they are free to dissolve the rebel government and establish a new one. Some of the ways that rulers may violate their trust are to take the legislative power into their own hands, to hinder the legislature from meeting, to change the composition of the legislature without the consent of the people and to neglect the administration of justice.

From one point of view this theory of what to do about tyranny may be considered a more radical version of Thomas's. For both philosophers the basic principle can be formulated "Those who may make may also unmake." But to apply the principle two questions must be answered. First, what is to be made and unmade? Thomas speaks of making and unmaking the king, but Locke speaks of making and unmaking the very form of government. Second, who *does* the making and unmaking? For Thomas the making and unmaking may be done by the people, the nobility or an external authority, depending on the constitutional traditions of the regime in question; for Locke constitutional traditions have nothing to do with it, for the making and unmaking may be done only by the people.

Tyrannical rulers, of course, are unlikely to take the attempt to dissolve their government lying down. Quarrels among the people are judged by the government, but if the quarrel lies between the government and the people because the judges themselves have become unjust, there is no further authority on earth to whom the people may appeal. In this case the people have no choice but to carry their appeal to the heavenly judge, God.

Here again we see how Locke has radicalized Thomas. In speaking of appeal to heaven, both thinkers mean that the outcome is to be trusted to God; but, whereas Thomas means the outcome of prayer, Locke means the outcome of revolution. Even so, the expression "appeal to heaven" is no euphemism. Locke devoutly believes that anyone who makes a revolution without weighty reasons will one day have to answer to the Almighty for it.

Locke's moral seriousness can be seen in the fact that he seems to have tried to adapt the principles of just war to the case of revolution:

☐ He believes that revolution may be initiated only by the majority of the people, not by a minority; furthermore he believes that the revolutionaries must not impose on the majority a form of government to which they do not agree. This seems to be an adaptation of the *jus ad bellum* principle of Competent Authority.

☐ He believes that before revolution may be initiated, the government must have exercised force contrary to right; furthermore, there must have been a long train of such actions, showing a settled plan of subverting the people's rights. This seems to be an adaptation of the *jus ad bellum* principle of Just Cause.

☐ He believes that all of the official channels of appeal must have been tried with no success. This seems to be an adaptation of the *jus ad bellum* principle of Last Resort.

☐ He believes that the aim of the revolutionaries must not be simply to dissolve the old government but to establish a new one. This seems to be an adaptation of the *jus ad bellum* principle of Right Intention.

Has anyone ever really cared about these *desiderata*? Absolutely. The American Revolution is the prime example, for the Declaration of Independence is a point-by-point application of Lockean criteria for revolution to the cause of the American colonies. In writing it Thomas Jefferson borrowed so extensively from the *Two Treatises* that he has been accused of plagiarism. The colonial pamphleteer Thomas Paine, on the other hand, seems to have thought that Locke was too strict, for he wrote years afterward in his *Dissertation on the First Principles of Government* that revolutionaries must sometimes act first and win the majority afterward.

Some historians do question whether most Americans were in favor of independence at the time of the break from England. Even if most were, the objection might be made that dissolving ties between the colonies and the motherland would require the consent of the majority of *all* British subjects, not just the consent of the majority of the colonists. Unfortunately Locke does not say enough in the *Two Treatises* for us to know how he would have answered the "Which majority?" question.

Questions for Reflection

1. Notice that Locke tells *how he knows* that there are natural rights, *how he knows* that they include life, liberty and property and *how he knows* what each of these means. How well or how poorly does contemporary rights-talk measure up to this standard?

2. Government X makes a law forbidding racial segregation in private lunchrooms. Government Y makes a law *requiring* racial segregation in private lunchrooms. Government Z makes a law requiring racial segregation in *public schools*. Under Lockean principles, how might the first two cases be similar, and how might they be different from the third?

3. As Locke explains in Chapter 11, Section 141, the redelegation of

a delegated power is a violation of trust. Just as a person to whom you have given your power of attorney cannot give it in turn to a third party, so the legislature, to whom the people have given their power to enforce the law of nature, cannot give it in turn to a third party. What would this imply about the legitimacy of the independent regulatory agencies set up by Congress, so numerous and powerful that they are now often called a "fourth branch of government"?

4. Locke's theory of property assumes that the earth, by God's gift, originally belongs to everyone in common, whereas my labor, under God, is my own. Why, aside from not believing it, *can't* he simply say that in the beginning nothing belonged to anybody?

5. After using money to buy a piece of land, survivalists raise what they need for themselves and stop using money altogether. What difference would it make to Locke if they could somehow have avoided *ever* using money? Why?

6. This chapter has shown that various Lockean criteria for revolution can be viewed as adaptations of the *jus ad bellum* principles now called Competent Authority, Just Cause, Last Resort and Right Intention. What other just war principles can Locke be viewed as adapting to the case of revolution?

7. Locke's expression "appeal to heaven" is an allusion to the biblical story of Jephthah's war against the Ammonites, which uses the same expression. Read the story in Judges 11:1-28, 32-33. Does it conform to his criteria for a just resort to arms?

UNIT IV

JOHN STUART MILL

TEN

THE PLEASURE PRINCIPLE

FAR AWAY ON THE OTHER SIDE OF THE WORLD IS A MARVELOUS LAND named Balnibarbi.[1] As you may have learned from *Gulliver's Travels,* its capital is the great city of Lagado, and in this place is an even greater Academy, filled with the most brilliant people in the world. Unfortunately, Mr. Gulliver was able to stay at Lagado Academy for only a short while, and there were many interesting things about the Academy that he did not have a chance to discover. Having recently taken the opportunity for a longer visit, I offer my findings to you.

Introduction to John Stuart Mill
The oldest and most honorable department in the entire Academy of Lagado is devoted to the study of color. Indeed, philosophy of color has been studied in Balnibarbi for something like twenty-four centuries. It was the Balnibarbian scholars, for instance, who first discovered that all the colors in the universe come from just three primaries—yellow, red and blue. The details are well known even in our part of the

world: orange is derived from red and yellow, green from blue and yellow, purple from blue and red, and so on. Of course the primary colors themselves are not derived from anything.

Unfortunately, over the last few hundred years the great tradition of Balnibarbian color philosophy has degenerated as wave upon wave of intellectual revolution has swept the Lagado Academy. Those few scholars who still believe in the doctrine of primary colors are now considered reactionary, retrograde, regressive—in a word, uncool. The three main parties of reform are the Monochromes, the Antichromes and the Neochromes.

The Monochromes object to the theory of primary colors because they do not think it goes far enough. In their view it's all well and good to say that orange comes from the primary colors red and yellow, purple from the primary colors red and blue, and so on—but what, they ask, is the *ultimate* basis of color? They reason that there must be an *even more* primary color than yellow, red or blue—a *fundamental* color from which even the primary colors are derived. For instance, some of the Monochromes think the color from which all colors come is chartreuse. Others think it puce. The latest Monochromes identify it as plaid.[2] Although these theories have disappointing consequences for interior decoration, they are bold and original, and to be bold and original is of course the goal of scholarship.

The Antichromes are the next party. Although they too reject the theory of primary colors, with their keener rods and cones they see right through the Monochromes. Chartreuse couldn't be the fundamental color, they observe, because all one can derive from it is various shades of greenish-yellow. Likewise puce couldn't be the fundamental color, because all one can derive from it is various shades of purplish-brown. Finally plaid couldn't be the fundamental color because it isn't a color at all.

The truth, say the Antichromes, is that there *is* no fundamental color from which even the primary colors can be derived. This is the crux. For if there is no fundamental color, then color has no ultimate basis; and if color has no ultimate basis, then color isn't real. This logic is so far beyond previous semblances of reason that it might almost be considered a new logic altogether. Its conclusions are equally breathtaking: Everything that we call a color is just a figment of our imagination, a projection of some desperate human desire onto a universe of cold and unvarying gray. For discovering the tragic truth, expressed in their motto, "Color is dead," the Antichromes are rightly praised as pioneers. They eat only burnt toast and milk and watch only black-and-white television.

Finally we come to the Neochromes, the most avant-garde party of all. They agree with the Antichromes that color has no ultimate basis; they agree that the universe is gray, the experiences of hue and tint existing only in our imaginations; they agree that we create the blue of the night and the blush of the rose in our own minds, rather than somehow discovering them in the order of things. But what, they ask, is so tragic about that? Is it not liberating? Smash the palettes! Pulverize the prisms! Away with the tyranny of yellow, red and blue! The creator of color is MAN!

Filled with revolutionary passion, the Neochromes, like the Monochromes, divide into factions. Some Neochromes say that every human being is entitled to his own primary colors. Other Neochromes object that permitting every human being his own primary colors would lead to difficulty with traffic signals and things of that sort; although every *country* is entitled to its own primary colors, they say, individuals must toe the line. Unfortunately no two Neochromes can ever agree upon the spectrum their country should use. In a sort of compromise, they usually wind up mixing all the colors together and painting everything a tepid shade of brown. Even so, they quarrel over whether to use sepia, beige or taupe.

We too have a great tradition. Just as the Balnibarbians learned long ago that all color in the universe is derived from just a few primary colors, so we learned long ago that all moral law in the universe is derived from just a few primary moral laws. Just as the primary colors are the same for everyone, so these moral laws are the same for everyone. Just as the primary colors are understood by all who hear of them, so these moral laws are recognized by all who hear of them. And just as the Balnibarbian philosophers have lost their ancient wisdom about color, so many of ours have lost their ancient wisdom about morality. The colorblind lead the colorblind. We touched on this parallel in chapter five, but now we'll explore it further.

In the first place, some of our thinkers treat moral law as the Monochromes treat color. They insist on some ultimate value which they rank as even more fundamental than the law of nature. But they are divided as to what that ultimate value is, some naming pleasure, some naming liberty, some naming another value such as privacy.[3] Despite all their disagreement, these thinkers have one thing in common: any moral law that cannot be traced to their ultimate value they simply ignore. In this way they manage to ignore quite a bit.

In the second place, some of our thinkers treat moral law as the Antichromes treat color. They insist that there is no real good and evil, no real right and wrong, and that the universe is merely an enormous screen onto which we project our desires and call them moral laws. According to Friedrich Nietzsche, the mentor of this dementia, God is dead, therefore everything is permitted.

Finally, some of our thinkers treat moral law as the Neochromes treat color. Just as the Neochromes think that human beings can create new primary colors, so these thinkers insist that human beings can create new and different moralities. Of course this is absurd. If someone claimed to have created new primary colors, you could be sure that he had merely made a new blend of the old ones, and the same is true for the primary principles of good and evil.

For instance, you can make up a new rule that taking the lives of infants is right instead of wrong. Nobody can stop you. But if you want to get pregnant young women to believe it, the only way to do it is to confuse them about the moral laws they already know—to tell them, for instance, that it isn't really killing but that it *is* somehow compassionate and prudent. Is it clear how this works? It is just like a painter who likes two primary colors, dislikes the third and, after a little mixing, claims to have invented a new one.

There still exist thinkers who are not Monochromes, Antichromes or Neochromes. I am one myself, a convert from the Antichromes—a point I emphasize because you have a right to know where the author stands. But the rise of these strange ideologies is the main story of nineteenth- and twentieth-century moral and political theory. To help you understand the story, the last few chapters before the intermezzo introduce you to just one of the characters—John Stuart Mill.

Here is the single most important thing to understand about John Stuart Mill: he is a Monochrome. The single primary moral "color" that he understands is pleasure. To make it look like an entire spectrum of colors, he distinguishes between many different kinds of pleasure—but always, and at every moment, pleasure is his sole concern.

The Arithmetic of Pleasure

What are some good things? Most people would be willing to nominate beauty, truth and God, their source. These things would be good even if there were no human beings to appreciate them, and they remain good whether human beings appreciate them or not. Because of their goodness a sane man desires them, but their goodness persists even if he turns his back—choosing not beauty, truth and God but ugliness, lies and self. My desire does not determine their goodness; their goodness determines the appropriateness of my desire. I may well desire things that aren't really good—but it isn't good for me to do so.

John Stuart Mill cannot speak this way. In his view feelings or sensations are the only things we can really be sure about;[4] therefore he does not know how to make sense of something good in itself. Instead he defines goodness strictly in terms of us. The good, in his view, is nothing but the desirable, and the desirable is nothing but what we actually desire.

What *do* we desire? According to Mill we ultimately desire only one thing. You may think you desire many things—love, skill, friendship, achievement, salvation—but according to Mill you're wrong. Everything we desire, he thinks, we desire either as *part* of our pleasure or as a *means* to our pleasure. Therefore the only thing we ultimately desire is pleasure itself. For instance, you may think you want to know the meaning of life, but what you really want is the pleasure of thinking that you do.

Superficially, this view may seem to be identical to the view of Aristotle and Thomas that the highest human good is happiness. Let's see if it really is.

1. Mill thinks happiness and pleasure are the same thing. Aristotle and Thomas sharply distinguish them.

2. Mill thinks happiness is a sensation—something we feel. Aristotle and Thomas understand it as an activity—something we do.

3. Mill thinks we don't need to consult the normative principles of human nature in order to understand happiness because there are none.[5] Aristotle and Thomas think we must consult them because there are.

4. Mill thinks we engage in reasoning either because we merely happen

to have acquired a pleasant taste for it or as a means to other pleasures. Aristotle and Thomas understand reasoning as something that pertains to the very essence of happiness, whatever the state of our tastes.

5. Mill thinks the only reason anyone ever does anything is to get pleasure. Aristotle and Thomas think this is a foolish way to act because some pleasures are bad. We should do things because they are worthwhile in themselves; pleasure is not the goal but the result.

6. Mill thinks that human reason is self-sufficient, so God has nothing to teach us about happiness. Thomas thinks that human reason is prone to error even about temporal happiness and knows nothing about eternal happiness but what God tells it.

Although Mill himself does not seem to recognize them, clearly these differences are profound. No one should be misled into thinking that just because these thinkers all speak of happiness they all mean the same thing.

Let's call Mill's claim that happiness is the same as pleasure the *Same-As Principle.* Then we can say that people who accept the Same-As Principle fall into two main groups. Some are *hedonists,* meaning that their fundamental principle of conduct is to maximize their *own* total of pleasure minus pain. Others are *utilitarians,* meaning that their fundamental principle of conduct is to maximize the *aggregate* total of pleasure minus pain—the grand total we get by throwing your sensations, my sensations and everyone else's sensations into one big pot.[6]

To understand the difference, suppose you and I have just pooled our money to buy a dish of ice cream. Just as we are about to share it, a hungry man approaches us and begs for food. We could ignore him and eat the ice cream ourselves, or we could give the ice cream to him. If I am a hedonist, I might weigh the pains and pleasures of each alternative like this:

	Give	Don't give
From eating	0	+4
From pity	0	-1
From disappointment	-3	0
TOTAL	-3	+3

Decision: DON'T GIVE

By contrast, if I am a utilitarian my calculations will include not only my pains and pleasures but also the pains and pleasures of the other two parties. Assuming that the beggar is hungrier than you or me, perhaps they will come out like this:

	Give	Don't give
You	-3	+3
Me	-3	+3
Beggar	+5	-5
TOTAL	-1	+1

Decision: DON'T GIVE

In both examples the decision turned out to be "Don't give"; with different sensations, it might just as easily have turned out "Give." Either way, moral decision reduces to an arithmetic of pleasure. However, whereas the hedonist is ultimately interested only in himself, the utilitarian claims to be interested in everybody.

Mill himself is a utilitarian. His reasoning is that if pleasure is the sole good for each individual, then the aggregate pleasure must be the sole good for the aggregate of individuals. Unfortunately this is merely a fallacy of composition—reasoning from the properties of parts to the properties of wholes. It's like saying that if each boy loves his mother, then the aggregate of boys must love the aggregate of mothers, or that if husbands are male and wives are female, then married couples are hermaphrodites. (Work it out.)[7]

The fact that Mill's proof is invalid does not by itself show that utilitarianism is false, because there might be some other argument for utilitarianism. However, the falsity of the doctrine is clearly shown by other problems, which are the subject of the next chapter.

Questions for Reflection

1. We saw in this chapter that according to Mill, the only thing we ultimately desire is pleasure itself; for instance, you may think you want to know the meaning of life, but what you really want is the pleasure of thinking that you do. Is this claim plausible? Once upon a time there was a man who wanted above all else to discover life's meaning. One

day a hypnotist said to him, "Join my cult, and you will forever lose your chance to discover it. However, I will use my powers to make you think you have discovered it already, and I can produce delusions to make you experience all other pleasures as well." What should the man have done?

2. In ethics, *rationalizing* is giving self-satisfying justifications for unethical behavior. An ordinary person rationalizes by playing with words: for example, "I know I shouldn't steal my neighbor's car, but I'm after the lawnmower."[8] A utilitarian rationalizes by playing with numbers: for example, "I know that you'd like some pie too, but since I want it so badly, more pleasure could be produced by giving it all to me." A university professor like me rationalizes by choosing a convenient philosophy: for example, "I know it has been said that adultery is wrong, but morals are relative to the individual." Is rationalizing just as easy for all three? For whom is it easiest? For whom is it hardest? Why?

3. Many nineteenth-century economists accepted a principle called the *diminishing marginal utility of wealth*. This principle means that the more wealth a person has, the less difference the gain or loss of a single dollar makes to his level of pleasure. Some observers of greed suggest the opposite principle, that the marginal utility of wealth *increases* rather than diminishes—that the more wealth a person has, the more wrapped up in it he is, so the *more* difference the gain or loss of a single dollar makes to his level of pleasure. Would a utilitarian who accepted the former principle recommend stealing from the rich to give to the poor, stealing from the poor to give to the rich, or leaving them both alone? How about a utilitarian who accepted the latter principle? (Hint: Given each principle, which person would have a greater change in pleasure from a given change in wealth?) Would these principles be *good* reasons to take from some and give to others? Why or why not?

4. Every Monochrome view of ethics has its own arithmetic or ranking system. For people who think everything can be reduced to individual pleasure, the ranking system is hedonistic calculation; for people who think everything can be reduced to aggregate pleasure, it is utilitarian calculation; for people who think everything can be reduced to dollars and cents, it is cost-benefit calculation. Have you come across any other Monochrome arithmetics or ranking systems? Describe them.

ELEVEN

THE PROBLEM WITH THE PLEASURE PRINCIPLE

IF MORALITY INVOLVES GETTING *BEYOND* MERE SELF-REGARD, THEN HE-donism is difficult to take seriously as a guide to moral decision. On the other hand, utilitarianism has numerous weaknesses of its own. To his credit Mill is aware of some of these weaknesses and tries to fix them. First we'll take a look at the blind spots of the "primitive," or unmodified, version of utilitarianism. Later in the chapter we will consider Mill's attempts at repair.

Blind Spots of Primitive Utilitarianism

First blind spot: The practical impossibility of utilitarian calculation. As our previous examples show, for every practical decision, however ordinary, a primitive utilitarian must do seven things: (1) Identify all the possible courses of action. (2) For each course of action, identify all the persons affected, however remote the effects on them may be. (3) For each person, identify every pain or pleasure likely to result from the course of action under consideration. (4) Assign each of these pains and pleasures a numerical value. (5) Calculate the net gain or loss for each person. (6) Sum up these gains and losses to arrive at a grand total for each course of action—its utility. (7) Carry out the course of action with the highest utility.

Consider step four alone. According to Jeremy Bentham, the founder of primitive utilitarianism, to rate even a single pleasure accurately *six* different factors must be taken into account: *intensity*—how strong it is in itself; *duration*—how long it will last; *certainty or uncertainty*—how likely it is to occur; *propinquity or remoteness*—how quickly it will occur; *fecundity*—to what degree it produces additional pleasures; *purity*—to what degree it is mixed with pain. To help his readers remember all six factors Bentham even composed some verses.

Intense, long, certain, speedy, fruitful, pure —
Such marks in *pleasures* and in *pains* endure.
Such pleasures seek if *private* be thy end:
If it be *public*, let them wide extend.
Such *pains* avoid, whichever be thy view;
If pains *must* come, let them *extend* to few.[1]

Yet the process of reckoning up the pains and pleasures of various courses of action is so complicated that in a later book Bentham devoted a number of paragraphs just to the investigation of whether and how to belch and pass gas![2] Is it reasonable to suppose that we can perform such elaborate feats of analysis and computation before making the simplest decisions? Or are we to hire utilitarians to calculate our choices as we hire accountants to calculate our taxes? Some people would say yes. "Ethicists," many of them utilitarian, now vie with lawyers as consultants to businesses, hospitals, and university and government bureaucracies.

Second blind spot: The incommensurability of different pleasures. Even if we do have the necessary computational abilities, can numbers be assigned to pleasures? Perhaps they can be assigned sometimes; I can tell you how much more pleasure of taste I get from a Snickers bar than from an Almond Joy. But surely they cannot be assigned always. I don't even know what is meant when I am asked whether the pleasure of tasting an Almond Joy is greater or less than the pleasure of finally getting my checkbook in balance. We can compare the latter two pleasures in quality, but we cannot compare them in quantity. If they can be measured at all, they must be measured on different scales, as temperature is measured in degrees and wind speed is measured in miles per hour.

Third blind spot: The distinctness of persons. It seems that the pleasures of different people cannot meaningfully be added together. Saying "Your pleasure is -3, mine is -3 and the beggar's is +5, so the pleasure of the aggregate is -1" makes about as much sense as saying "Iowa's temperature is 75°, Wisconsin's is 70° and Minnesota's is 68°, so the temperature of the tristate area is 213°." Society is not a megaperson; it is a collection of distinct persons. For the utilitarian, however, all persons seem to run together, like gingerbread men placed too close on the cookie sheet or lead soldiers melting down in the furnace.

Fourth blind spot: The moral irrelevance of aggregate pleasure. If we say that what we should do with people depends only on the quantity of aggregate pleasure that results from each alternative, then anything goes so long as the numbers come out right. To see this, consider a utilitarian sex offender. He has cornered a woman in a dark alley. Should he rape her or not? Here is how the moral decision looks to him:

	Rape	Don't rape
Rapist	+50	-50
Woman	-40	+10
TOTAL	+10	-40

Decision: RAPE

You may be thinking that I have doctored the numbers to make the rapist's pleasure greater than the woman's pain and the rapist's frustration greater than the woman's relief. There are several ways I might reply. For instance, the rapist, being a utilitarian, may have knocked the woman out to spare her some of the horror of the experience. Or she might be a mentally ill street person, incapable of fully understanding what is going on. Perhaps he ought to kill her first; then her distress wouldn't enter into the totals at all. If the numbers don't justify rape in this instance, perhaps they would in another. Invading armies have often employed rape as a means of subduing an enemy population through terror. If the cause is important enough, don't such means become legitimate?

If these answers make you angry, that is a good sign. But ask yourself: Do you really want to quibble with me over numbers? Aren't they irrelevant? Wouldn't rape be wrong no matter *how* they came out? Isn't it wrong to "do evil that good may result" (Romans 3:8)? This utilitarianism denies. Apart from results, it *has* no concept of good and evil.

Fifth blind spot: The specialness of being human. Several years ago at a political science conference I heard a scholar present a talk on ethics and ecology. One of his opinions was that all moral thinking before our time was unjustly biased in favor of either God or human beings; this was unjust, he said, because other living things deserved equal concern and respect. During the question period I posed him a problem: "I am driving in my automobile. A little girl darts into the road from the right, and at the same moment two dogs dart into the road from the left. Should I swerve to the right to miss the dogs and hit the girl? After all, they have equal rights, and there are two of them and only one of her." His reply: "I admit that there are some unresolved problems in ecocentric ethics."

One does not have to believe in cruelty to animals to see that there is something deeply wrong with his answer. Yet can the utilitarian answer differently? Remember that the only thing his arithmetic takes into account is pain and pleasure. But dogs, snakes and presumably cockroaches experience pain and pleasure too. From the utilitarian point of view, the fact that we treat human beings as somehow special is arbitrary and indefensible. Apparently I *ought* to hit the girl.

Mill's Attempts at Repair

As you learned earlier, Mill is not a primitive utilitarian but a souped-up utilitarian. He recognizes some of the blind spots of primitive utilitarianism and tries to fix them.

What does Mill do about the practical impossibility of utilitarian calculation? Mill does two things about this blind spot. One of them is intended to reduce the number of calculations, the other to reduce their scale and difficulty.

The change that is supposed to reduce the *number* of calculations is to shift their basis. Mill does not ask us to envision a person asking whether he should commit this act; rather he asks us to envision a person asking whether he should adopt such-and-such a rule concerning all such acts. Suppose, for instance, that over the course of my lifetime, twelve occasions arise in which I see some advantage to myself in killing someone. Primitive utilitarianism forces me to perform a new calculation each time: What is the net change in aggregate pleasure if I murder my father? What is the net change in aggregate pleasure if I murder my boss? What is the net change in aggregate pleasure if I murder my wife? What is the net change in aggregate pleasure if I murder my unborn child? And so forth. Rule-utilitarianism simplifies things because it allows me to reduce the number of calculations to one: What is the net change in aggregate pleasure if I adopt a rule that says I will not murder anyone at all?

The problem is that the change from an "act" to a "rule" basis for calculation may not actually reduce the number of calculations at all. In fact it may increase it. The reason is that the rules produced by utilitarian calculation are only rules of thumb—they tell what will *usually* increase aggregate utility, not what will *always* increase it. There may be exceptions, and one may have strong motives to investigate them.

For instance, even if she is assured that most murders reduce aggregate pleasure, a woman may wonder whether it would really reduce aggregate pleasure to kill her husband; he drinks too much, he philanders, and his habit of sucking his teeth is getting worse and worse. For a utilitarian, there is only one way to find out the answer: to perform the calculation. So even if she does perform the calculation for the rule, she may end up performing the other twelve calculations anyway. Instead of going from twelve calculations to one, she has gone from twelve calculations to thirteen.

The change that is supposed to reduce the *scale and difficulty* of utilitarian calculations is to accept long-established traditions as evidence of what produces happiness. After all (as Mill reasons in several works), people have been calculating utilities for centuries, so the rough outlines of inherited rules are pretty good and need only refinement, not overhaul or abolition.

In considering this proposal we need to distinguish two points as carefully as possible. One is whether there is something to be said for tradition; the other is whether a *utilitarian* can hold that there is something to be said for tradition. The former is not at issue here; the latter is. For two reasons Mill *cannot* consistently admit that there is anything to be said for tradition. In claiming that there is, he is being unfaithful to his own premises.

The first reason is that however many the centuries over which tradition has accumulated, it certainly hasn't accumulated through utilitarian calculation. On the contrary: utilitarianism is something new. Mill's answer to this objection is that although people throughout history have not been *conscious* utilitarians, they have been *unconscious* utilitarians; the only really new development is that at last our unconscious utilitarian assumptions have been brought out into the open. But this reply is weak because a utilitarianism which is merely unconscious is bound to make serious errors. There must then be many traditions which are altogether wrong—traditions which need to be not merely refined but overhauled or thrown away.

The second reason Mill's openness to tradition is inconsistent with his premises is that he does not believe in a fixed human nature. In his thinking we have no essence; whatever experience makes us, that we are. There may be instincts, but even if so, they are like a broad platform on which almost anything can be built. Whether this strange view is true or false is not the point just now. The point is that if it *were* true, what made people happy or unhappy centuries ago could not possibly tell us anything about what would make us happy or unhappy today, for their experiences and ours have been different. Therefore, ancient traditions would have to be thrown away *even if those ancient people had been conscious* utilitarians; in every generation utilitarianism would have to be redone from the ground up.

Mill seems to recognize this point himself. For instance, he looks forward to socialism because he thinks that the advance of civilization diminishes selfishness and increases fellow-feeling. But complete socialism would mean the complete abolition of such traditions as privacy and property. Abolishing traditions is not the same as refining them.

If some traditions do have to be thrown away, then nothing is gained by the fact that others, perhaps, do not. The only way to know which are which is to perform the utilitarian calculation all over again for each one. Thus we are back where we started; the burden of calculation is just as great as it was before.

What does Mill do about the incommensurability of different pleasures? Mill squarely admits that pleasures come in different kinds that cannot be measured in the same units. How then does he perform utilitarian calculation at all? In the same way that porcupines give hugs—very carefully. The arithmetic works all right, he thinks, so long as we are speaking of only one kind of pleasure at a time. For instance, we can subtract a sensual pain from a sensual pleasure, or we can subtract an intellectual pain from an intellectual pleasure. What we can't do meaningfully is subtract an intellectual pain from a sensual pleasure. That would be like subtracting the barometric pressure in the music hall from the number of minutes the orchestra played. Nothing stops you from doing it—but the resulting answer makes no sense.

How then *does* Mill balance pains and pleasures of different kinds? For instance, suppose that only two ways of life were open to him: to live like Socrates but dissatisfied, or to live like a pig but satisfied. How would he choose between them?

	Like Socrates	Like pig
Sensual pleasure	-50	+50
Intellectual pleasure	+1	-1
TOTAL	No meaning	No meaning

Decision: LIVE LIKE SOCRATES

A primitive utilitarian would have pretended that the units of sensual and intellectual pleasure were units of the same scale so that he could do arithmetic with them. For him, the choice would be between -49 units of pleasure and +49 units of pleasure; therefore, he would conclude, it is better to be a satisfied pig than a dissatisfied Socrates.

Mill proceeds differently. The numbers -49 and +49 are meaningless. What is really at stake is which kind of pleasure a being capable of both kinds *prefers*. The fact is that no being capable of both human pleasures and pig pleasures *can* be satisfied living like a pig. Any rational being recognizes that even the smallest amount of intellectual pleasure (measured in intellectual-pleasure units) is preferable to even the greatest amount of sensual pleasure (measured in sensual-pleasure units). So the decision rule seems to be this:

When comparing pleasures and pains that are all of the *same* kind, go ahead and do the arithmetic, choosing the course of action with the highest total. But when comparing pleasures and pains that are of *different* kinds, don't even attempt the arithmetic. Choose the course of action that yields the greatest amount of the higher pleasure. Don't even consider which yields the greatest amount of the lower pleasure, unless in the higher kind the two courses of action are tied.[3]

Whether Mill can make the second part of the decision rule work depends on one thing and one thing only: being able to tell which kinds of pleasure are higher and which kinds of pleasure are lower. How is he to do this? Remember what we said earlier: In his view the desirable is nothing but what we actually desire; the preferable is nothing but what we actually prefer. This is the very foundation of utilitarianism. He is *not* saying, as Thomas would, that whatever kind of thing is higher, people *ought* to prefer it; rather he is saying that they *do* prefer it and that we call it higher for no other reason. So to order the different kinds of pleasures from highest to lowest, we merely have to observe their actual choices.

Easy! Or is it? It isn't. The first thing we notice in observing actual choices is that people do not all prefer the same kinds of pleasure. Some prefer the pleasures of human beings, whereas others prefer the pleasures of pigs. Some prefer the pleasures of intellectual conversation, but others prefer the pleasures of sniffing glue. Some prefer the pleasures of kindness, whereas others prefer the pleasures of cruelty. How does Mill reply to this objection?

Explicitly he doesn't reply at all. Implicitly, however, he does, and his reply has three parts. First, he's not talking about all preferences but only about "decided" preferences. Second, he's not talking about the preferences of ordinary people but only about the preferences of people qualified to judge. Third, he's not necessarily talking about the preferences of all such people; if almost all share a preference, that's enough.

Of these three points, clearly the most important is the second—that only qualified judges count. Indeed, chapter two of his well-known book *Utilitarianism* is in large part a list of their qualifications! The fact is easy to miss because Mill does not call attention to them; the chapter about various objections to utilitarianism, and each of the various qualifications that judges of pleasure must have is buried in one of Mill's responses. Following are the most important of these buried qualifications:

1. In order to be qualified to judge between two different kinds of pleasure a person must have had "experience of both."

2. In order to be qualified to judge between two different kinds of pleasure a person must be able to block out any "feelings of moral obligation" he may have to choose one over the other. His goal ought to be to *reach* a moral principle, not to *act* on one.

3. In order to be qualified to judge between two different kinds of pleasure a person must not be in a state of "extreme unhappiness." Otherwise he might be so desperate that he would choose something "undesirable in his own eyes" just to escape his condition.

4. In order to be qualified to judge between two different kinds of pleasure a person must not suffer from "infirmity of character"—that is, from weakness of will. Otherwise he might choose the "nearer" pleasure even though he knows it to be the less valuable of the two.

5. In order to be qualified to judge between two different kinds of pleasure a person must not have "killed" the very capacity for the "nobler feelings" by pursuing a way of life which has given them no "exercise."

Unfortunately, grave objections can be raised to each of these supposed qualifications.

1. If no one is qualified to judge between pleasures unless he has experienced both, then only the depraved will be qualified to judge. For instance, only a person who has experienced sex with both children and adult spouses will be qualified to judge between the pleasures of pederasty and of marriage.

2. If no one is qualified to judge between pleasures unless he is able to block out his moral feelings while he is doing it, then once again the advantage is given to depravity. A morally sound person can reconsider whether his moral feelings are reasonable, but he cannot simply block them out and would never agree to try.

3. If it is really possible for a person to choose something undesirable in his own eyes, then Mill is wrong in equating the desirable with what is actually desired. But in that case the entire exercise of

observing actual choices is pointless.

4. If desirability *is* in the eye of the desirer, how does Mill know that it is *not* rational to desire nearer pleasures over farther ones? Isn't he slipping nonutilitarian moral concepts into the list of qualifications for utilitarian judges? Indeed, Bentham thought that it *was* rational to desire nearer pleasures over farther ones, as we saw previously.

5. Every way of life kills *some* capacities for pleasure; there are no exceptions. A malicious life kills the capacity for enjoying kindness; a kind life kills the capacity for enjoying malice. Therefore it is impossible to have lived a life that kills *no* capacities for pleasure. We'll have to allow a judge to have killed certain capacities for pleasure but not others. But in order to know which he can have killed and yet be qualified to judge, we have to know *already* which ones are higher and lower. Finding that out was the whole point of asking for a judge in the first place. So the test is circular.

We conclude that Mill has not solved the problem of the incommensurability of different pleasures after all. Although it makes perfect sense to distinguish between base and noble kinds of pleasure, his way of telling which are which can never work. He must abandon the notion that the desirable is nothing but what we actually desire, and this he cannot do without giving up utilitarianism itself.

What does Mill do about the distinctness of persons? Little time need be spent on this problem, for Mill does nothing about the distinctness of persons. He simply does not recognize the difficulty. If failure to notice the distinctness of persons is a blind spot of primitive utilitarianism, then it is a blind spot of Mill's souped-up version too.

What does Mill do about the moral irrelevance of aggregate pleasure? At first it may seem that moral monstrosities, such as a utilitarian justification for rape or murder, would be prevented by the fact that Mill is willing to accept long-established traditions as evidence of what produces happiness. After all, these traditions include traditional moral rules, and among these rules are firm prohibitions of rape and murder. As we saw previously, however, this line of reasoning does not work. (1) Previous generations may have made mistakes. (2) Even if they haven't, given Mill's strange belief that there is no such thing as human nature, then what produced happiness for previous generations may not produce it for us. Therefore, (3) as Mill himself admits, any moral rule, no matter how traditional, may be challenged. (4) When it is, the utilitarian calculation must still be performed—with all the attendant risk of monstrosity.

It may also seem that moral monstrosities such as a utilitarian justification for rape or murder would be prevented by the fact that Mill changes the basis of calculation from individual acts to general rules. After all, it hardly seems likely that the effects on aggregate pleasure could ever justify adopting the rule "Anyone may take innocent human life for personal advantage." Unfortunately, this change is not as helpful as it may appear. Even though rule utilitarianism might not justify the rule "Anyone may take innocent human life for personal advantage," it may well justify such rules as "Anyone may take innocent human life *provided enough people agree*" or "Anyone may take innocent human life *provided the victim is unwanted*." The reason? In such cases utilitarian calculation would probably show that murder improves the balance of pleasure over pain.

Think this is silly? Think again. As I write, the courts in Allegan County, Michigan, are considering Mary Martin's request for doctors to starve and dehydrate her husband Michael to death by withdrawing his feeding tube. Although Michael is brain damaged, he is not terminally ill and is not being kept alive by machines. He lives in a nursing home where he enjoys television and country-western music. Doctors testify that he is fully conscious, that he is able to communicate, that he understands the difference between living and dying and that he desires to live. On an alphabet board he has spelled out his satisfaction with the care he is receiving in the nursing home and his fear of being taken from it. Nevertheless a judge has ruled that he is not competent to make decisions for himself.[4] Indeed, from a utilitarian point of view it would not matter who made the decision—so long as aggregate pleasure were increased.

What does Mill do about the specialness of being human? At first Mill seems to have solved the problem of being unable to distinguish between higher and lower *creatures* by distinguishing between higher and lower *pleasures*. Animals can experience only the sensual pleasures; human beings can experience not only the sensual pleasures but also higher pleasures such as the intellectual and the aesthetic. Although our lower pleasures are not worth any more than theirs, our higher pleasures are worth infinitely more than their lower ones. Therefore wherever one of a human being's higher pleasures comes into play, his desires trump those of the animal. Yet there are two problems with this supposed solution. In one way it goes too far; in another it does not go far enough. The supposed solution goes too far in that it permits actual cruelty. No, that is imprecise. Hurting an animal "just for the hell of it" is permitted even under primitive utilitarianism, provided that the human's pleasure exceeds the animal's hell. But after the Millian modification, the range of permissible cruelty becomes even wider! What the modification means is that higher pleasures trump lower pleasures. Therefore so long as the human being takes even the slightest intellectual interest in the amount of pain the animal can withstand, what he does is all right no matter *how* terrible its hell becomes.

The way in which the supposed solution fails to go far enough is that it draws the line between the higher and lower creatures in the *wrong place*—allowing some human beings to treat other human beings the same way they treat animals. Suppose, for instance, that there are three different kinds of pleasure, ranked in order as follows.

Lowest: Sensual pleasure—the enjoyment of bodily feelings.

Middle: Aesthetic pleasure—the enjoyment of beauty.

Highest: Intellectual pleasure—the enjoyment of understanding.

Now consider the following arguments. First, aesthetic pleasure trumps sensual pleasure. Although animals are capable of only sensual pleasure, humans are capable of both. Therefore whenever aesthetic pleasure comes into play, a human being can treat an animal as he pleases. Second, intellectual pleasure trumps aesthetic pleasure. Although some human beings are capable only of sensual and aesthetic pleasure, other human beings are capable of all three. Therefore whenever intellectual pleasure comes into play, a human being who is capable of it can treat a human being who is not capable of it as *he* pleases.

If the first argument is valid, the second must be too: Some human beings may treat some others the same way that all human beings may treat beasts. Think I'm being silly again? Once more I ask you to reconsider. The Nazi "doctors" used just this sort of reasoning to justify performing inhumane "experiments" on Jews, whom they considered a lower kind of human being. From time to time such reasoning is heard closer to home too.

Consider for example the 1982 case *New York v. Ferber*, in which, at the same time that the U.S. Supreme Court agreed that a state could make child pornography illegal, it specified conditions under which the same kinds of sexual abuse could not be considered pornographic and would therefore have to be allowed. The forms of abuse of which we are speaking are those listed in the challenged New York law: making children engage, on film, in actual or simulated sexual intercourse, deviate sexual intercourse, sexual bestiality, masturbation, sadomasochistic abuse, or lewd exhibition of the genitals.

Said Justice White, such filming would have to be allowed if it had "serious literary, artistic, political, or scientific value." He wrote that he was not sure how often conduct of the sort the New York law prohibited would be necessary "in order to produce educational, medical, or artistic works"—but when it was necessary, it could not be prohibited. *What this really means is that child sexual abuse must be permitted if it is done for highbrow purposes.*[5]

Apparently it has been. Consider the research of Alfred Charles Kinsey, the famous sex researcher. As E. Michael Jones points out,

Tables thirty through thirty-four in chapter five of Kinsey's book *Sexual Behavior in the Human Male* document the incidence of orgasm in pre-adolescents. One four-year-old was "specifically manipulated" for twenty-four hours around the clock. This child achieved twenty-six orgasms in this time period. Another eleven-month-old infant had fourteen "orgasms," according to the Kinseyan definition, in a period of thirty-eight minutes, or one orgasm every 2.7 minutes. . . . In addition the Kinsey team making these observations noted various types of reaction on the part of the children involved. One of the six types of reaction involved: "Extreme tension with violent convulsion: Often involving the heaving and jerking of the whole body . . . gasping, eyes staring or tightly closed, hands grasping, mouth distorted, sometimes with tongue protruding; whole body or parts of it spasmodically twitching . . . groaning, sobbing, or more violent cries, sometimes with an abundance of tears (especially among younger children)." Not until thirty-three years had passed did any other researcher ask where Kinsey had got his data. This question has never been satisfactorily answered.[6]

The grown-up human beings who understand such things are permitted to treat the little human beings who don't understand them like animals; perhaps it is because the grown-ups are capable of higher pleasures.

Has Mill any other ideas about how to fix primitive utilitarianism? Yes, he has. Although our discussion has been confined to the doctrinal changes made by Mill in *Utilitarianism,* in other works he does make others. The most important of these is an alteration in the definition of utility: in his essay *On Liberty* it becomes "the permanent interests of man as a progressive being." Unfortunately the grandiose new definition does not go anywhere. In the first place, Mill never tells us what these "interests" are: Are we still talking about the things that bring about aggregate pleasure, or are we talking about something else? In the second place, the contradiction of a "progressive" being that has "permanent" interests seems to be merely Mill's way of saying, "I reject the belief in an unchanging law of nature—*but I refuse to accept the implications of doing so!"*

Questions for Reflection

1. The only way we can tell that utilitarianism needs fixing is by applying nonutilitarian moral standards we *already* know and that *don't* need fixing. In the very act of trying to do without these moral standards Mill unconsciously slips some of them back in, for instance in his notion that some feelings are "nobler" than others. Suppose he let them *all* back in. Would anything be left of utilitarianism?

2. Utilitarianism is sometimes defended as an *impartial* and *compassionate* doctrine because it requires us to sympathize with the pains and pleasures of everyone, making no distinctions. But is that really what impartiality and compassion require? For instance, should we really sympathize just as much with the frustration of a foiled rapist as with the relief of his would-be victim?

3. As we have seen, Mill fails to recognize the specialness of being human. Following the book of Genesis,[7] Jews and Christians claim that it is special to be human "because only human beings are made in the image of God." Following the gospel, Christians add, "And because God, in the incarnation, further ennobled humanity by taking it upon Himself—not by conversion of the Godhood into flesh, but by the taking of the Manhood into God."[8] But the pagan philosopher Aristotle

thinks there is something special about being human too. What reason does he give? In what respects is it compatible or incompatible with the Jewish and Christian reasons? In what respects does it fall short?

4. This chapter has remarked that "ethicists," many of them utilitarian, now vie with lawyers as consultants to businesses, hospitals, and university and government bureaucracies. Far fewer of these consultants are believers in natural law. Why might that be the case?

5. Although Mill recognizes that pleasures of different *kinds* are incommensurable, he assumes that the arithmetic works fine so long as we are speaking of only one kind of pain or pleasure at a time. Is that claim true? Let's test it in the case of physical pains and pleasures. Positive ten plus negative ten is the same as zero. Therefore, if I get ten units of physical pleasure from kissing my wife and ten units of physical pain from biting my tongue, I should just as soon do both as neither; biting my tongue *while* kissing my wife should have the same value to me as neither biting my tongue *nor* kissing my wife. I find this implausible—but what do you think? Why?

6. Some neo-utilitarians have tried to escape the absurdities involved in adding up pleasures by speaking instead of "combining preferences." Suppose, for instance, that Sam, Fred and Mary are planning a meeting and have to decide which beverage to serve. Their preferences are as shown in the following table:

	Serve coffee	Serve tea	Serve milk
Sam	1	2	3
Fred	2	3	1
Mary	3	2	1

The numeral 1 indicates the first-ranked action, the numeral 2 the second-ranked action and the numeral 3 the third-ranked action. For instance, Fred would best like having milk served and worst like having tea served. There are many methods of combining preferences. One is *adding ranks:* in this case coffee scores 6, tea 7 and milk 5, so we serve tea. Another is *voting:* in this case milk beats tea, coffee beats tea and milk beats coffee, so we serve milk.

The neo-utilitarians who believe in "combining preferences" instead

of "adding pleasures" quarrel over which method of combining preferences to use. Here are your questions: Do these ways of making
decisions suffer from the particular blind spots we have studied? Do
they suffer from any others? (In thinking over your response, feel free
to change the problem, the alternatives and the rankings in any ways
that you please. For instance, perhaps Sam and Mary have found Fred
unconscious in an alley. They are trying to decide whether to rob him,
ignore him or help him, and the rankings are as shown in the table
above. But be imaginative.)

TWELVE

UTILITY &
JUSTICE

YOU MAY HAVE BEEN WONDERING WHY MILL CALLS HIMSELF A UTILITARIAN
rather than, say, a pleasuretarian. In ordinary language, for an act to
have utility is for it to be useful, to be expedient. So by calling himself
a utilitarian Mill is telling us that he regards expediency as the ultimate
consideration in personal and social life—that he regards the end as
justifying the means. Where then does pleasure come in?

If you are going to make expediency your ultimate consideration,
you have to have some way to measure it, don't you? You have to have
some basis for saying "This is more expedient than that." But Mill thinks
that pleasure is the only good thing there is. For him, then, measuring
the expediency of something can mean only one thing: finding out
how much pleasure it causes, net pain. So *utility, usefulness, expediency*
and *aggregate pleasure* all turn out to be synonyms.

Where Is Justice?
Where in all of this is there room for *justice*, the last topic Mill covers?

Common sense replies, "Nowhere." If the just is the right and the expedient is the useful, then justice and expediency are two different things. Sometimes they may even come into conflict with each other such that what is right is not useful and what is useful is not right. When this happens we must be willing to give up expediency for the sake of justice. For instance, it may be expedient to hang an innocent man in order to placate the mob and prevent a riot; but it cannot be just, and so it must not be done.

Utilitarianism rejects this common sense. It holds that the rules of justice *are* rules of expediency—that the only reason for following them is that they *do* tend to increase utility. Now the utilitarian may mean either of two things by this statement. Which one he means makes a great difference.

Claim one: The commonly accepted rules of justice are rules that *always* increase utility. In this case justice and expediency can never come into conflict, so the common-sense question "What should we do when the just is inexpedient?" simply does not arise. That makes the rules of justice unbreakable. The innocent man must not be hanged.

Claim two: The commonly accepted rules of justice are rules that *usually* increase utility but sometimes fail. In this case justice and expediency *can* come into conflict, so the common-sense question "What should we do when the just is inexpedient?" arises after all. In the utilitarian view this makes the rules of justice *breakable.* Go ahead and hang the man.

Which of these two claims is Mill's? Claim two. This puts him under an even heavier burden of proof than if he maintained claim one. In order to convince us of his theory he must do three things: (1) *list* the commonly accepted rules of justice (this merely gets the conversation going); (2) for every single rule, *prove* that following it increases utility in most cases but not all (this sets up the conflict between justice and expediency); (3) for every single case in which following the rule does *not* increase utility, *prove* that it ought to be broken (this justifies putting expediency first).

Does Mill do all three things? No. As to the first, he does list the rules of justice. As to the second, he *asserts* that for every single rule, following it increases utility in most but not all cases—but he makes no effort to prove the point. As to the third, he *asserts* that for every single case in which following the rule does not increase utility, we ought to break it—but again he makes no effort toward proof. To be sure, he does offer a few examples. But, in the first place, the examples themselves depend mostly on assertion rather than argument, and, in the second, even if we accepted his examples they would not count as proof because there may be counterexamples. The bottom line is that Mill comes nowhere near establishing the truth of the utilitarian theory of justice.

But if he does not prove the theory, what *is* Mill up to in his discussion of justice? Are all those pages of argument for nothing? Not exactly. Mill is up to a sophisticated game of bait and switch: after luring us into the department store with the promise of product X, he offers us product Z instead. The success of the switch depends on our not noticing that whether something is unjust is a different question from whether we *feel* it to be unjust—for instead of a proof of the utilitarian theory of justice, he offers us a fanciful explanation of the origin of the *feeling* of injustice (a species of the feeling of moral indignation).

Why does Mill want to make the switch? Probably because he cannot tell the difference between product X and product Y himself! Remember what we said back in section two: in Mill's view feelings or sensations are the only thing we can really be sure about. Even as Mill does not know how to make sense of something good in itself, so he does not know how to make sense of something just in itself. Therefore, even as he has to define goodness strictly in terms of us, so he has to define justice strictly in terms of us. The good becomes nothing but what we desire; in the same way the just becomes nothing but what we have a feeling of justice about. Ethics is boiled down to emotions; the moral is boiled down to the nonmoral. To make matters worse, his explanation of where the feeling of injustice comes from does not work anyway! We are about to see why not.

Elementary Feelings and Compound Feelings

Even as Mill's theory of *justice* attacks common sense about justice itself, so his speculation about the *feeling* of injustice attacks common sense about the feeling of injustice. It does so by rejecting the view that this feeling is an *elementary* feeling. What does he want to put in its place? The view that he proposes is that it is a *compound* feeling.

You see, Mill views feelings as a chemist views chemicals. Hydrogen is just hydrogen, oxygen is just oxygen, but to a chemist water isn't just water; it's a molecular partnership of the other two. Hydrogen and oxygen are elementary chemicals, whereas water is a compound chemical. Mill believes that feelings too may also be either elementary or compound. Some feelings are like hydrogen and oxygen; others are like water.

This is not how the commonsense reasoner views feelings. To be sure, he may have all sorts of insights. He may be able to *classify* them. For instance, he may notice that the feeling of hunger is associated with a desire, whereas the feeling of joy is not. He may be able to *evaluate* them. For instance, he may encourage the feeling of generosity, while discouraging the feeling of malice. He may be able to analyze their *causes*. For example, he may see that the sheer feeling of anger arises from the perception of harm, whereas the feeling of moral indignation arises from the perception that the harm is wrong. He may be able to see how one leads to *another*. For instance, he may see that if one acts on cruel feelings, he will usually start having contemptuous feelings toward the people he has treated cruelly. He may even be able to *unmask* them. For example, he may observe that a compliment can appear to express the feeling of admiration while concealing the feeling of envy.

But here is where the commonsense reasoner stops: to treat feelings as compounds or molecules that must be dissolved into their atomic components just does not seem to him a useful exercise. Each feeling is elementary; each is itself. Envy is envy, anger is anger, joy is joy, and that is just the idea that Mill rejects.

Mill is not trying to develop a general theory of compound feelings. All he wants to do is prove that *one* feeling is compound—the feeling of injustice. The commonsense reasoner says that the feeling of injustice is an elementary emotional response to the perception of an injustice in the real world, a world that is what it is no matter what we perceive or feel. Mill does not believe in a real world, a world that is what it is no matter what we perceive or feel. So he tries to explain the feeling of injustice in another way—not as an emotional response to a perception but as a mere compound of other emotions.

Explaining something by deriving it from something else which is supposedly more elementary is called *reduction*. So another way to express Mill's strategy is to say that it is reductionist. First, he tries to *reduce* the feeling of injustice to other feelings. Next he claims that such an explanation is *simpler* than the commonsense one that leaves the feeling of injustice unreduced. Then he asserts that whenever we have two competing explanations of the same facts, all other things being equal the simpler one is better. Finally he says that because his explanation actually is simpler, it must be better. The easiest way to reconstruct Mill's argument is to put it in question-and-answer form:

1. *What does the feeling of injustice involve?* Mill's answer: It involves a desire to punish a person who has done harm to some individual.

2. *What other human feeling involves the same desire?* Mill's answer: The same desire is involved in the feeling of resentment modified by the feeling of sympathy.

3. *How is this the case?* Mill's answer: Ordinary resentment makes me desire to punish someone who has done harm to *me,* and sympathy makes it possible for me to feel resentment on behalf of someone *else.*

4. *Is it possible then that resentment modified by sympathy is all that the feeling of injustice is?* Mill's answer: Yes, because both sets of feelings involve the same desire to punish.

5. *Is this explanation simpler than the commonsense reasoner's, which treats the feeling of injustice as elementary?* Mill's answer: Yes, because it allows us to cross off the feeling of injustice from the list of elementary feelings. And, being simpler, it must be better.

Unfortunately for Mill, his reductionist explanation is invalid. Steps two, four and five all fail.

Step two does not work because resentment modified by sympathy does *not* involve the same feeling as injustice. What resentment involves is the mere desire to hurt someone else, and the true desire to punish differs from the mere desire to hurt in at least two respects. First, a true desire to punish presupposes consciousness that the original harm was wrong and therefore that retribution is deserved. Mere desire to hurt does not. Second, a true desire to punish intends the wrongdoer's own good—if nothing else, the good of acknowledging his wrongdoing. Again, mere desire to hurt does not.

Step four does not work because Mill thinks that in order to show the plausibility of reducing the feeling of injustice to the feeling of resentment modified by sympathy, all we need to show is that both involve the same desire to punish. But that is not true; we need to show something else as well: that no *other* feelings involve the same desire to punish. If some other feeling involves this desire too, there is more than one thing to which the feeling of injustice might be reduced.

Step five does not work because Mill's explanation works equally well in the opposite direction. He, of course, reduces the feeling of injustice to the feeling of resentment. But turnabout is fair play: the commonsense reasoner can counter by tracing the feeling of resentment to the perception of injustice! After all, when a person feels resentment over deserved treatment, we blame him. Challenged, he replies that the treatment is *not* deserved, so his resentment is reasonable. Obviously, *both* sides agree that the reason for resentment is perception of injustice—not the other way around.

Now which explanation is simpler—Mill's, which treats the feeling of injustice as the thing to be explained, or the commonsense reasoner's, which treats the feeling of resentment as the thing to be explained? Obviously the common sense reasoner's is simpler. Both explanations assume the same number of elementary feelings, but the commonsense reasoner needs to mention only two of them—the feelings of justice and resentment—while Mill has to drag in a third—the feeling of sympathy. Thus by Mill's own test—that if all other things are equal, the simplest explanation is best—Mill loses, and the commonsense reasoner wins.

Questions for Reflection

1. Self-interest is not the only thing that tempts us to put expediency in the place of justice, for sometimes justice requires allowing bad things to happen to others. If we refuse to allow the hanging of an innocent man, the mob may break out in a riot. If we refuse to allow the bombing of population centers, the war may be prolonged. If we refuse to allow the theft of honest earnings, the poor may lack warm clothes. Surely it isn't right that there are riots, war deaths and nakedness, so in all these cases we are tempted to do evil that good may result.

a. Can you suggest other cases in which the temptation arises?

b. In each case, what specific injustice arises from giving in?

c. When people do commit injustices, which of the following rationalizations is more effective, and why? (i) "I know it's unjust, but it's necessary." (ii) "Because it's necessary, it's not really unjust."

2. For the reasons given in the previous question, one of the strongest motives to commit large-scale political injustice is the desire to *fix everything* on our own. Christian faith undercuts this desire through conviction of the helplessness of man and confidence in the providence of God: in other words, through certainty that only God can set all to rights and that in the end he will. Many Christian thinkers have wondered whether it is even possible to resist the urge to fix everything on our own if we lack this conviction and confidence. Has secular society any resources of its own for resisting the urge? Explain.

3. If the just is defined as the expedient, then it would seem to leave no room for mercy. How is justice understood in biblical tradition, which teaches that mercy as well as justice is a virtue?

INTERMEZZO

THE ART
OF TEACHING

*We have now sunk to a depth at which re-statement of the
obvious is the first duty of intelligent men.*
G E O R G E   O R W E L L

THIS BOOK IS WRITTEN FOR SEVERAL DIFFERENT AUDIENCES. BEFORE GOING
on to Unit V, I should like to address students.

We have finished our selective survey of the ethical and political
classics, and it may have been quite different from other surveys you
have read. The differences, I imagine, have become more and more
noticeable as we went along, culminating in the chapters on Mill. There
is a reason for that, and you deserve to know what it is. Because a writer
ought to respect his readers, I lay my cards on the table. You may not
like or believe what I am going to say, but I don't require you to.

Everyone carries around a personal baloney-meter in his mind. I'm
speaking of the useful little instrument that lights up and beeps when
you hear plain nonsense, prompting you to say to yourself, *That's
baloney.* The baloney-meter is factory-installed, not an option. You have
one, I have one, we all have one—ever since reaching the age of reason.
Each of us depends on it constantly. "Tell you what," says your friend.
"Let's pool our life savings and invest them in the lottery. One of us is
sure to win, and we can split the take." Beep! Beep! "That's baloney."

One would be a fool not to recognize how much better off we are having baloney-meters than we would be without them. Yet even the most appreciative among us must recognize that baloney-meters aren't perfect. Sometimes they light up and beep when the words we hear are not baloney, and sometimes they fail to light up and beep when they are. Because you have to use your baloney-meter to recognize a defect in a baloney-meter, the malfunction is easiest to notice in the baloney-meter of another person. Perhaps you haven't noticed it in your own, but I can assure you that others have.

What causes baloney-meters to malfunction? Is there something wrong with the factory programming?[1] No. Think for a moment about what it would take for your baloney-meter to be infallible. The factory would have to program it with a sample of every possible piece of baloney that anyone might ever try to feed you—libraries upon libraries of samples. In life, whenever another person spoke to you (or you spoke to yourself), the baloney-meter would look for a match. If it found one, it would light up and beep. You can see what's wrong with this design. Baloney is infinitely various. Not even libraries upon libraries could hold all the necessary samples.

The only practical way to build a baloney-meter is to give it just that *basic* programming which will allow it to learn more about baloney from experience. This basic programming is what philosophers have called the first principles of practical and theoretical reasoning. We have also called the first principles of practical reasoning the natural law.

Reflection on the design of the baloney-meter explains several important facts.

In the first place, the factory programming explains why the baloney-meters of different people, even in different cultures, tend to light up and beep about pretty much the same things in certain areas of life. High-minded men among both the Greeks and the Chinese condemned disrespect for the dead; those among both the Vikings and the Babylonians have condemned stealing a neighbor's wife; those among both the Hindus and the Egyptians have condemned treachery—not just men *we* call high-minded but men *they* called high-minded. As C. S. Lewis remarked, "Think of a country where people were *admired* for running away in battle, or where a man felt *proud* for double-crossing all the people who had been kindest to him. You might just as well try to imagine a country where two and two made five."[2]

In the second place, the fact that the factory programming is only basic explains why the baloney-meters of different people light up and beep about *different* things in other areas of life—and also why they can go off over what is *not* baloney and fail to go off over what is. For although you do know certain things without having to learn them, you learn most things from experience. But any being that can learn from experience can learn incorrectly—partly because his experience is not complete, and partly because he may rebel against the lesson.

We see then that any baloney-meter, however perfectly programmed in the factory, will tend to get out of correct calibration. Originally the purpose of a higher education was to recalibrate it. A secondary purpose was to teach it to perform further recalibration on its own.

Courses of study such as logic and mathematics trained the mind to think clearly. Courses of study such as history, literature and politics immersed the mind in the experience of centuries so that it was not isolated on the little island of its own experience. Courses of study such as ethics recalled the mind to what it knew already so that it did not drown in its own new depths. Courses of study such as theology directed the mind to consider what was deeper and greater than itself. And courses of study such as *revealed* theology exploded the mind's self-deceptions and enabled it to know what it could not have discovered solely through its own resources.

This attitude toward higher education was humble. A teacher such as Aristotle or Thomas respected the baloney-meter. He always started with the common sense of mankind, something he did not invent, then went on to refine it and gently correct its errors. You may feel that such humility is impossible, because in our own culture common sense seems largely to have disappeared. We have come to feel it normal to have disagreements about fundamental issues of morals, just as we might have them about politics and other areas more distant from the factory programming. This condition, in turn, changes the *kind* of disagreements we have in politics. But this condition is not normal at all; it is a symptom of a civilization in an advanced state of decay.

Unlike classical higher education, modern higher education is *not* humble. It both reflects and contributes to the decay of civilization by insisting on the *disconnection* of the baloney-meter and its replacement

by "theory" of its own devising. Of course it cannot really be disconnected—we have seen that earlier in the book—but it can be obscured
by having another hooked up alongside it. What educated people now
call their common sense is largely a collection of dogmas pumped in
from the outside. Because these dogmas are often pumped in under
the guise of liberation from dogma, they pass unrecognized. We are
entering a strange era in which, in some respects, the educated know
less than the completely uneducated.[3]

The methods used in higher education for disconnecting the
baloney-meter are many. One method is false anthropology, whereby
young people are taught the wholly spurious idea that the human race
is in complete disagreement about all the elementary points of right
and wrong. Another method is outright attack, about which you have
learned quite a bit from observing John Stuart Mill. An especially subtle
method is teaching ethics by *quandaries*—imaginary occasions for
moral decision which are deliberately contrived to baffle—the common result being that students lose their confidence that moral law
tells them anything at all.[4]

In turn, the usual method for replacing the baloney-meter is *meta-
ethics*—in which we no longer talk about right and wrong but instead
talk about the talk about it, or maybe even talk about the talk about the
talk. In this way we get further and further from the data. If mentioned
at all, the natural law itself is presented as but one of many competing
theories of ethics. This is like treating the existence of light as but one
of many competing theories of vision. Actually light is presupposed in
any theory of vision. In the same way, the law written on the heart ought
to be presupposed in any theory of ethics. Just as in geometry, if we
don't already know something, we can't even get started learning the
rest.

How would a classical moral teacher go about teaching under such
circumstances? As we have seen, his humble goal is to recalibrate the
baloney-meter, not to replace but to refine the common sense of
mankind. But one cannot recalibrate a baloney-meter that receives
continuous interfering signals from another installed alongside it. The
ersatz baloney-meter implanted by modern education cannot be cali-
brated at all. It lights up and beeps at the very mention of an objective
moral law. "Aren't we beyond all that now?" "Aren't morals just rela-

tive?" "Aren't good and evil up to the individual?"

In the classroom I answer such questions, "Tell that to the man who is trying to rape or murder you." This is a much more aggressive response than Aristotle and Thomas would make to their students, but their students did not ask such questions. Today a classical teacher must be aggressive before he can exercise his humility. Before the students' original baloney-meters can be recalibrated, the ersatz baloney-meters that have been installed alongside them must be disconnected. So students must unlearn before they can learn. A classical teacher today is first, though not last, an unteacher.

That's why I've been so blunt with examples and rebuttals at some points in Units I through IV. I hope I have taught and untaught well enough that if anything in my own understanding of things is wicked or perverse you will be able to tell—and, should this be the case, I hope you will let me know.

Questions for Reflection

1. How do Aristotle and Thomas signal the reader that their intention is to respect and recalibrate the baloney-meter?

2. How does Mill signal the reader that his intention is to disconnect and replace it?

3. What difference does it make to their respective attitudes toward the baloney-meter that Thomas is a Christian and Aristotle is not?

4. Can any traces of the respect and recalibration ideal still be found in Mill?

5. Where does Locke stand on respect and recalibration versus disconnection and replacement?

UNIT V

WRITTEN ON THE HEART

THIRTEEN

A CHRISTIAN APPRAISAL OF NATURAL-LAW THEORY

THE PURPOSE OF THESE LAST THREE CHAPTERS IS TO COMMENT ON SOME of the voices in the contemporary debate about natural law and to state my own position. The most convenient procedure is to reverse the prescription by stating my position first. I am primarily addressing those who share it, but I am glad for anyone who pleases to listen in.

Before anything else I am a Christian; this means, among other things, that I am a Christian before I am a philosopher. The fact might be thought to mar my objectivity, as though to be intellectually honest one ought to be a philosopher before anything else. But every philosopher is something else first. So long as arguments depend on premises the matter cannot stand otherwise. There is a foundation in every house of thought, a prephilosophical faith in every philosophy. Mine is the gospel of Jesus Christ.

The gospel is the story of a rescue, of a path of salvation which God has opened up to a world that has forsaken him and cannot save itself.

How has this God made himself known? One way, of course, is special revelation (2 Timothy 3:14-17). Examination of Scripture, revelation's record, shows at least four kinds: (1) the works of God in history, by which he set apart for himself a people of promise and delivered them from oppression (Joshua 24:1-18); (2) the law of Moses, which told his people what sin is, though without giving them power to escape it (Romans 7:7-13); (3) prophecy, which foretold the coming of a Messiah who would save his people from their sins (Isaiah 52:13—53:12); (4) that Messiah, Jesus Christ, who took their sins upon himself (John 3:16; Romans 3:23-24; 5:6-8; 7:4-6).

Each of these revelations paved the way for the later ones. For example, Scripture teaches explicitly that the works of God in history prepared his people to receive the law of Moses (Exodus 20:2 as prelude to 20:3-17; Deuteronomy 29:2-9). It also teaches that the law of Moses prepared them to receive the gospel of Jesus Christ (Galatians 3:23-24).

Now it may be asked why a Christian should be interested in natural law at all. If one already has the Bible, what use is it? At best it would merely repeat in cursive a small part of what God had already written in great block letters. Moreover, like any other person the Christian may well doubt whether there is such a thing as natural law at all. If there were, wouldn't people act more as though they knew it? It may seem as though the Bible is not only the surest and most complete but the *only* source of moral knowledge.

Surprisingly, Scripture itself gives a different account of the matter. The Bible maintains that God has not left himself without a witness among the pagans (Acts 14:17). In contrast to special revelation, provided by God to the community of faith, this may be called *general* revelation because it is provided by God to all mankind. According to Scripture it comes in at least five forms: (1) the testimony of creation, which speaks to us of a glorious, powerful and merciful Creator (Psalm 19:1-6; 104; Acts 14:17; Romans 1:20); (2) the fact that we are made in the image of God, which not only gives us rational and moral capacities but also tells us of an unknown Holy One who is different from our idols (Genesis 1:26-27; Acts 17:22-23); (3) the facts of our physical and emotional design, in which a variety of God's purposes are plainly manifest (Romans 1:26-27); (4) the law of conscience, written on the heart, which, like the law of Moses, tells us what sin is but does not give us power to escape it (Romans 2:14-15); (5) the order of causality, which teaches us by linking every sin with consequences (Proverbs 1:31).

So it is that unconverted Gentiles, who have neither waited at the foot of Sinai nor sat at the feet of Jesus, are still accountable to God. This makes general revelation tremendously important to Christians who are speaking to their nonbelieving neighbors. They do not start out believing in Scripture; if it does make sense to them, it will do so by illuminating what God has already made partly known to them by other means.

The doctrine of natural law is grounded by the second, third, fourth and fifth of God's ways of general revelation. Because of the influence of the pre-Christian thinker Aristotle, most natural lawyers focus on the third. For two reasons I focus on the fourth—the law of conscience, written on the heart. One reason is that Scripture is especially clear and emphatic about it. The other is that although we profess Christ in a world that seems bent on repaganizing itself, the new sort of pagan is very different from the old sort.

The old sort knew about the law written on the heart; he heard about it in the plays of Euripides, he read about it in the philosophy of the Stoics, and he studied it in the commentaries of the Roman lawyers. The new sort does not know about the law written on the heart. Don't misunderstand—he still feels it pressing upon him inwardly, just as it pressed upon the inwards of the old sort of pagan. However, with a head filled with false sophistication that tells him that right and wrong are invented by culture and are different everywhere, the new sort of pagan mistrusts his own conscience and views guilt as a sign of maladjustment that therapy will remove.

Because of this difference, speaking with the new sort of pagan is much harder than speaking with the old sort. Not only that, the false sophistication that bewitches him has wormed its way into certain parts of the church itself. All these are good reasons to take a closer look at the law written on the heart.

Let us begin this closer look by reviewing what Scripture says about it. Paul writes these words in the letter to the Romans:

Indeed, when Gentiles, who have not the law, do by nature *[physei]*

things required by the law, they are a law for themselves, even though
they do not have the law, since they show that the requirements of
the law are written on their hearts, their consciences also bearing
witness, and their thoughts now accusing, now even defending
them. (Romans 2:14-15 NIV)

That is the bright side of the story. It also has a darker side. Although
Scripture confirms the reality of general revelation, it also holds that
general revelation is obscured—more precisely, that we have obscured
it through our rebellion against the Revealer. All have sinned and fallen
short of the glory of God (Romans 3:23). Rather than accepting God
as our god, we want to be gods to ourselves (Genesis 3:1-6). To do this
we "hold down" *(katechontōn)* the truth—we pretend to ourselves that
we do not know what we really do know (Romans 1:18-19). Persistence
in such pretense darkens or perverts such natural knowledge as God
has given us. Paul explains the problem in this way:

For although [men] knew God, they neither glorified him as God
nor gave thanks to him, but their thinking became futile and their
foolish hearts were darkened. . . . Furthermore, since they did not
think it worthwhile to retain the knowledge of God, he gave them
over to a depraved mind, to do what ought not to be done. . . . They
invent ways of doing evil. . . . They not only continue to do these
very things but also approve of those who practice them. (Romans
1:21, 28, 30, 32 NIV)

In sum, the very heart on which God has written his law is estranged
from itself. Jeremiah laments that it is "deceitful above all things and
beyond cure. Who can understand it?" (Jeremiah 17:9 NIV). Indeed it
needs to be written upon again, this time with transforming power
(31:33). Until this is accomplished, by grace through faith in Jesus
Christ, we discern the law of God more through the consequences of
its violation than through the witness of clear conscience. Unfortunately even that instruction may be ignored when we need it most
(Proverbs 1:7). We are "by nature"—by fallen nature—"children of
wrath" (Ephesians 2:3). "Quarry the granite rock with razors, or moor
the vessel with a thread of silk," said John Henry Newman; "then may
you hope with such keen and delicate instruments as human knowledge and human reason to contend against those giants, the passion
and the pride of man."

What then shall we say of the natural law? On the tablets of the heart a law is written indeed, the same for all men (as Thomas Aquinas said) not only as to rectitude but as to knowledge. But it is a far cry from knowing something to acknowledging it, and the human race has been in the condition psychologists call "denial" ever since the Fall. Acknowledging what we really know is now an act of faith.

Care is needed here, for two opposite mistakes must be avoided. In the face of human rebellion against the law written on the heart, one mistake is to believe that the aspiration to a philosophy of natural law is futile. Some Protestant theologians hold that when Paul spoke of a law written even on the heart of the pagans, he meant only that even the pagans were conscious of guilt—not that they knew what they should do.[1]

My own view is that this is unscriptural. One notices in the New Testament that the apostles always begin with the Scriptures when they are talking to Jews but that with Gentile nonbelievers they always begin somewhere else—with the testimony of creation, with the Gentiles' own sense of the insufficiency of their gods or with the Gentiles' consciousness of the law written on their hearts. Although these things are insufficient for salvation, the apostles clearly think they prepare Gentile nonbelievers to *receive* the gospel of salvation in the same way that the law of Moses prepared the Jews. Moreover, Paul simply does not teach that what is written on the heart gives nothing more than a vague consciousness of sin; he states explicitly that what is written there is *law*.

The other mistake is to believe that the doctrine of natural law can be *demonstrated* through ordinary philosophical method. But philosophy is not a remedy for denial of the obvious; the more we learn, the better we are at rationalizing. Joy Davidman spoke of "the lie of the skeptic bound hand and foot in despair, who rather than face his own sins will even doubt his own reality."[2] We meet with it every day—famous philosophers get away with saying that truth is whatever their peers will let them get away with saying.

Poised between these two errors is what I take to be the verity. There is a natural law, and it can be known and philosophically analyzed. But that which is beside the Scripture can be vindicated only with the help of Scripture; that which is revealed before the gospel can be secured against evasion only in the light of the gospel. The doctrine of natural law is best grounded not in the study of nature independent of God's Word but in the Word of God itself. I do not mean that natural law is the same as Divine law; I do mean that Scripture is our foremost authority about both.

But what is the use of the natural law? The main use of general revelation, including the natural law, is apologetics: giving a reason for the hope that lies within us. I do not mean that in apologetics we always *refer* to the natural law but that we depend on its existence.

Apologetics, in turn, comes in three main varieties. Though in practice they overlap and intersect in various ways, they can be distinguished in principle. The evangelical variety of apologetics finds its occasion whenever a believer shares his faith. You have to know the bad news before you can grasp the good news; you have to know your sins before you can want to be delivered from them. A person with no conception of these things could not be reached with the gospel. Yet God's preparations cannot ultimately fail: our nonbelieving neighbors do know of such things before we even begin to speak. Though our hearts are made of stone, his carvings on them remain, and they are not so easy to write over as the Enemy would like us to think.

The moral variety of apologetics finds its occasion when we engage in ethical persuasion or counsel. We use the political variety, its special case, to leaven the civil law we share with our nonbelieving neighbors—for instance, when we seek agreement that life in the womb should not be destroyed, that sodomy should not be granted legal equivalence with marriage, or that sick people should be cared for and comforted instead of starved or pressured into suicide. In this area we can hardly get far by proclaiming to nonbelievers "The Bible says!" But we can get somewhere by proclaiming extrabiblical truths which we know, on biblical authority, that the nonbeliever really knows too.

A difficulty arises here. Karl Barth holds that because every term and every proposition gains its meaning from the system of thought to which it belongs, the affirmations of believers and nonbelievers will have no meaning in common even when they use identical terms. They might both speak of "God" and "spirit," for example—or for that matter of "love" and "forgiveness"—but there is no common ground, no point of contact, no real connection between them. Stanley Hauerwas and William H. Willimon make a similar point in the context of politics:

Big words like "peace" and "justice," slogans the church adopts under the presumption that, even if people do not know what "Jesus Christ is Lord" means, they will know what peace and justice means, are words awaiting content. The church really does not know what these words mean apart from the life and death of Jesus of Nazareth. After all, Pilate permitted the killing of Jesus in order to secure both peace and justice (Roman style) in Judea. It is Jesus' story that gives content to our faith, judges any institutional embodiment of our faith, and teaches us to be suspicious of any political slogan that does not need God to make itself credible.[3]

If Barth had expressed the *whole* truth there could be no common converse with nonbelievers; a Christian in the American public square might just as well be speaking in Farsi as in English. Often enough it feels as though we are. To believe that, however, is to take the world's pretense of ignorance at face value. Barth's thesis is incomplete. He is certainly right to suppose that our respective systems of thought do not *in themselves* supply a point of contact with nonbelievers, but he is wrong to suppose that there *is* no point of contact.

Our point of contact with nonbelievers is established by God himself. That point is general revelation, which "penetrates the very mind of man even in his revolt" so that his conscience bears witness despite himself. Natural law is but the moral aspect of this penetrating arrow.[4]

Notice that the same two things are necessary in all three kinds of apologetics. First we must know what is known already, then we must know how this knowledge is repressed; first we must learn the heart's inscription, then we must learn its devices. My thesis is that a bright light on the text and devices of the heart is precisely what we should demand from any philosophical analysis of natural law.

From this perspective, most modern ethical thinking goes about matters backwards. It assumes that the problem of human sin is mainly *cognitive*—that it has to do with the state of our knowledge. In other words, it holds that we don't know what's right and wrong and are trying to find out. But natural-law theory assumes that the problem is mainly *volitional*—that it has to do with the state of our will. It holds that by and large we know what's right and wrong but wish we didn't, and that we try to keep ourselves in ignorance so that we can do as we please.

How then shall we uncover the text and devices of the heart? Through self-examination? No. Not many of us are honest enough for that. Of course all hearts do have the same text. But just because they also practice the same devices, something more than self-examination is necessary to bring either the text or the devices fully into the light. Our analysis must be anchored in God's Word, which has the power to explode self-deceptions. "Test everything," says Paul (1 Thessalonians 5:21).

Christians then have a standard for the philosophy of natural law: as to the goal, uncover the text and devices of the heart; as to the test, rely on the Word of God. Even among Christian philosophers the doctrine of natural law often fails to measure up. Either it focuses on matters peripheral to the text and the devices of the heart, or it wanders from its scriptural foundation. To one degree or another these have been flaws of almost all previous natural-law theorizing, including my own—and nearly all books about it, probably including the present one. The survey presented in the next two chapters is intended to indicate where we might do better.

FOURTEEN

A REPRISE OF THE OLDER THINKERS

WE HAVE ALREADY CONSIDERED WHAT ARISTOTLE, THOMAS AQUINAS AND John Locke have to say for themselves. But what shall we say about them?

Aristotle
As we saw earlier in the book, Aristotle is only a natural-right thinker, not a natural-law thinker. He is also a pagan. These two facts are connected.

The universe, for Aristotle, is a self-existent order of causes. Logically, he believes, there must be a "first" cause, but he thinks of it as merely part of the system—not distinct from and superior to it as Creator. Therefore, although he knows that there are objective standards of goodness and justice over and above what this or that society happens to call good and just, he nowhere says that these standards are given or sustained by a sovereign God; nor does he say that they can be expressed in the form of law.

One result of this blindness is that he misses the specifically moral *point* of the moral virtues, seeing them not as qualities that men ought to have but only as qualities that happy and noble men actually do have. In the same way he cannot see a difference between mere accomplishments, such as wittiness, and true virtues, such as courage.

So it is that although he understands the baseness and absurdity of vice, he cannot fathom its sheer guiltiness. However disgusting and ridiculous it may be, it is not *sin;* he has never heard of the One who commands, "Be holy; for I the LORD your God am holy" (Leviticus 11:44; 19:2).

To be sure, the gravitational pull of true law can often be felt in Aristotle, and it is easy to see why natural-law thinkers have found him suggestive. For instance, he knows that there cannot be any moral deliberation at all unless certain "first" principles are taken for granted. Moreover, although he cannot really make sense of guilt, at least he knows that there is such a thing. In one passage on natural justice he even maintains that he is speaking of the same thing as Euripides' character Antigone—a tragic heroine who justifies her defiance of royal command by appeal to the law of the gods! But Aristotle probably means only that both he and Antigone recognize a standard prior to and higher than the law of the king.

I should say that the usefulness of Aristotle for the theory of natural law owes not to his grasp on very truth but to his being the supreme example of general revelation "penetrating the mind of man even in his revolt." Particularly brilliant is his habit of always beginning moral reflection with the general opinion of mankind (or of men whom mankind has generally accounted wise). Like his other habits—sifting and synthesizing competing opinions, rummaging for the mean—it presupposes a single mark that is missed in many ways. *If there were no special revelation,* no better method could be devised for disentangling the text on the heart of man from the evasions and subterfuges of men. The human race has dimmed and weakened the good of marriage in a dozen directions, but marriage is nearly everywhere accounted good; it has blurred and confused the wrong of murder in a dozen ways, but murder is nearly everywhere accounted bad.

For this reason some people have considered Aristotelian method to be *the* method of natural-law thinking. Here Christians must dissent, for of course we have only God's assurance that the common text *is* true. Moreover God *has* granted us other assurances; there is, after all, the rest of special revelation. On the other hand, within limits Aristotle's method is useful even for Christians. Scripture is not an encyclopedia that tells us everything we need to know about every subject. For instance, it does not give us a comprehensive doctrine of politics. Our only guarantees are that its teachings are truthful, foundational and sufficient for salvation. Therefore, although all propositions must be tested by Scripture, they need not all be *found* in Scripture. For probing general revelation in domains of the heart where special revelation, though sure, is incomplete, Aristotle's method is suggestive.

Yet it is often misleading, and this in four ways. The first is that all human beings seek excuses for distorting the natural law, and some excuses are so versatile and convenient that they pass into general usage—for example, "the end justifies the means." The second is that because of their permanent advantages, certain groups are able to get away with the same sorts of wrongdoing in almost all times and places, so that their mottoes also pass into general usage—for example, "the government is above the law." In both these cases, taking the general usage of mankind as an infallible test of the law written on the heart would beguile us into accepting the formulae of wrongdoing as parts of the law itself.

The third and fourth problems with Aristotle's method are somewhat different. By the very nature of the universal human revolt against God and his requirements, until we submit to his grace we are apt to believe anything rather than the truth about him. In this domain nothing passes into general usage, for, although all nations worship, their objects of devotion have nothing in common. True, none of the nations is satisfied, from which a daring Aristotelian might hazard the guess that all of them know they are wrong; but as to what is right he could have no idea. In turn, by the same universal revolt not one of God's laws is observed in its purity. In this sense their violation passes into general usage, so no matter how many remain visible under the crust of diverse desecrations, they can never be recognized by Aristotle's method *as laws.* They will always seem more like rules of thumb. True, all men know guilt, from which a daring Aristotelian might guess that there is something wrong with this picture; but he could never be sure.

These problems, I think, are why the great pagan philosopher was never able to pass beyond natural right. His method, so useful to one who already knows that the heart's text is law, kept him from admitting that there is any such thing. We pass now to one who did.

Thomas Aquinas

There is much for a Christian to complain of in Thomas Aquinas, and I speak as one who loves him. Though he knows that everything other than God is utterly dependent on God, he sometimes gives the impression that what goes on in nature is somehow less dependent on him than are the effects of his grace. Though he knows that there can be no sin without the complicity of the mind, he sometimes gives the impression that the mind has not fallen as far as the rest of us. Though he knows that the text on our hearts is overwritten by sin, he sometimes gives the impression that it is just as plain to the sinful eye as a traffic light in the middle of the road.

Some of these obstacles may result from his having borrowed a subscriptural ontology from pagan philosophers and modified it in the light of Scripture, rather than grounding it on Scripture in the first place.[1] Though Thomas is extremely conscientious, at times his reliance on pagan sources seems to lead him into misinterpretation of Scripture itself. For instance, in the *Treatise on Law*, Question 91, Article 1, he cites Proverbs 8:23 in support of the Platonic view that the orderliness of existent things reflects the orderliness of eternal, *un*created ideas in God's mind. Not only is the Platonic view unsupported by this verse, it seems to be contradicted by the preceding one, which declares the very Wisdom or pattern according to which God created the universe to be his creation:[2] Wisdom speaks for herself:

The LORD *created* me at the beginning of his work, the first of his acts of old. Ages ago I was set up, at the first, before the beginning of the earth. When there were no depths I was brought forth, when there were no springs abounding with water. Before the mountains had been shaped, before the hills, I was brought forth; before he had made the earth with its fields, or the first of the dust of the world. When he established the heavens, I was there, when he drew a circle on the face of the deep, when he made firm the skies above, when he established the fountains of the deep, when he assigned to the sea its limit, so that the waters might not transgress his command, when he marked out the foundations of the earth, then I was beside him, like a master workman; and I was daily his delight, rejoicing

before him always, rejoicing in his inhabited world and delighting in the sons of men. (Proverbs 8:22-31, emphasis added)
Fortunately not all of Thomas's work is vitiated by questionable ontology, and the parts of his natural-law theory which are most important for moral apologetics are strong enough to survive its excision. Indeed in many ways Thomas is his own best critic. Far from being unaware of how we repress and deny the law written on the heart, he gives perhaps the best short analysis of repression and denial to be found anywhere in philosophy or theology. I mean, of course, the discussion we have seen previously of how some precepts are suppressed and others blotted out through passion, evil habit, evil disposition of nature, vicious custom and evil persuasion. More of his critics should read these parts of his work. So should some of his defenders, who prefer him to Calvin for the bad reason that they would rather paint the Fall in softer colors than the true ones.

At this point my only criticism of Thomas would be that although his excellent analysis of repression and denial presupposes a distinction between principles we can't not know and other principles derived from them, he does not tell us how he knows which are which or exactly how the derivation works. In fact he seems a bit unsure himself, for, as we saw in chapter four, he sometimes classifies the principles of the Decalogue among the primary precepts of the natural law but at other times classifies them among the secondary.

What causes him difficulty, I think, is that God's commands are so concrete, so singular. God utters not just clean abstractions but messy particulars. His word is not "Thou shalt not covet" but "Thou shalt not covet thy neighbour's house, thou shalt not covet thy neighbour's wife, nor his manservant, nor his maidservant, nor his ox, nor his ass, nor any thing that is thy neighbour's" (Exodus 20:17 KJV). Thomas is torn. In one ear whisper the prophets, saying that all God utters is real; in the other whisper the Greeks, saying that messy concrete things are not *really* real—certainly not matter for first principles.

The best work on Thomas Aquinas is done by professional philosophers and theologians. The best work with him, though, has often been done by amateurs. By working *with* him I mean putting his insights to use—turning them into the field and using them to plow. To this genre belong *The Abolition of Man*, a series of lectures on teaching English by

C. S. Lewis, and *Degenerate Moderns,* a collection of biographical essays by E. Michael Jones, both cited previously. Neither is perfect—in particular, the latter is erratic and sometimes uncharitable—but they add greatly to our understanding. Jones quotes a passage from Augustine's *Confessions:* "Even those who set themselves up against You do but copy You in a perverse way." In their different ways both books set out to show how, and I drew from both in chapter five.

Lewis teaches what it means that the natural law constitutes the first principles of practical reason. We tend to think we can escape from the law and make up new moralities for ourselves. The truth is that the mutinous heart can find no other tenets on which it might base its insurrection but those written upon it already. Its revolt is a sham, for all it can do is pull a few ordinances from the ranks, fatten them up and use them to beat down the others. It derives the very strength of its rebellion from the law itself; it exploits the fact that the moral precepts qualify each other to make them suppress each other. I believe that this is what Paul meant in Romans 2:15 when he said of the Gentiles not only that "what the law requires is written on their hearts" but also that "their conflicting thoughts accuse or perhaps excuse them." The first is about the heart's text; the second about its devices.

Jones teaches what it means that conscience has the character of law. We tend to think we can escape from conscience because we can escape guilty feelings. The truth is that "moral realism is predicated upon moral absolutes, and one quickly comes to realize that one of the qualities of an absolute is that its effects are achieved absolutely, which is to say, without regard to the intentions of those who act on them." Guilt therefore works on us whether there are guilty feelings or not. Contra Freud, for instance, it is not true that the mind in general is "condemned to project its concerns on the outside world." On the other hand, "the guilty conscience is." The man who will not admit his sins "still tells the truth in a way, but not the truth about reality. He can only tell the truth about himself, in spite of himself, in a way that he himself is condemned not to understand."[3]

John Locke

Though John Locke speaks of principles of action written on the heart by God himself,[4] this is lip service; by such language he means something far different from what Scripture does. He views the mind as a blank slate on which letters can be written only by sense data. To be sure he thinks that there are such things as innate desires, but he does not believe in such a thing as underived knowledge.[5] Therefore, if we are to know the natural law, we must *infer* it from sense data in the manner sketched out in chapter seven. It would seem to follow that those who are lazy or unskillful in inference do not know the natural law at all. Something of the sort seems to be hinted at in the *Second Treatise*, Section 6. Locke might there have said that reason teaches all mankind; rather he says that it teaches all mankind *who will but consult it*. The problem, apparently, is not that we hold down our knowledge but that we do not all acquire it in the first place.

This is no small mistake. To distinguish between wise men and fools is one thing; to imply that poor reasoners have no conscience is another. Besides, the blank-slate theory is incoherent. If everything we know had to be learned from sense data, then of course everything in the way we learn would also have to be learned. But if everything in the way we learn had also to be learned, then we could never begin to learn in the first place. Yet we do begin to learn. Therefore there must be some knowledge that is not learned from sense data, knowledge on which even our ability to learn from sense data depends. Locke uses this knowledge no less than any other thinker. He has no choice.

Yet one can see how Locke's mistake arises. Although the mind is not a blank slate in his sense, it is certainly a blank slate in another—for although even a baby's mind is somehow structured by underived first principles, the baby certainly cannot be said to *know* them yet. The ability to *articulate* the deep structure of the mind comes much, much later than the structure itself does; that ability presupposes experience, even though it goes beyond experience. The root problem is simply that Locke fails to distinguish between innate knowledge and underived knowledge.[6]

Unfortunately this theoretical error has practical consequences. They emerge not all at once but by degrees. Convinced that he must ground every moral duty solely on the lessons of sense experience, Locke naturally emphasizes the moral duties he *thinks* he knows how to ground in that way. These turn out to be chiefly the ones that safeguard other people: we might express the formula "I have a duty to honor your liberty so long as you stay within the bounds of the natural law yourself." Unfortunately, if we are cloudy about duties *other* than honoring liberty, then it is hard to see what staying within the bounds of the natural law could *mean* but honoring liberty. Gradually then the formula becomes "I have a duty to honor your liberty so long as you honor mine." At this stage liberty is bounded by nothing but itself, which is to say that it is not bounded at all.

To be sure, Locke would be horrified by this fatal progression. The problem is that he cannot easily stop it. Though he correctly views rights as something we deduce from the demands of morality rather than something that protects us against them, his wrong choice of emphasis *within* the moral law threatens to destroy the moral law itself.

On the other hand, Locke performs a signal service to the natural-law tradition by providing a counterweight to something in Thomas Aquinas that ought not be there. There is a defect in the Thomistic way of speaking about the common good, a defect which comes not from the natural law itself, but from Aristotle—in particular, from the way Aristotle thinks about parts and wholes. Aristotle says that the whole is prior to its part. What this means is that although we can speak about a whole without presupposing its division into parts, we cannot speak of a part without presupposing the whole to which it belongs. In this sense, the whole provides the part with all its meaning and identity—just as the puzzle is what gives meaning and identity to the piece.

The difficulty comes when we try to apply this talk about parts and wholes to the relation between the state and its citizens. We all know that true statecraft promotes the common rather than the individual good. But why is that true? The reason, thinks Aristotle, is that the whole is prior to the part—*and the citizen is a part of the state.*

This is a view which no Christian can accept. We do not reject all talk of parts and wholes; we say, for instance, that believers are parts of the community of the faithful, the body of Christ. But that means that our meaning and identity come from him, not from the state. In fact, though citizens and subjects of the earthly city, we cannot call ourselves *parts* of it at all. The Bible calls us exiles in the world. We are in it but not of it; we participate in it, but we do not belong to it. Our true commonwealth is Heaven. We agree with Aristotle that true statecraft promotes the common rather than the individual good—but our reason is that we are commanded to love our neighbors, not that the whole is prior to the part.

The difference makes a difference. To hold that citizens and subjects belong to the City is not an ennobling imitation of the idea that believers belong to Christ but a debasing perversion of it. It is, in the most literal sense, an idolatry. The one idea says that for the sake of my neighbor I should sacrifice myself; the other implies that for the sake of the state I may have to sacrifice my neighbor.

In talking about politics I believe that Thomas and his followers have far too readily accommodated themselves to the Aristotelian idea about parts and wholes. Now people of good sense often hold surprisingly bad ideas, but they prevent them from poisoning judgment by watering them down with other ideas that are more wholesome. Thomists do this when they say things such as "The individual is a part of the state, but not only a part" or "The individual is a part of the state in some respects, but not in others." More power to them! But the strategy of adulteration is risky; it would be better to give up the bad idea altogether. As pointed out by Yves R. Simon, himself a Thomist and practitioner of the strategy, even good ideas become dangerous when shorn of their necessary qualifications.[7]

John Locke too fends off the bad effects of the citizen-as-part-of-the-state idea, but in a different way than good Thomists do: for although his view of the relation between the citizen and the city is equally distorted, it is conveniently distorted in the opposite direction. The introduction of this counterweight is his chief contribution to the tradition of natural law. So long as the tradition's two tendencies were opposed—one threatening to diminish the individual, the other to distend him—there was a chance of muddling through to the right way of acting, of finding the mean in practice even while missing it in theory.[8]

The American republic was long the beneficiary of this tension; it was like a string pulled tight between the cult of the individual and the cult of the state. Unfortunately the public philosophy of our own century has made the string go slack. It glues the two cults together rather than pulling them apart: it distends the individual in some ways while diminishing him in others. The lesson for those who love the tradition is that we can no longer rely on a balance of errors. From now on, nothing less than truth will suffice.

FIFTEEN

A SAMPLING OF RECENT THINKERS

ALTHOUGH SOME HAVE CLAIMED THAT IT DID, AND OTHERS MIGHT WISH that it had, the philosophy of natural law did not end with the classical and early modern writers. It is enjoying a hard-won renaissance. Because I view this renaissance from a Christian perspective, the most convenient way to group its various schools of thought is theological: Roman Catholic, Jewish, Protestant, and finally secular. As we shall see, the secular way of thinking is just as full of theological commitments as the other three—just as full of faith, but of a different sort.

Roman Catholic Reconsideration of Natural Law
The works of Catholic thinkers Germain G. Grisez, John Finnis and Joseph M. Boyle represent minor variations on what is really the same approach to natural law. Although it bears a family resemblance to the scholastic doctrine epitomized by Thomas Aquinas, it departs from Thomas in several important ways and is best described as a brand-new theory. For purposes of the following summary, I draw most heavily on Grisez.[1]

The basic structure of the new natural-law theory is simple. First, we have "pre-moral practical principles" that identify the various kinds of human good as self-evident objects of pursuit. Second, we have "modes of responsibility," equally self-evident, that tell us how to pursue them. Third are ordinary moral rules, which result.

Category one begins with a First Principle of Practical Reason: that in all choices, good is to be done and evil avoided. All the other premoral principles result from plugging in specific forms of good where the First Principle simply says "good."

What then are the forms of good? Grisez lists them as follows: (1) *Self-integration* is harmony among the parts of the person who is doing the choosing. (2) *Authenticity* is harmony among how one judges, how one chooses and how one carries out his choices. (3) *Justice and friendship* are aspects of communion among good people who choose to act in harmony with each other. (4) *Holiness* is harmony with God—we might say "the Unknown God," because the authors do not assume that the natural man knows who God is. (5) *Life,* a broad category, includes health, safety, bodily wholeness and procreation. (6) *Knowledge* is knowing the truth as well as appreciating beauty and excellence. (7) *Exercises of skill* are those activities of work and play that enrich people in the very act of doing them.

These seven forms of good are supposed to be both mutually exhaustive and irreducible. They are mutually exhaustive in that they are supposed to cover all the possibilities of human goodness. They are irreducible in that each is to be valued for itself, not as an aspect of another. For instance, the goodness of life does not arise from the goodness of knowledge; the goodness of knowledge does not arise from the goodness of life; and the goodnesses of life and knowledge do not arise from some yet more fundamental good different from both.

Category two begins with another first principle, this time called a First Principle of Morality: that all choices must be compatible with a will toward "integral human fulfillment." What this awkward term means is that we are to avoid "unnecessary self-limitation": each of us must live his life in a coherent way that gives each of the seven forms of good its due. The other eight moral principles spell out the ways of making choices that we must avoid for this idea to be honored. Grisez likes to call them "modes of responsibility."

We may paraphrase his list as follows: (1) Never neglect any human good because of sloth. (2) Never be selfish; integral human fulfillment requires *partnership* in human goods. (3) Never pursue emotional satisfaction for its own sake; although the human goods are emotionally satisfying, emotional satisfaction is not what *makes* them good. (4) Never allow choices to be guided by bad feelings about things that are not really bad. (5) Never *arbitrarily* treat different persons differently; treat them differently only for reasons that arise from the basic goods themselves. For instance, friends should be treated differently from nonfriends, but only in matters that pertain to friendship alone. (6) Never sacrifice reality to appearance—for instance, by seeking the *feeling* of knowledge instead of knowledge or the *feeling* of holiness instead of holiness. (7) Respect every human good in every act. (8) Never sacrifice any human good to any other; in other words, never do evil that good may result.

Each mode of responsibility corresponds to a particular virtue, and each excludes a particular kind of *ir*responsibility—a particular kind of unnecessary self-limitation. Not all of them are exactly what they seem. For instance, the usual interpretation of the principle never to do evil that good may result, confirmed by Scripture at Romans 3:8, is that we are never to do *moral* evil that good may result. Not every evil is a moral evil; for instance, the pain of being spanked or grounded is an evil but not a moral one. If we were never to inflict *any* evil that good may result, we could not even discipline our children.

Grisez, Finnis and Boyle cannot take "evil" as meaning only moral evil, because doing so would make their argument circular; they are trying to find out what counts as moral evil in the first place. So they take "evil" as meaning harm to *any* basic good. But this broadens the principle enormously, perhaps distorting it.

Just how to derive ordinary moral rules from all of this apparatus is also somewhat mysterious. The problem may be illustrated with the seventh mode of responsibility, which directs us to respect every good in every act. What does that mean? The authors say it has the same meaning as the second version of Kant's Categorical Imperative—"Act so that you treat humanity, whether in your own person or in that of another, always as an end and never only as a means." But the emptiness of the Categorical Imperative is notorious. Which is true: that mothers should not be "means" to their babies' survival, or that babies should not be "means" to their mothers' control of their pregnancies? That speakers should not be "means" to their listeners' purity, or that their listeners should not be "means" to the speakers' pleasure in filth? That patients should not be "means" to the quiet of their doctors' consciences, or that their doctors should not be "means" to their patients' desire to die? The mere idea of Not Using Others cannot produce a moral code, for only by the light of a moral code can we tell what counts as using others.[2]

The authors think that Kant was on the right track but failed to go far enough. Some of his impotence they attribute to the fact that he knew *only* the seventh mode of responsibility; the rest they attribute to the fact that he was unable to explain even this mode correctly. Its correct explanation, the authors say, is that we should never deliberately injure any of the human goods or go along with such injury. Why then was Kant unable to grasp this point? Because he stubbornly refused to regard most human goods as goods at all. Nothing is truly good, he said, except a good will.[3]

Very well: let us grant that a better explanation of the seventh mode of responsibility helps show why it is so hard to derive ordinary moral rules from the Kantian apparatus. Our question, though, was how to derive them from the *authors'* apparatus. Perhaps we will get further with an example. A young woman goes to college, commits illicit sex and gets pregnant. May she have an abortion? The authors would say no. Why not? Because it would be a deliberate injury to life, in violation of mode seven. Could she plead the importance of continuing her schooling? Again the authors say no. Why not? Because then she would be sacrificing life to knowledge, in violation of mode eight. So we have a deduction: no abortion. That was easy.

On the other hand, deriving equally simple moral rules sometimes requires some pretty fancy philosophizing. For instance, the authors think that the young woman of the previous example *may* choose to remain unmarried and chaste in order to serve God without the distractions of domestic life. Now obviously celibacy does forestall certain possibilities of human good, such as marital friendship and the procreation of new life. Why then is it permitted? Most people would say that marital friendship and procreation may be sacrificed because holiness is more important. But because of modes seven and eight—the same ones cited a moment ago—the authors cannot give this reason. Mode seven says no good is more important than any other, mode eight that no good can be sacrificed for another. What the authors must do then is find a way of saying that although the woman's decision has indeed forestalled certain possibilities of friendship and procreation, it is permissible because these goods have not been *deliberately* harmed.

Perhaps they haven't been. But we ought to be uneasy about the argument anyway. Do such mundane decisions as the one we have been considering really *require* such delicate distinctions? And is it always clear how to apply them? We know that hairs must be split in the hard cases. For instance, just-war theorists must distinguish between deliberate and nondeliberate harm to innocents in order to decide whether it is permissible to bomb a rocket launcher located on the roof of an orphanage. The difficulty is that the authors threaten to make even the easy cases into hard ones. "If there really is writing on the heart," runs the oldest jibe against natural law, "why don't people know the ordinary moral rules better than they do?" But from now on the jibe may have to be reversed: "If the writing on the heart is like *that*, why do people know the ordinary moral rules *even as well* as they do?" It is hard to see how ordinary reasoners could bridge such a canyon of conscience— even with the most generous allowances for the donation of accumulated wisdom that each generation passes on to the next.

There is an even deeper problem with the new natural-law theory. Is it really true that each form of human good is just as important as every other? The intention behind the claim is certainly praiseworthy. The authors wish to explode the claim of the utilitarians that nothing is sacred—that every good may be sacrificed. But to show that these blind men are wrong, is it really necessary to go to the opposite extreme of holding that everything is sacred—that no good may be sacrificed? Is it true, for instance, that an opportunity for play may never be sacrificed for life? That an opportunity for skill may never be sacrificed for justice? That an opportunity for beauty may never be sacrificed for holiness? *Why* must we regard every form of good as equally important?

According to the authors, the reason we must regard each form of good as equally important is that taken from its own perspective each seems to be *most* important; from A's perspective all non-A are derivative, from B's perspective all non-B are derivative and so forth. This is a strange argument. The premise is true; it is almost a tautology. From the perspective of play, a friend does seem merely someone to play with, and from the perspective of friendship, play does seem merely a thing that friends do. Unfortunately the conclusion does not follow. All that such examples really show is that each form of good becomes an idol if we let it. How does it cure idolatry to let them all be idols?

Scripture is clear that idolatry must be rejected, not universalized. One good really is supremely important: the good of holiness, for everything must be done for the sake of God. "Seek first his kingdom and his righteousness," says Jesus, "and all these things shall be yours as well" (Matthew 6:33). The cure of idolatry is there and nowhere else. Amazingly Grisez, Finnis and Boyle quote the verse themselves but fail to see that it contradicts their doctrine.[4] Their view seems to be that holiness has priority in one sense but not in another.

The argument has two stages. First, the authors say that although no form of good may be sacrificed for the others, so long as that is not demanded there is no reason why a person may not pursue a particular possibility of goodness more ardently than the others. It will not be more important *in itself* than the others, but it may certainly be chosen as the integrating thread of a plan of life in which all of them are given their due. Next they ask whether any form of good might serve equally well as an integrating thread. The answer is no, because there is such a thing as empty goodness. We cannot be satisfied in the pursuit of work, play, truth and so on unless there is some *point* to it all. But the point of it all is God, and the only good which speaks to this point is holiness. Therefore only holiness can serve as the integrating thread.

The problem with this argument is that it gives but half the story. That only God can give my life its point is a truth of the faith. But if I pursue holiness only to give my life a point, am I really serving God? I seem to be still serving myself; I am only doing so in a more high-minded way than before. Jesus does not say that we are to seek first God's kingdom and righteousness *so that* all other things shall be ours as well; he says we are to seek first God's kingdom and righteousness *and* all other things shall be ours as well. Only by death shall we live;

only by laying all goods down shall we pick them all up; only by abandoning the idea that they have value apart from God shall we enjoy, unstained, the value they have *from* God. This transformation of motive is possible only by grace, which opens the way through faith to participation in the death and risen life of Christ.

To be sure, we should not demand too much from the natural law, for what we need most is made known to us only in the gospel. I am not trying to smuggle the gospel into the natural law; my point is that the doctrine of natural law should not hold the gospel hostage. We cannot expect it to point the way to self-transcendence, but at the same time we must not allow it to rule out self-transcendence. Unfortunately that is just what the doctrine of integral human fulfillment seems to do.

Jewish Reconsideration of Natural Law

Opinion differs among Jews as to whether the doctrine of natural law is compatible with Jewish faith. Those who reject it do so on grounds that the Torah is divine revelation—the commandments of God, not the cogitations of philosophers. He who is devoted to "the books of the Greeks," said Rabbi Solomon ibn Adret in 1305, "makes them the root and uproots the Torah of the Lord!"[5] Those who do accept the doctrine of natural law offer three points in reply: (1) natural law too is revelation; (2) Torah presupposes natural law; (3) Judaism already teaches natural law, but under a different name.

Natural law is *revelation* because it too comes from God. Its content is rationally evident only by virtue of the order God has placed in creation and in the mind of man. Natural law is his indirect revelation; Torah is his direct revelation. This parallels the Christian distinction between general and special revelation.

Torah *presupposes* natural law because otherwise it would be unintelligible. In Deuteronomy 4:8 God asks the people of Israel, "And what great nation is there, that has statues and ordinances so righteous as all this law which I set before you this day?" Had the people not had some idea of righteousness already, his question could not even have been understood.

Judaism *teaches natural law under a different name* because it includes the ancient rabbinical tradition of the Noachian commandments—

very general laws given by God to Noah and his "sons," or descendants, a group which of course includes every subsequent generation of human beings. Some rabbis held that up to six of these commandments had previously been given to Adam. Either way, the point is clear: no people now can claim to be ignorant of them; no nation now can claim to be exempt. This gives the Noachian commandments special importance for understanding relations between those who do accept biblical revelation and those who do not. As the focus of all rabbinical reflection on natural law, the Noachian commandments deserve our close attention.[6]

How many Noachian commandments are there, and what do they include? The rabbis differed about their number; some said one, some said three, some even said thirty. Most, however, said that they numbered seven. In the classical enumeration, the first commandment concerns adjudication: there must be courts for the administration of justice. All of the other six commandments are prohibitions: there must be no idolatry, no blasphemy, no sexual immorality, no bloodshed, no theft and no eating of flesh torn from living animals.

In Talmud each of these laws receives further specification. For instance, the Noachian commandment concerning sexual immorality is always understood as forbidding incest, adultery, sodomy and bestiality. As the minimal setting for sexual intercourse, something like marriage is always presupposed too, although it is not understood as *qiddušin*—a covenant between the spouses, undertaken in the sight of God—for outside of Torah, marriage in the full sense of the term is unknown.[7]

The first written formulation of the Noachian laws is found in the *Tosefta*.[8] Although this work is believed to have been edited late in the second century, it would have drawn from oral tradition of much greater antiquity. When the Christian apostle Paul writes in Romans 2:14-15 of a law written on the hearts of the Gentiles, we can be all but certain that this earlier oral tradition is exactly what he has in mind.[9] He was, after all, a Pharisee, brought up in Jerusalem, trained "at the feet of Gamaliel" (Acts 22:3). Of course we need not assume that the form in which he knows the tradition is identical to the form it takes in later works, but the central point is the same: even though the Gentiles do not have Torah, they have enough knowledge of God's requirements to be accountable for disobedience.[10]

Paul's claim raises a question. *Was* it the rabbinic teaching that the way in which God gave his commandments to the sons of Noah was (as Paul puts it) to write them on their hearts? In other words, was the Noachian doctrine really about *conscience?* Milton R. Konvitz thinks so and gives two arguments in support of his view. One is that Hebrew Scripture itself speaks of laws written on the tablets of the heart; the other is that although the concept of conscience is not explicitly formulated in Hebrew Scripture, it is clearly presupposed.[11]

Argument one seems invalid. In Proverbs 7:3, the first of the passages cited by Konvitz, God does not declare that he has written his commandments on the tablets of the heart; rather he instructs his people that *they* should write his commandments on the tablets of their hearts. In the second passage, Deuteronomy 30:14, God does say that his commandments are in the people's hearts, but he is speaking to Israel about the Sinaitic commandments—not to all people about the Noachian commandments. In the third passage, Jeremiah 31:33, God is not talking about what he has done but about what he will do when Messiah comes: in a new covenant, different from the old one, he will write his commandments on the people's hearts in such transforming fashion that they will finally be able to obey them.

Argument two is more to the point. "The story of Cain and Abel," says Konvitz, "would have no point unless conscience were assumed; for there had been no [special] supernatural revelation of a law against murder before one brother killed the other, nor was there at that time an enacted criminal code." He continues that the same point may be made about other instances of judgment, for example, the judgment on the Cities of the Plain and the judgment on the generation of Noah himself.

Granted the claim that something is written on the heart even prior to Sinai, how do we arrive at the particular seven commandments of which the rabbis spoke? One point is that the created human mind is able to see some (though not all) of the reasons for each of them. Indeed, explaining the reasons for God's commandments was one of the great projects of rabbinical Judaism. For instance, Rabbi Saakyah Gaon declares that if all relied on theft instead of work for livelihood, "even stealing would become impossible, because, with the disappearance of all property, there would be absolutely nothing in existence that might be stolen."[12] In similar fashion Maimonides says that the eating of flesh torn from living animals "would make one acquire the habit of cruelty,"[13] and Rabbi Hanina explains about the administration of justice that "were it not for the fear of it a man would swallow his neighbor alive."[14]

Insofar as these rabbinical arguments refer to basic human goods, one is tempted to compare them with the new natural-law theory of Grisez, Finnis and Boyle. However, there is a sharp difference. The new natural lawyers assume that we have immediate intuitive knowledge of the human goods and the modes of responsibility and only afterward connect them with ordinary moral rules, such as the prohibition of murder. The rabbinical procedure is the opposite: we have immediate intuitive knowledge of the ordinary moral rules and only afterward connect them with human goods. It is from enduring the horror of murder that we face up to the sanctity of life.

Another way to arrive at the particular seven commandments of which the rabbis spoke is to search the Hebrew Scriptures. Can it be shown that all seven were generally known even before the Sinaitic revelation? Only two of them are expressly declared in this period—the prohibition of bloodshed in Genesis 9:6 and the eating of flesh taken from living animals in verse 4. As to the other five, two different modes of argument can be found in the classical rabbinical literature.

In the first mode of argument all seven commandments are derived from a single verse, Genesis 2:16: "And the LORD God commanded the man, saying, 'You may freely eat of every tree of the garden; but of the tree of the knowledge of good and evil you shall not eat, for in the day that you eat of it you shall die.'" The method of derivation is to link each word or phrase with a scriptural passage on another subject in which the same word or phrase appears. From the first word, for instance, one tradition derives the commandment to establish courts of justice, whereas from the same word another tradition derives the prohibition of idolatry. David Novak explains:

> The first word in the Hebrew is *vayitzav*, "and He commanded." In the *Gemara* [to] the Palestinian Amora, R. Johanan connects this word with the word *yetzaveh* in Genesis 18:19 where Abraham is anticipated as commanding justice; hence for him *dinin* (adjudica-

tion) is the first law. On the other hand, the *Gemara* presents a
Tannaitic tradition quoted by R. Isaac that the first word refers to
idolatry. The *Gemara* connects this word with Exodus 32:8 where the
worshippers of the Golden Calf are described as straying from the
path God has commanded them *(tzivveetim)*. The *Midrash* connects
this word with the word *tzav* in Hosea 5:11, where idolatrous decrees
are condemned.[15]
This method of derivation seems artificial, and some rabbis came to
reject it. In the twelfth century, for instance, Rabbi Judah Ha-Levi
remarked that "there is a wide difference between these injunctions
and the verse. The people, however, accepted these seven laws as
traditions, connecting them with the verse as an aid to memory."[16]

The second mode of argument therefore uses Scripture in a different way, calling attention to the many passages about pre-Sinaitic times
which make sense only on the assumption that the people of that time
were expected to know the Noachian commandments. In Genesis 34:7,
for instance, the sons of Jacob are enraged by the rape of their sister
Dinah, not because "it is not so done *in our country*" (a phrase used in
Genesis 29:26) but because "such a thing *ought not* to be done." Their
reason presupposes knowledge of the wrong of sexual crime. Similarly
knowledge of the wrong of theft is presupposed by Abraham's complaint to Abimelech about the seizure of his well by Abimelech's
servants (Genesis 21:25), and knowledge of justice is presupposed by
Abraham's complaint to God, "Shall not the Judge of all the earth do
right?" (Genesis 18:25). Numerous passages of this sort can be cited.[17]
The only difficulty they place in the way of the Noachian doctrine is
that they demonstrate pre-Sinaitic knowledge of many more commandments than seven; then again, some rabbis did think there were more
Noachian commandments than seven.

The precise number of the commandments may not be important.
What is important is that according to Jewish tradition, certain first
principles are known, and known *as laws,* even apart from Torah. For
the theory of natural law, one part of the significance of the doctrine
is that these principles are known immediately rather than depending
on prior considerations about human goods; law, in other words, is not
just a fancy name for prudence. Another part is that they include not
only general rules, such as the administration of justice, but also

detailed rules, such as the prohibition of specific modes of sexual immorality.

Although the general and detailed rules illuminate each other, their status is exactly the same: the latter are not derived from the former, nor are the former derived from the latter. Both stand in complete and immediate dependence on God. In this way the Noachian doctrine seems to avoid the derivation difficulties we saw earlier in the theory of Grisez, Finnis and Boyle—a difficulty that Thomas Aquinas also escapes, but only at the cost of ambiguity.

Finally, although the Noachian doctrine falls far short of philosophical analysis, it comes much closer than some philosophical analyses we have examined to satisfying the double criterion stated earlier. In the first place it does at least try to ground itself in Scripture, concerning which the rabbis said, "The clear meaning cannot be overridden."[18] In the second place, although it sheds no light on the heart's devices, it does illuminate the inscription.

Protestant Reconsideration of Natural Law

The early Reformers believed in natural law. At any rate, they said they did. In the final chapter of the *Institutes* John Calvin announces, "It is a fact that the law of God which we call the moral law is nothing less than a testimony of the natural law and of that conscience which God has engraved upon the minds of men." Martin Luther is more emphatic, as well as more consistent: "There is no one who does not feel it," says he:

> Everyone must acknowledge that what the natural law says is right and true. . . . If men would only pay attention to it, they would have no need of books or of any other law. For they carry along with them in the depth of their hearts a living book which could give them quite adequate instruction about what they ought to do and not to do, how they ought to judge, and what ought to be accepted and rejected.[19]

Again,

> Experience itself shows that all nations share this common ordinary knowledge. . . . I feel in my heart that I certainly ought to do these things for God, not because of what traditional written laws say, but because I brought these laws with me when I came into the world.

... For although the decalogue was given in one way at a single time and place, all nations recognize that there are sins and iniquities.

He does not mean that in our fallen state the law written on the heart is sufficient for moral guidance: "The devil so blinds and possesses hearts that they do not always feel this law. Therefore one must preach the law and impress it on the minds of people till God assists and enlightens them, so that they feel in their hearts what the word says." Even so, he insists that the natural law is real and active:

Otherwise, were is not naturally written in the heart, one would have to teach and preach the law for a long time before it became the concern of conscience. The heart must also find and feel the law in itself. Otherwise, it would not become a matter of conscience for anyone.

These affirmations would seem to be clear. The tendency among some Protestants, however, has been to dismiss them as "occasional remarks" inconsistent with the theology of the Reformation. Thus according to Helmut Thielicke:

Luther says, "We are not so thoroughly inclined toward evil that there is not left to us a portion which is affected toward the good." He is thinking above all—as he says here—of conscience, *synderesis.* Here, as in certain of Luther's statements concerning natural theology, what we have are relics of Scholastic thinking which cannot be reconciled with his real theological intent as we have described it. One must be on guard precisely at this point against quotations torn from their context in the very heart of Luther's theology.[20]

Whatever Luther and Calvin themselves may have meant, there can be no uncertainty about the views of their followers today. Some do speak of natural law, although they are careful to explain that they are not Thomists. Others insist that such talk be rejected root and branch.

What objections to the doctrine of natural law do the rejectionists advance? We will glance at the thirteen most prominent.[21] The first five have no particular relationship to Christianity; indeed they resemble the arguments of secular thinkers who deny that there is any moral truth at all. We have taken up some of them earlier in this book.

1. *Natural-law doctrine claims to articulate moral principles that are accepted by everyone, everywhere. Yet different principles are held in different places.* But everyone does know certain principles: there is no land where murder

is virtue and gratitude vice. Moreover natural lawyers admit diversity in moral practice too. Such diversity can exist for both good and bad reasons: (1) not all moral rules are universally known, but only first principles; (2) under different circumstances the same rule may have to be applied in different ways; (3) right application requires the exercise of practical wisdom, which cannot itself be exhaustively characterized by any list of rules; and (4) as everyone knows, there is a difference between knowing something and admitting it to oneself.

2. *Although different people and cultures do believe in many of the same moral principles, their agreement is merely verbal; each one gives these principles a different meaning.* What counts as theft will certainly vary according to the property arrangements of different societies, but within limits natural-law theory allows such variation. The meaning of the precept to do unto others as I would have them do unto me will be distorted if what I would have them do unto me is foul, but the fact that a precept can be distorted is no argument against its truth.

3. *Even natural-law theorists disagree about what the natural law includes; whereas Emil Brunner thought that the institution of private property is derived from natural law, Philip Melanchthon held that by nature everything is owned in common.* The appearance of disagreement among such authors results mostly from failure to read their works closely. Quite a few natural lawyers have thought that everything would be owned in common *had it not been for the Fall,* but they have also agreed that under present circumstances property is necessary and that taking the property of another is wrong.

4. *In the name of natural law many false and horrible beliefs have been propounded. Didn't Aristotle and many others justify slavery as natural?* But in the name of every good evil has been done, and in the name of every truth lies have been propounded. That is how sin works; having nothing in itself by which to convince, on what other resources but good and truth can it draw to make itself powerful and plausible?

5. *The doctrine of natural law is supposed to tell us what to do, yet it finds the hard cases just as hard as the rest of us.* No proponent has ever presented the natural law as a magic that makes moral judgment easy; the object is to make it right. One might as well complain that time and motion problems are difficult even after one has learned algebra. The critic has a point against any theory that makes the *easy* cases hard, but, unless

there really is a natural law, how can there even be an easy case?

Now we turn to the other eight objections, which do have a Christian flavor. Most of these result from thinking that what is true of some natural-law theories must be true of them all.

6. *Apart from revelation there cannot be any moral knowledge. In its arrogance natural-law doctrine holds that there can be.* Some thinkers have indeed distinguished natural law from revelation, but the error is more common among the critics than the proponents of natural law. I have defended the view that natural law is general revelation, whereas Scripture is special revelation. Though the latter is superior, both are true and both derive their authority from God alone. Anything from an authority less than this is less than law.

7. *There is a moral law that all men know, but it is prephilosophical, "written on the heart." By contrast, natural-law doctrine tries to deduce it entirely from other considerations.* Again, some natural-law theories have done so. To be sure, although "other considerations" are insufficient, they are not necessarily invalid; as explained earlier, Scripture itself attests to at least five modes of general revelation. But I have argued that the primary aspiration of natural lawyers should be a philosophical analysis of what is prephilosophically known—that they should study the heart's inscription, not invent a substitute.

8. *Although natural-law doctrine admits that there is a law written on the heart, it refuses to admit that this law has been obscured by sin.* Thomas did not refuse to admit that the law written on the heart has been obscured by sin, nor did Luther or Calvin.

9. *There is no law written on the heart; fallen conscience is merely a battleground of competing voices.* This objection presents a false alternative. There is a law written on the heart *and* the fallen conscience is a battleground of competing voices because it tries to deny its own inscription. For this reason I have maintained that an adequate analysis of natural law would illuminate not only the heart's text but also its devices. Several such devices have already been discussed.

10. *Natural-law doctrine views creation as though God put his order into it once and for all such that now it need only be discovered. Rather he acts continually to maintain it and preserve its order in the face of the Fall.* The greatest natural-law thinkers do not make this mistake. For instance, Thomas Aquinas declared that "as every created thing has its being

from another, and, considered in itself, is nothing, so does it need to be preserved by another in the good which pertains to its nature. For it can of itself fail in good, even as of itself it can fall into nonexistence, unless it is upheld by God."[22] Though I agree with the rejectionists that the gracious God acts continually to preserve creation order in the face of the Fall, I would ask: Isn't the writing on the heart one of the things that he preserves? Despite all our efforts to erase it, all we can do is obscure it.

11. *If we are to speak of "nature," then we must recognize that nature includes evil as well as good; if we are to speak of "law," we must recognize that sin also has its laws. The doctrine of natural law denies both points.* Although the first point is not wrong per se, it is perilously ambiguous. Does the critic mean that the laws of a good creation are perverted to serve evil, or does he mean that the creation is not all good? If the former, the claim is orthodox, and a Christian natural-law theory can accept it. If the latter, the claim is not orthodox at all, and a Christian natural-law theory must reject it. Although the second point is ambiguous too, the right way to take it has already been explained in the natural-law theory of Thomas Aquinas: the "law of sin" is not a law in the strict sense but a natural consequence of *violating* the order that ought to have prevailed. By analogy, because of the body's surviving order, there is a certain horrible regularity even in the course of sickness, yet sickness *as such* is disorder.

12. *Christianity maintains that we are reconciled with God by grace alone, through faith alone; natural-law doctrine maintains that salvation can be earned by human moral effort.* Of course anyone who does think we sinful human beings can earn our way into heaven will import this belief into his explanation of natural law. Rabbinical Judaism, for instance, maintains that Gentiles who follow the Noachian commandments will have a share in the life to come.[23] However, the idea of salvation by works is neither implied nor presupposed by the natural law itself and was not believed by Thomas, Calvin or Luther.

13. *The gospel liberates us from bondage to law, whether the law of Moses or the law of nature.* The gospel liberates believers from bondage to law in the sense that they no longer groan under its condemnation; that does not mean they are liberated in the sense of being set free from obedience. "For this is the love of God, that we keep his command-

ments" (1 John 5:3). Therefore, although believers are not saved *by* the moral works of the law, they are certainly saved *for* them.

Because of these misunderstandings of the doctrine of natural law, rejectionists put various other moral doctrines in its place. Among Lutherans, for instance, the favored alternative is "creation orders." But all such labor seems unnecessary. Though not every alternative theory is laid out in full, those that are laid out look suspiciously like natural-law theories doing business under an alias. They scrupulously avoid speaking of the law written on the heart, but they recognize all of its functions. Sometimes they merely reassign them to the *imago Dei*, as though "the image of God"[24] were not man's very definition but only one of his faculties. The good news is that the mostly Catholic proponents of overt natural-law theories and the mostly Protestant proponents of covert natural-law theories are finally coming to the table to iron out their differences.[25] If each of these Christian traditions resolves to talk *to* the other instead of past it, perhaps the coming years will see a gain in clarity.

Secular Reconsideration of Natural Law

Most recent secular thinkers reject the natural law. Yet there is a modest countertrend in secularism too, a cautious groping *back* to the idea of a moral standard known by all and right for all. *The Moral Sense,* an important book by sociologist James Q. Wilson, illustrates both the possibilities and the limits of this trend. "My understanding of our moral confusion," says Wilson, "is a bit different from that of many others."

> To some, the central problem is that modern man has lost his moral bearings or religious commitments so that he is now governed only by immediate impulse or calculating self-interest. Though examples of such a mentality abound, I do not think it is an accurate characterization of the general problem. I will argue in this book that most of us have a moral sense, but that some of us have tried to talk ourselves out of it. It is as if a person born to appreciate a golden sunset or a lovely song had persuaded himself and others that a greasy smear or a clanging gong ought to be enjoyed as much as true beauty.[26]

By those who have tried to talk themselves out of the moral sense,

Wilson means mainly contemporary intellectuals. He comments on just how far this talking can succeed:

> If our passing intellectual and cultural fashions made a vast differ-
> ence, it would follow that there could not be a natural moral sense
> of much consequence. If they made no difference, then the moral
> sense would be so strong that it would govern our actions regardless
> of the circumstances. The correct position, I think, is the middle
> one: we have a moral sense, most people instinctively rely on it even
> if intellectuals deny it, but it is not always and in every aspect of life
> strong enough to withstand a pervasive and sustained attack.[27]

So far Wilson's view sounds much like the doctrine of a law written on the heart which can be obscured but never erased. One who does believe in that law can learn a good deal from his survey of the literature in sociology, anthropology and developmental psychology. He even uses a similar figure of speech: "The teachings of the heart," says Wilson, "deserve to be taken as seriously as the lessons of the mind."[28]

But by the teachings of the heart, does the author mean the same thing as the law written on the heart? Not quite. The great difference is that he calls the moral sense a matter of moral *feelings*. Let us consider this matter more closely.

Wilson offers four examples of moral feelings: sympathy, duty, self-control and fairness. He means by these terms pretty much what most of us do. Sympathy is "the human capacity for being affected by the feelings and experiences of others."[29] Duty is "the disposition to honor obligations even without hope of reward or fear of punishment."[30] Self-control is the ability to defer the "immediate and tangible" for the sake of the "future and uncertain."[31] Fairness, the most complex, is a composite of equity, reciprocity and impartiality—equity being distribution according to worth or merit,[32] reciprocity being repayment of debts and favors,[33] and impartiality being treatment "without prejudice and with an opportunity to present our side of the story."[34] The author assembles an impressive array of evidence to show that the four feelings are active in every culture. In two different senses of the term they are also natural: "They are to some degree innate, and they appear sponta-neously amid the routine intimacies of family life."[35]

The puzzle is why Wilson calls these four things *feelings* at all. As his own language signifies, they are not feelings at all. Rather they are capacities and dispositions—states of character. All four deal with feelings, but that does not make them feelings.

We need not seek far for the solution to the puzzle. That he is talking about states of character Wilson never denies. He uses the language of feelings, impulses, senses and sentiments for another reason: to deny that he talking about *universal rules or laws*. To be sure, he is ready to concede that a few such rules exist: "It would be odd if there were *no* universal rules, since their absence would imply that the moral sense is so weak as never to lead to a rule."[36] But, as the following passages show, he repeatedly avows that rules are not his subject:

Let me . . . stress that these are four aspects of the moral *sense,* not laws.

My saying that people have a moral sense is not the same thing as saying that they have direct, intuitive knowledge of certain moral rules.

If we find such common inclinations, we will not have found a set of moral rules.

Deciding that mankind has at some level a shared moral nature is not the same thing as deciding that men are everywhere in possession of a set of moral absolutes.

The existence of a natural moral sense does not require the existence of universal moral rules.

[Parents care for children] not because a rule is being enforced, but because an impulse is being obeyed.

I agree that there is a universal human nature, but disagree that one can deduce from it more than a handful of rules or solutions to any but the most elemental (albeit vitally important) human problems.

I am reckless enough to think that many conducting [the search for moral universals] have looked in the wrong places for the wrong things because they have sought for universal rules rather than universal dispositions.[37]

Though the author works hard to banish universal rules, it cannot be said that he succeeds. There is no *ought* without a rule, so if Wilson is serious about banishing rules, he must do without the *ought* as well. For instance, he might imitate Aristotle, who saw the virtues as states of character that admirable men do have rather than as states of character that all men ought to have. But Wilson keeps the *ought:* "By a moral sense, I mean an intuitive or directly felt belief about how one *ought* to act when one is free to act voluntarily." As though to remove any doubt that *ought* means rules to him too, he adds "by 'ought,' I mean an obligation binding on all people similarly situated."[38] On a later page he seems to concede the point himself: "What [researchers] find to be binding everywhere are those *rules* governing the fundamental conflicts of everyday, intimate life—keeping promises, respecting property, acting fairly, and avoiding unprovoked assaults—*that have been the subject of earlier chapters in this book.*"[39]

Seeing that Wilson is really talking about rules after all, why is he so insistent that he isn't? There seem to be at least four reasons.

The first is that Wilson falls into Aristotle's trap. Like Aristotle, he discovers human moral nature by consulting the general opinion of mankind (or of men whom mankind has generally accounted wise). Earlier we saw that if there were no special revelation, no better method could be devised for disentangling the text on the heart of man than the evasions and subterfuges of men. But we also saw that in four different ways the method is often misleading. One of them is that precisely because of the universality of the human revolt against the law written on the heart its *violation* passes into general usage so that no matter how many laws remain visible under the crust of diverse desecrations, they can never be recognized by Aristotle's method *as laws.*

For example, Wilson recognizes the universal moral impulse to care for one's children—nay, he insists on it. But he denies it the status of law, just because it is often violated; infanticide, he says, has been practiced throughout history, sometimes even tolerated.[40] The problem here is put well by Augustine when he says that a person must believe something to know anything. In this case a person must believe in the law written on the heart even in order to recognize its instances.

The second reason the author thinks he is talking about something other than rules and laws is his quirky way of using terms such as *rules* and *laws.* The more narrowly he defines them, the fewer instances he is likely to find. The most important quirk is that he gives the name *rules* only to *explicit* rules, rules stated in the form of rules, rules of the sort that people cite when you ask them to list their rules. Because of this quirk, when he meets the most obvious rules of all, rules so clear they don't even need to be mentioned, he casts them out of ruledom and calls them something else. Ironically, in the passage that best illustrates this tendency the author is complaining about an almost identical tendency among anthropologists:

> Much of the dispute over the existence of human universals has taken the form of a search for laws and stated practices. But what is most likely to be universal are those impulses that, because they are so common, scarcely need to be stated in the form of a rule, and so escape the notice of anyone scanning indexes to ethnographic studies.[41]

Though he chides anthropologists for not noticing universals unless they are stated in the form of rules, Wilson does not notice that they are *rules* unless they are stated in the form of rules. The two universals that he mentions on this page are the "impulse" to care for one's children and the "impulse" to avoid incest. Although he says that the former is more important, he calls only the latter a rule.[42]

The third reason for Wilson's aversion to talking about rules is that he thinks the moral feelings which are his subject come into conflict in a way that moral rules cannot. To understand his mistake we need to consider the way in which moral rules do come into conflict. There are three cases.

Case one is rules that have no exceptions. Ordinarily such rules cannot come into conflict at all; if they could, we would assume that some *did* have exceptions and that we had made a mistake in classification.[43]

Case two is rules that have unspecified but specifiable exceptions. Such rules can come into conflict, but the conflict can always be resolved by rewriting them more precisely. Suppose, for instance, that a kidnapper who is threatening to kill his hostages can be stopped only by being shot. We have an obvious conflict between the rules "Kill no one" and "Protect the innocent," but it arises only because the exceptions to the former rule have not been specified. If we specify these exceptions so that the rule reads *"Deliberately kill no innocent human being,"* the conflict disappears.

Case three is rules that have exceptions which *cannot* be fully specified. Such rules can also come into conflict, but we cannot always resolve it just by rewriting them more precisely. Their exceptions are of such a nature that they cannot be exhaustively listed: they are either too numerous, too subtle or too dependent on the infinite varieties of circumstance. This does not mean, as people often think, that there is no right way to resolve the conflict at all. What it means is that resolving it requires a circumstantial exercise of moral judgment that cannot *further* be reduced to rules.

Type three rules are exactly the kind that Wilson's "moral sentiments" involve. For instance, the rule "Have sympathy for the feelings of others" belongs to type three, because on the one hand not every feeling deserves sympathy, but on the other the exceptions are too multifarious to be listed in advance. Three things follow: first, sympathy can come into conflict with other moral rules; second, further moral rules cannot always resolve these conflicts; third, in such cases resolution requires an exercise of moral judgment.

Now here is the problem: Wilson does not recognize the existence of type three rules, nor does he recognize the kind of moral judgment their application requires. From the fact that clashes between one moral sense and another cannot always be settled by further rules, he mistakenly concludes that they do not involve rules in the first place. From the fact that the resolution of their clashes requires judgment, he then concludes that it must be some other kind than moral judgment:

> If the moral senses can conflict with one another and with what prudent action requires under particular circumstances, then living a good life requires striking a delicate balance among those senses and between them and prudent self-interest. Common sense, to say nothing of modern philosophy, shows that there is no single rule or principle by which that balance can be struck.
>
> The balance among the moral senses is, to me, more an aesthetic than a philosophical matter. It is aesthetic in two senses: it is a balance that is struck without deliberation or reasoned justifications, and in the character thereby formed there is no clear distinction between form and content.[44]

Unfortunately the view expressed in the preceding passages is not even consistent with the author's previous statements. Though here he says that balance among competing moral claims is struck without deliberation, just seven pages earlier he praises those who balance competing moral claims precisely through deliberation.[45] The only way to clear up this confusion would be to recognize the specific kind of deliberation that the application of type three rules requires.

The fourth and last reason Wilson does not want to talk about laws and rules is that he is a materialist. One hesitates to say so because he speaks of moral obligation, which seems to be neither a material property nor reducible to material properties. But who says so? Apparently the author thinks it *is* either a material property or reducible to material properties. In his view explaining moral obligation is the same as explaining certain feelings, and explaining these feelings is telling how a creature capable of experiencing them could have arisen in a universe with nothing in it but matter and energy.

Making the story convincing turns out to require two things. First, one must talk about the central nervous system, for the author assumes that even if we can't see how, the mind must be nothing but the brain. Second, one must talk about natural selection, for the author assumes that even if we can't see how, that brain must have been a product of natural selection. In such a universe we might well find something rumbling in our hearts! But it could not be a law—because there is no Law Giver.

I do not believe that the mind is nothing but the brain *or* that we are mere products of natural selection.[46] But there is no need to make these arguments here. Wilson's explanation of morality is incoherent even on its own terms.

"The passions of man are in conflict," he says. To base morality on feelings such as sympathy, duty and fairness is therefore to *prefer* them to their "wilder rivals" such as avarice, ambition and vanity.[47] Wilson of course admits this: "Morality . . . rests on sentiment, but morality does not rest on *mere* sentiment, because there is nothing 'mere' about certain sentiments."[48] That is why he speaks not just of sentiments but of "moral" sentiments, not just of motives but of "nobler" motives, not just of nature but of "better" nature.[49]

But there is something puzzling here. For what is the basis for this judgment? How do we know which sentiments are "moral," which motives are "nobler" or which aspect of nature is "better" if the only tool we have for judging is sentiment or motive or nature itself? Notice

Wilson's criticism of Bentham and Mill:

> Utilitarianism reminded us of the truism that men choose pleasure over pain, but its founder, Jeremy Bentham, added the dubious corollary that the pleasures they choose are equal in value if they are equal in their intensity, duration, certainty, and propinquity. His wary disciple, John Stuart Mill, tried to correct this by discussing the pleasures that were better than others, but of course saying one pleasure is better than others implies the existence of some standard other than pleasure by which to judge things.[50]

Of course Wilson is right, but he is hoist with his own petard. If saying that one pleasure is better than other pleasures implies the existence of a standard other than pleasure by which to judge things, then saying that some sentiments are better than other sentiments implies the existence of a standard other than sentiment by which to judge things.[51] There is a real standard for judgment, and that standard is law: the law written on the heart.

APPENDIX

Elementary Reasoning

MODERN WRITING IS FILLED WITH SENTENCES SUCH AS THIS: "THOMAS Aquinas felt that so-and-so was true." He *felt* that it was? Nonsense. The mind is an instrument for thinking, not for feeling; what one ought to write is "Thomas Aquinas *thought* that so-and-so was true." Our modern writers are so confused about the difference between feeling and reasoning that they wrongly attribute the same confusion to the classical philosophers.

Am I suggesting that feelings and intuitions are irrelevant to thinking, that they should be ignored? No, they should be taken seriously. To ignore human feelings is as dangerous as to have no human feelings. However, there is a right way and a wrong way to take feelings seriously. The right way is to recognize them as part of the *data* with which any account of human matters will have to reckon. The wrong way is to treat them as though our feelings about a subject proved anything about it all by themselves. In order to follow the right way and avoid the wrong way, we need to reason logically. I hope you will find the experience bracing.

"But I don't know anything about logical reasoning!" That can be remedied; here is a short lesson in applied logic. Whenever someone makes a claim to you about politics or morals—anything from "Morals are all relative anyway" (which you might hear at the corner convenience store) to "No one should be required to surrender his autonomy" (which you might hear at a political theory conference)—ask these three questions: (1) What do you mean by that? (2) How do you know it's true? (3) What difference does it make?

When you ask the second question—"How do you know it's true?"—the person to whom you are speaking should reply by giving a *reason* for his claim. The reasons are the *premises;* the claim they are supposed to support is the *conclusion.* Taken together, the premises and the conclusion make up an *argument.* Here are three tests for arguments: (1) Do the terms used in the premises have clear meanings? (2) Is the reasoning free of fallacies? and (3) Are the premises true? If it passes all three tests, you can be sure that the conclusion is true. But if it fails even one of the three tests, you know no more about whether the conclusion is true than you knew before.[1]

I have been asked, "What if I just *know* the conclusion of an argument is false, but no matter how hard I try, I can't find anything wrong with the terms, the premises or the reasoning?" The answer is, "Then you change your mind."

Several of the examples of logical fallacy that follow are borrowed from Douglas J. Wilson's *Introductory Logic.*[2] The responsibility for any foolishness, of course, is mine.

Informal Fallacies (Also Called Fallacies of Distraction)
Ipse dixit ("he said it himself"). Definition: Illegitimate appeal to authority. Example: "Scientific people don't believe in God, so there must not be any God."

Not all appeals to authority are illegitimate. For instance, there is nothing wrong with consulting a geologist about the chemical composition of limestone. Such consultation is legitimate when (a) the person has reasonable assurance of the supposed authority's honesty, reliability and qualifications, (b) the question concerns his own field of expertise and (c) among experts in the same field, the point about which he is asked is not a matter of serious dispute.

Argumentum ad populum ("argument to the people"), short name *ad populum*. Definition: Illegitimate appeal to popular opinions. This fallacy takes many forms, three of which are so important that they have names of their own. *Argumentum ad verecundiam* is illegitimate appeal to shame; *argumentum ad invidiam* is illegitimate appeal to envy; and *argumentum ad captandum* is substitution of a flattering manner for a valid argument. Examples: "How can you be so unpatriotic as to criticize the president's proposal?" "The best reason for being an atheist is that it annoys those disgusting fundamentalists." "You are too sensible to doubt what I say."

Not all appeals to popular opinion are illegitimate. For instance, if conscience really is a gift of God, then the fact that almost all people in all times and places have called murder wrong is a strong argument that it really is. Shame too has legitimate uses; if you have done wrong, then those who arouse your conscience are doing you a favor.

Argumentum ad baculum ("argument to the stick"), short name *ad baculum*. Definition: Illegitimate appeal to fear, especially in the form of a threat. "If you don't agree with me about this, I'll never be your friend again."

Not all threats and appeals to fear are illegitimate. True, the mere fact that laws are backed up with threats of punishment does not prove that they are just. But this does not make it wrong to back up laws with threats of punishment.

Argumentum ad hominem ("argument to the man"), short name *ad hominem*. Definition: Avoiding the issue by criticizing the speaker rather than his argument. Examples: "Why should we read Plato? He's just a dead white European male." "You don't believe that openly practicing homosexuals should be allowed to teach children? How could you be such a homophobe?" "What a hypocrite you are. Your real reason for trying to get me to stop drinking is that you want all the liquor for yourself." Notice that *ad hominem* is a fallacy even if the opponent really does have the motives or personality traits of which he is accused.

Criticizing the speaker is not always a way of avoiding the issue. For example, if a speaker persists in statements that are already known to be false, their truth is no longer the issue; the issue now is probably why he persists in them. A statement such as "He says his products are safe only to make a sale" would be a fallacy of distraction if we had no idea whether they were safe; but if we know that he knows they aren't, the statement merely answers the question "Then why does he say they are?"

Argumentum ad misericordiam ("argument to pity"), short name *ad misericordiam;* also known as false compassion. Definition: Treating a person's suffering as automatically justifying his desires or opinions. Examples: "How could it be wrong to give the poor little fellow a fourth piece of chocolate cake? Look how much he wants it!" "How can you criticize the way gays have sex? Must you add to their shame?"

Not all compassion is false compassion. The definition does not imply that it is wrong to practice acts of mercy; it does suggest that what the sufferer wants may be different from what he needs.

Tu quoque ("you too"). Definition: Defending your own wrongdoing by pointing out that your opponent does the same thing you do. Examples: "So what if I cheated on the examination? So did you." "So what if Republicans buy votes? So do Democrats."

Self-justification is not the only possible motive for pointing out that your opponent commits your sins too. It would not be a fallacy but an act of courage to say, "Yes, we both cheated, and it was wrong. I'm going to turn myself in; will you join me?"

Equivocation. Definition: Confusing different senses of the same term. Example: "I know that peace is possible in the world; why, everyone in my meditation group has achieved peace already." A common form of equivocation is *accent,* in which the meaning of a sentence is changed not through differing definitions but through differing emphases. I cannot improve on Wilson's examples: "*We* should not steal our neighbor's car, but it is fine if someone else does." "We *should* not steal our neighbor's car, but we will anyway." "We should not *steal* our neighbor's car, but it's okay to vandalize it." "We should not steal our *neighbor's* car, but the folks across town are fair game." "We should not steal our neighbor's *car,* but we are after the lawnmower."

Using terms in different senses is not itself fallacious; we just have to keep track of them. For example, there is nothing faulty about the statement "Personal peace is possible, but world peace is not."

Formal Fallacies (Also Called Fallacies of Form)

Contradiction. Definition: Maintaining two contrary claims in the same sense at the same time. Examples: (a) At the beginning of *A Tale of Two Cities,* author Charles Dickens declares, "It was the best of times, it was the worst of times." If Dickens means (as he does) that it was the best of times in one sense but the worst of times in another, then this is not a contradiction, but if he means that in one and the same sense it was both best and worst, then it is one. (b) A poet declares, "The sun rises, the sun sets." If he means (as he does) that the sun rises at one time and sets at another, then this is not a contradiction, but if he means that it rises and sets at the same time, then it is one. (c) A painter remarks, "The house is both black and white." If he means that the house is black in some parts and white in others, then this is not a contradiction, but if he means that it is both black all over and white all over, then it is one.

The principle of noncontradiction is fundamental to all valid reasoning; it must be true for truth and falsity to have any meaning at all. Amazingly, however, it is often attacked. A former colleague taught her students that two contradictory statements could simultaneously be true because "*convex* and *concave* are contrary properties, yet every curve has both." Her error was that the statements "The curve is convex" and "The curve is concave" do not have clear meanings; they do not specify from which side we are looking at the curve. A more adequate description is that the curve is convex when viewed from an exterior point and concave when viewed from an interior point. In this case the terms *convex* and *concave* are not being used in the same sense, so the principle of noncontradiction has not been violated after all.

One also hears sometimes that Hegel's "dialectic" has made the principle of noncontradiction obsolete by showing that thesis and antithesis come together in synthesis. If Hegel did believe that he had refuted the principle of noncontradiction, he was confused. Of course any given "thesis" may be true in one sense or at one time even though its "antithesis" is true in another sense or at another time. In such a case a "synthesis" may indeed sum up the senses in which or the times at which each is true. This is exactly what we have achieved by analyzing such examples as "It was the best of times, it was the worst of times." But that is not real contradiction.

Contradiction is not the only kind of incoherency; for instance, the sentence "There is no such thing as a sentence" is incoherent even though it is not contradictory. For a brief discussion of other coherency requirements, see Roy A. Clouser, *The Myth of Religious Neutrality,* pp. 68-73.[3]

Petitio principii ("little principles"), also known as circularity or begging the question. Definition: Assuming what must be proven; including the conclusion among the premises, usually in camouflage. Wilson's example: "Of course George Washington crossed the Delaware! Otherwise, how could he have made it to the other side?"

A common form of petitio principii is Tendentious Definition. A good example may be found in a textbook on "racism and sexism" by Paula Rothenberg, once proposed for use at the University of Texas in the required course on rhetoric and composition but dropped because of charges of classroom indoctrination. Rothenberg defines racism not as racial prejudice but as racial prejudice *plus power.* Adding that all black people are powerless, she concludes that no black person can be a racist. The fallacy is obvious: rather than carry the burden of justifying black racism while condemning white racism, she simply defines black racism out of existence.

Complex question: Wording a yes-or-no question in such a way as to exclude a legitimate response. The classical example: "Have you stopped beating your wife?"

False alternative. Definition: Oversimplifying the alternatives; forcing a choice when the alternatives are either nonexhaustive or nonexclusive. When oversimplification has reduced the apparent options to just two false alternatives it is often called false dichotomy, bifurcation or the either-or fallacy. Examples: "Are you a liberal or a moderate?" "Do you go to school or work?" The problem with the first example is that the alternatives are nonexhaustive, for one may be other than a liberal or a moderate. The problem with the second is that the alternatives are nonexclusive, for one may go to school and work at the same time.

Notice that false dichotomy is often used in a way that resembles complex question. For instance, the query "Are you liberal, or do you have a brain?" excludes a legitimate response by intelligent liberals, and the query "Are you conservative, or do you have a heart?" excludes a legitimate response by compassionate conservatives. These questions would escape fallacy only if it were literally impossible for a liberal to be intelligent or a conservative to be compassionate.

Not all dichotomies are false dichotomies. For example, "Are you a liberal or a moderate?" proposes a false dichotomy, but "Are you a liberal or a nonliberal?" does not.

Appeal to the excluded middle, also known as neutralism. Definition: Reasoning as though a meaningful statement could be some third thing besides true or false. Example: "I don't have a position on the morality of abortion; I'm prochoice." Obviously between the two mutually exclusive alternatives "Permitting abortion is ethical" and "Permitting abortion is unethical," the speaker *does* have a position: he is committed to the former. Unfortunately, entire political and ethical philosophies are based on the illusion that one never really has to take sides.

Like the principle of noncontradiction, the principle of excluded middle is sometimes attacked. The objection runs, "Don't we speak of 'half-truths'? Aren't truth and falsehood just the endpoints of a continuum?" Although the expression "half-truth" is useful, it is not to be taken literally; its meaning has nothing to do with fractions. For instance, if a painter calls the statement "The house is black" a half-truth, what he probably means is that the statement is completely true about one part of the house but completely false about another.

Post hoc ergo propter hoc ("after this, therefore because of this"). Definition: Establishing causation by solely chronological sequence. Examples: "When I crow, the sun comes up; therefore, I am the cause of the sunrise." One paradise for *post hoc ergo propter hoc* reasoning is politics. For example, if the economy improves immediately after a new president takes office, most people give him the credit. Actually, (a) it takes time for the government to make changes in policy, and (b) even after the government has made them, their economic effects generally do not kick in for at least eighteen months.

Don't think that chronological sequence has *nothing to do* with causation; the problem is that chronological sequence *by itself* is no proof of causation.

Composition. Definition: Attributing to the whole the properties of the parts. Examples: "Chlorine and sodium are both poisons, so salt must also be poisonous." "All of the floor tiles are square, so the floor itself must be square."

The converse of composition is *division,* attributing to the parts the properties of the whole, as in the statement "Salt is wholesome, so chlorine and sodium must be wholesome" or the statement "The floor itself is square, so all of the floor tiles must be square." The hazard of these two fallacies is great in political theory, where properties of individuals and of communities are often thoughtlessly interchanged. For example, the utilitarian John Stuart Mill incorrectly reasoned that if individual happiness is a good for an individual, then aggregate happiness is a good for an aggregate of individuals. In the same way, some writers on diplomacy incorrectly reason that since every individual in the nation has a will, the nation as a whole has a will.

Apriorism, also known as sweeping generalization. Definition: Leaping to conclusions from limited or selected instances. Example: "Every Baptist I know is uneducated, so I guess all Baptists are uneducated."

Affirming the consequent, also known as substituting the converse for the proposition. Definition: Reasoning that if P implies Q, then Q implies P. Example: "If there were no heaven, people would believe in it anyway; they do believe in it, so there must be no heaven."

Substituting the inverse for the proposition. Definition: Reasoning that if P implies Q, then not-P implies not-Q. Example: "The instructor said that if I didn't write the essay, I wouldn't get an A. Well, I wrote the essay, but I still didn't get an A. He lied."

Failing to distribute the middle term, also known as faking the connection. Definition: Reasoning that if all A are X and all B are X, then all A are B. Example: "All Christians go to church, and all religious phonies go to church, so all Christians must be religious phonies."

Special pleading. Definition: Claiming for someone an exemption from a rule even though the person exempted falls within the category to whom the rule rightly applies. Examples: "I know I told you not to exceed the speed limit, but when I do it, that's different." "I know I said that censorship is wrong, but that guy just has to be shut up."

Not every exemption from a rule is special pleading. One must ask "To whom is the rule meant to apply?" Speed limits are not meant to apply to policemen in pursuit of speeders, and laws against the use of drugs are not meant to apply to persons taking them by prescription because of medical conditions.

Compound Fallacy

Compound fallacy is combining several different fallacies in the same statement. The combination may be complicated, as the following examples show.

A quadruple compound fallacy. After sympathetically describing the efforts of guidance counselors in a public high school to set up "support groups" for homosexual teenagers, a television reporter in my town concluded, "This isn't about right and wrong; it's about saving the lives of these students." The statement combined the following fallacies: *contradiction,* because although the reporter implied that the guidance policy was right, she also insisted that right and wrong were not at issue; *appeal to the excluded middle,* because to say that right and wrong were not at issue was to suggest that the statement "The guidance policy is right" may have been some third thing other than true or false; *false alternative,* because although she presented listeners with a choice between saving lives and considering right and wrong, one can save lives at the same time as considering right and wrong; and *ad misericordiam,* because the fact that teenagers who practice deadly behaviors should be pitied does not demonstrate that the kind of "support" that these groups would provide would save them.

Another quadruple compound fallacy. A student reports to me that in a graduate seminar on public policy the professor asked, "All of you here are too intelligent to be prolife, right?" The statement combined four fallacies: *ad hominem,* because it attacked the intelligence rather than the arguments of the defenders of unborn children; *ad invidiam,* because it appealed to a widespread attitude of contempt without justifying that contempt; *ad captandum,* because it used flattery rather than reasoning to persuade; and *ad baculum,* because it appealed to the personal anxieties of students who did not want their teacher or classmates to consider them stupid.

Notes

Chapter 1: Politics & the Human Good
[1]At stake here is his idea that material, formal, efficient and final properties are the *causes* of all other properties that a thing may have.

[2]Aristotle *Politics* 1.2.1252b.

[3]I am giving what is called a *subsidiarist* interpretation of Aristotle. Another interpretation is possible: see question 5 at the end of the chapter. Further discussion may be found in chapter fourteen.

[4]Plato's *Republic* 436 is its first known use in philosophy.

[5]Even Rolling Stone Mick Jagger knows this. In that philosophical classic "I Can't Get No Satisfaction" he doesn't mean that he can't experience pleasure. Had he read Aristotle he might have had a better idea what to do about the problem.

[6]By the way, one should not assume that when Aristotle uses the term *soul* he means what Christians mean by it—or even what Plato meant by it! In another work he defines the soul as merely "the form of the body," which may be roughly paraphrased "the characteristic pattern of an embodied human life."

[7]Plato *Republic* 352-53.

[8]Compare G. K. Chesterton, *Heretics* (New York: John Lane, 1905), chap. 20.

[9]He does not say that government is unnecessary: see Romans 13:1-7.

Chapter 2: Moral Excellence & Regime Design
[1]Following the terminology of Thomas Aquinas, some writers call these the *rational*, the *irascible* and the *concupiscible* powers. You should remember these terms because you will encounter them again in Unit Two. We are not here distinguishing between powers and other things, such as characteristics, though Aristotle does that too.

[2]*Sehnsucht* is the longing for "that unnameable something, desire for which pierces us like a rapier at the smell of a bonfire, the sound of wild ducks flying overhead, the title of *The Well at the World's End*, the opening lines of *Kubla Khan*, the morning cobwebs in late summer, or the noise of falling waves" (C. S. Lewis, *The Pilgrim's Regress* [New York: Bantam, 1986], preface to 3rd ed., p. xii). Although Aristotle doesn't talk about *sehnsucht*, it seems to be nearly universal. Lewis and many others have thought that it is the longing for God.

[3]C. S. Lewis, *Mere Christianity* (New York: Macmillan, 1952), p. 71.

[4]Aristotle *Nicomachean Ethics* 3.5.1115a.

[5]I discuss the virtue of tolerance at greater length in "The Illusion of Moral Neutrality," *First Things*, no. 35 (July/August 1993): 32-37, and in *True Tolerance: Liberalism and the Necessity of Judgment* (New Brunswick, N.J.: Transaction, 1992).

[6]Aristotle *Nicomachean Ethics* 2.6.1106b-7a. It would seem that such rational principles brook no exceptions. However, Aristotle does *not* take this position about the rules of

natural justice, which we will consider later on.

[7]This does not mean that you can be thoroughly immoral and still have practical wisdom. See the later discussion of the "Unity of the Virtues."

[8]See Thomas Aquinas *Summa Theologica* I-II, Question 65, Article 1. I explain only the second of Thomas's two arguments.

[9]For further discussion, see my article "The Politics of Virtues, the Government of Knaves," *First Things*, no. 44 (June/July 1994).

[10]Most of the material in this section is drawn from Aristotle *Politics* 3-4.

[11]This ancient saying holds true not only in politics but also in many other realms of life. I believe it was C. S. Lewis who said that a bad man is worse than a bad dog precisely because a man is better than a dog; there is more in him to be twisted.

[12]Charles W. Colson, "Why Women Like Big Government," *Christianity Today* 40, no. 13 (November 11, 1996): 112.

Chapter 3: Friendship, Justice & the Moral Significance of Law

[1]Aristotle does *not* say that the principles of natural justice can be stated in a form that does not require exceptions. Thus, unlike the "natural laws" which we will study in the unit on Thomas Aquinas, they fall short of perfect universality. That is also why he thinks that submission to just men (if you could find them) would be better than submission to just laws. On the other hand, we saw in the last chapter that Aristotle *does* speak of "rational principles" that *do* seem to be universal in describing how the man of practical wisdom reaches judgments. In fact what Thomas calls the first precepts of natural law turn out to be the same as what Aristotle calls the first principles of practical reason.

[2]John T. Marshall, "Rebuilding the American City: Bonds of Friendship as Bricks and Mortar," master's report, University of Texas at Austin, May 1994.

[3]A reader protests that proponents of the graduated income tax merely think it is *fairer* than the alternatives. That is correct, but it does not contradict the point. They believe that some people ought to be made to pay for the benefits that others receive *because* they consider it fair, not *instead* of considering it fair.

[4]Because I am sure to be challenged on this one, some documentation is in order. Whether a particular act of killing counts as *murder* is, of course, an ethical question, but *whether it kills* is a biological question. To kill is to take life, and the unborn child is alive. You needn't take this from me; the following quotations come from congressional testimony in 1981, in which not a single expert witness held that human life begins at any other point in time than conception or implantation. Each speaker is a medical doctor or researcher. Alfred Bongioanni, professor of pediatrics and obstetrics at the University of Pennsylvania: "I am no more prepared to say that these early stages [of fetal development] represent an incomplete human being than I would be to say that the child prior to the dramatic effects of puberty . . . is not a human being." Jerome LeJeune, professor of genetics at the University of Descartes, Paris: "After fertilization has taken place a new human being has come into being." This is "no longer a matter of taste or opinion" and "not a metaphysical contention, it is plain experimental evidence." Micheline Matthews-Roth, Harvard University Medical School: "It is incorrect to say that biological data cannot be decisive. . . . It is scientifically correct to say that individual human life begins at conception." Watson A. Bowes, University of Colorado Medical School: "The beginning of a single human life is from a biological point of view a simple and straightforward matter—the beginning is conception."

The fact that the unborn baby is alive is not seriously disputed even by those who believe that abortion should be legal. Both of the following quotations come from abortion advocates:

Since the old ethic has not been fully displaced it has been necessary to separate the idea of abortion from the idea of killing, which continues to be socially abhorrent. The result has been a curious avoidance of the scientific fact, which everyone really knows, that human life begins at conception and is continuous whether intra- or extra-uterine until death. (Editorial in *California Medicine*, September 1970, p. 68)

There clearly is no logical or moral distinction between a fetus and a young baby; free availability of abortion cannot be reasonably distinguished from euthanasia. Nevertheless we are for it. (Editorial in *The New Republic*, July 2, 1977)

In a more recent article in *The New Republic* (October 16, 1995), feminist Naomi Wolf goes so far as to describe abortion as real sin that incurs real guilt and requires atonement; yet she is for it too.

[5]See Aristotle *Politics* 1.2.1252b.

[6]Aristotle *Nicomachean Ethics* 10.9.1180a.

[7]Aristotle *Politics* 8.4.1338b.

[8]For instance, the textbook *Changing Bodies, Changing Lives* tells high-school students, "If you feel your parents are overprotective . . . or if they don't want you to be sexual at all until some distant time, you may feel you have to tune out their voice entirely" (quoted in William Kilpatrick, *Why Johnny Can't Tell Right from Wrong* [New York: Simon & Schuster, 1992]).

Chapter 4: The Grand Design of Law

[1]*The Apostle*, by the way, is St. Paul, who wrote most of the letters in the New Testament, and *the Jurist* is Ulpian, a Roman lawyer whose writings are excerpted in the *Corpus Juris Civilis*. The *Corpus Juris Civilis* is a short law library commissioned by the Emperor Justinian to bring some order to the sprawl of Roman civil law. It has four main parts: the *Institutes*, a brief textbook; the *Pandects*, or *Digest*, an anthology of the writings of the classical jurists (especially Ulpian himself); the *Codex*, a collection and reconciliation of imperial pronouncements issued before the *Corpus Juris Civilis*; and the *Novels*, a collection and reconciliation of imperial pronouncements issued subsequent to the *Corpus Juris Civilis*.

[2]Notice, however, that Darwinism can also be challenged insofar as it rests on dogmatic materialism rather than on actual evidence. See Michael J. Behe, *Darwin's Black Box: The Biochemical Challenge to Evolution* (New York: Free Press, 1996); Phillip E. Johnson, *Darwin on Trial* (Downers Grove, Ill.: InterVarsity Press, 1993); and Michael Denton, *Evolution: A Theory in Crisis* (Bethesda, Md.: Adler & Adler, 1986).

[3]Thomas understands God to be the self-existent Being from which all else comes. Therefore it does not logically follow that God himself must also have "come from" something. Anything else might have never been, but he is the one thing that can't not be.

[4]Pronounce the first syllable "soon," not "sin" or "sine."

[5]This word has two syllables: *fom-es*.

[6]Mentioned in the Bible in Romans 2:14-15.

[7]The clearest statement of these "three grades" of moral precepts is found in *Summa Theologica* I-II, Question 100, Article 11.

[8]In *Summa Theologica* II-II, Question 122, Article 1, for instance, Thomas says, "The precepts of the decalogue are the first principles of the Law; and the natural reason assents to them at once, as to principles that are most evident."

[9]I have borrowed this analogy from Peter Kreeft and Ronald K. Tacelli, *Handbook of Christian Apologetics* (Downers Grove, Ill.: InterVarsity Press, 1994), p. 135.

Chapter 5: The Law of Nature & the Law of Man

[1]The cover was finally blown by another anthropologist, Derek Freeman. See his book

Margaret Mead and Samoa: The Making and Unmaking of an Anthropological Myth (Cambridge, Mass.: Harvard University Press, 1983). Be sure to get the point. It would be an ad hominem fallacy to argue that because Mead had grave character flaws, she must have been wrong about the Samoans. But if we *already know* that she was wrong about the Samoans, then it is *not* a fallacy to take character into account in order to understand how she could have made such a huge mistake.

[2]See E. Michael Jones, *Degenerate Moderns* (San Francisco: Ignatius, 1993).

[3]Follow-up studies of abortion have shown significant increases in nervous disorders and behavior disorders in other areas of life. One major study found that a minimum of 19 percent of postabortion women suffered from diagnosable posttraumatic stress disorder (PTSD); half had many but not all PTSD symptoms. Symptoms of abortion-related PTSD include hyperarousal (for instance, anxiety attacks, irritability and outbursts of anger or rage), intrusion (for instance, recurrent, unwanted thoughts, flashbacks or nightmares about the abortion or the baby) and constriction (for instance, the inability to recall the abortion in whole or part and avoidance of activities which might arouse such memories). See J. R. Ashton, "The Psychosocial Outcome of Induced Abortion," *British Journal of Obstetrics and Gynecology* 87 (1980): 1115-22; H. David et al., "Postpartum and Postabortion Psychotic Reactions," *Family Planning Perspectives* 13 (1981): 88-91; Catherine Barnard, *The Long-Term Psychological Effects of Abortion* (Portsmouth, N.H.: Institute for Pregnancy Loss, 1990); Judith Lewis Herman, *Trauma and Recovery* (New York: BasicBooks, 1992), p. 34; and David C. Reardon, "Psychological Sequelae of Abortion," in *Abortion Malpractice* (Lewisville, Tex.: Life Dynamics, 1993), pp. 5-11.

[4]To avoid quibbles about what term to use for natural law—for instance, "right reason," "traditional morality" or "first practical principles"—Lewis deliberately used a term from another language: "the Tao," which means roughly "the Way." However, his argument has nothing to do with the Eastern philosophy called Taoism.

[5]C. S. Lewis, *The Abolition of Man* (New York: Macmillan, 1947, 1955), pp. 54, 56. Some consider this book the profoundest defense of natural law written in our century, and it is certainly the easiest to read.

[6]Lewis, *Abolition of Man*, pp. 54-55.

[7]Ibid., p. 56.

[8]One forgets the self in caring for friends and children too, but these are not erotic unions.

[9]I take Thomas to mean all general precepts, but he may mean only primary precepts (see note 13).

[10]The view that Thomas thinks that *no* secondary principle can be general—put another way, that to *any* secondary principle there may be exceptions—is common but mistaken. For instance, in *Summa Theologica* I-II, Question 77, Article 2, he identifies the secondary principle "no fornication is lawful" as general.

[11]Obstacles may be met in *who* does something, *what* he does or *where, why, how, when*, or *by what aids or instruments* he does it. This follows from the "circumstances" declared relevant to the nature of an act in *Summa Theologica* I-II, Question 7, Article 3.

[12]Another name for evil persuasion might be "depraved ideology." One of the most remarkable phenomena of our century is the rise of entire political movements devoted to the rationalization of particular sins.

[13]If we do take him to mean all secondary precepts, then his previous references to general precepts must refer only to the primary precepts (see note 9).

[14]See Question 94, Article 4. Yet Thomas seems to contradict himself at Question 100, Article 1, holding that the precept against theft is not secondary but primary.

[15]Question 95, Article 1.

[16]Some people have misunderstood Thomas on this point because although he does not believe that human law may enforce religious observances in the case of nonbelievers such as Jews, Muslims and atheists, he does believe that it may enforce them in the case of fallen-away Christians. But he does *not* see this as an effort to advance the spiritual goal of salvation, viewing that as the church's affair, not the state's. Rather he sees it as advancing the earthly goal of enforcing public promises. The state may enforce baptismal vows in the same way and for the same reasons as business contracts.

[17]In practice this is less a qualification than it seems, for once we consider indirect hurts, such as the harm of bad example or the harm of reducing one's ability to fulfill one's duties, we realize that there may be no such thing as an act of vice that does *no* public injury. Nevertheless it is a limit, for not all injury is significant injury.

[18]Joseph Califano, "Fictions and Facts About Drug Legalization," *America* 174, no. 9 (March 16, 1996): 7.

Chapter 6: Human Law & Regime Design

[1]Thomas does not mean that a person can earn his way into heaven. He teaches the New Testament doctrine that all sin and stand in need of reconciliation with God, which is possible only through faith in Christ, the sin bearer.

[2]Several of the following paragraphs incorporate verbatim quotation from pp. 61-64 of my book *The Nearest Coast of Darkness* (Ithaca, N.Y.: Cornell University Press, 1988).

[3]At least after the passage of the law called the *Lex Hortensius.*

[4]This famous definition comes from Harold Lasswell's book *Politics: Who Gets What, When and How* (New York: McGraw-Hill, 1938).

[5]Thomas himself would go further because he is not satisfied that market prices are always just. I do not deal with that question in this book because the theoretical apparatus used to study markets has advanced since Thomas's time, and several chapters of explanation would be necessary before the question could even be posed correctly.

[6]Edmund Burke, *Reflections on the Revolution in France,* Part VI, Sections 2(a) and 3(b).

Chapter 7: The State of Nature & the Social Contract

[1]*We the People* (New York: Coronado, 1983), pp. 20-21.

[2]This sort of move—holding that if you do X you have implicitly consented to Y—is characteristic of Locke. You will find at least two other examples of it in the pages that follow. Look for them.

[3]Get in the habit of turning its use *against* its abuse. Whenever someone commits the Biographical Fallacy, ask him, "What in *your* life might explain your refusal to face the argument fair and square?" This is an example of legitimate use number two.

[4]For another account of how the principles of natural law may be derived from sense-experience, see Locke's *Essays on the Law of Nature,* chap. 4.

[5]For a brief discussion of each, see Peter Kreeft and Ronald K. Tacelli, *Handbook of Christian Apologetics* (Downers Grove, Ill.: InterVarsity Press, 1994), pp. 47-88.

[6]Even in Locke, individuals consent to the social contract not as solitary atoms but as heads of households.

[7]We are speaking here only of *proximate* causes for holding office. Locke agrees with Thomas Aquinas that parents and rulers hold office *ultimately* by the will of God, for God created nature and can overrule the will of the people.

Chapter 8: Two Views of Natural Law

[1]See chapter fourteen.

[2]A few natural-law thinkers may seem to have denied this last point, notably Hugo

Grotius, who held that even if God did not exist—which, he added, it would be wicked to concede—the natural law would still have "a degree of validity," but apparently in a different and lesser way. What he seems to have meant was that the judgment expressed in the law would lose the force of law proper but retain the force of prudence. If this interpretation is correct, then even Grotius agreed that the authority of natural law *as law* is rooted in God. His statement may be found in *De Jure Belli ac Pacis Libri Tres*, Prolegomena, paragraph 11.

[3]Romans 2:14-15.

[4]William Ames, *Conscience* (1639), Question 8, quoted in A. S. P. Woodhouse, *Puritanism and Liberty* (London: Dent, 1992), p. 190.

[5]*Table Talk* (written during the Long Parliament, but published in 1689), quoted in David Wooten, *Divine Right and Democracy* (New York: Viking Penguin, 1986), p. 450. I take Selden to mean that the natural law can be known only by the written law of God, but he might mean merely that the natural law is itself an unwritten law of God.

[6]John Locke, *Second Treatise*, Section 6.

[7]Ibid., Section 16; compare Section 8.

[8]Ibid., Section 5.

[9]In the English of Locke's day, to "dispose of" matters did not mean to get rid of them, but to arrange them or set them in order.

[10]See Locke's *Letter Concerning Toleration*. He does put certain limits on religious liberty, but none of them apply here.

[11]The legal basis of the decision was that Mr. Swanner had violated city and state laws prohibiting landlords from discriminating on grounds of marital status. Mr. Swanner, who rents to single, married and divorced persons, replied that his objection was not to the fact that the applicants were unmarried but that they proposed to use his apartments for sexual cohabitation with other unmarried persons. As I write this, Mr. Swanner is making plans to press an appeal to the U.S. Supreme Court on grounds that the Alaska decision violates the Religious Freedom Restoration Act passed by Congress in 1993.

[12]This example is adapted from Robert Nozick, *Anarchy, State, and Utopia* (New York: Basic Books, 1974).

[13]My list follows *The Challenge of Peace: God's Promise and Our Response*, a pastoral letter by U.S. Catholic bishops.

[14]One must consider not only ordinary good and evil but also spiritual good and evil, and one must consider not only what will happen but also what might happen. It's also important to understand that the proportionality principle does *not* suppose that all goods and evils *can* be weighed on the same scale; however, where they can be, they should be.

Chapter 9: Private Property & Revolution
[1]Because he says that almost all value comes from labor, many first-time readers think Locke is defending a "labor theory of value." Not so. By "value" economists mean price. Locke, by contrast, is using the term to mean only usefulness. *So far* he has made no effort to ascertain the relation between usefulness and price.

Chapter 10: The Pleasure Principle
[1]The following section is virtually identical to several pages in my article "The Balnibarbian Heresies," *First Things*, no. 46 (October 1994).

[2]A compromise faction, the Polychromes, works hard to miss the point: it tries to reconstruct the spectrum with primary colors of chartreuse, puce *and* plaid.

[3]As before, a compromise faction works hard to miss the point, trying to reconstruct

the moral law from fundamental values of pleasure, liberty and privacy.

[4]See his *Examination of Sir William Hamilton's Philosophy*, chaps. 11-12 and the appendix that follows them. Indeed, not only does Mill say that all we can be sure about is sensation, he gets as close as he can to saying that nothing even exists but sensation. The experience of mind brings him to a halt because he doesn't know how to make sense of a series of sensations which is aware of itself as past and future; however, rather than admitting that his way of explaining is incoherent, he merely calls mind inexplicable.

[5]Mill's disbelief in normative human nature is easy to miss because his language is so evasive. He says that a certain feeling *has the characteristics that we associate* with being natural, that a certain want *makes us feel* that it is natural, that a certain conception *is more and more felt* to be natural—all the time giving the impression that he thinks they really are natural, either in the sense of being constants or in the sense of being norms. Yet as to constants, he seems to think that our feelings, wants and conceptions are infinitely plastic; and as to norms, his essay *Nature* mocks the very idea of following natural law. (In it he argues that following nature means either acting as we have no choice but to act or imitating the way nonhuman things act. Then he points out that the admonition "Follow nature!" is unmeaning if taken in the first sense and foolish if taken in the second. His error is that neither sense corresponds to what the great natural-law thinkers have actually meant.)

[6]Mill himself is careless about these distinctions. For instance, in various works he calls Epicurus a utilitarian even though he is really a hedonist, and he calls Aristotle a utilitarian even though he is neither a hedonist *nor* a utilitarian.

[7]Mill commits other logical fallacies as well. For instance, consider his answer to the charge that utilitarian doctrine is "godless" in the sense of being inconsistent with Christian revelation. The gist of his reply is that if the God of Christianity has any sense he will be a utilitarian himself. This assumes, without proving, (1) that what utilitarianism teaches about morality, happiness and their relation is the same as what Christianity teaches about them and (2) that what utilitarianism teaches about them is true. But these are the very points that Christians deny. Thus Mill commits the fallacy of *petitio principii*, or begging the question.

[8]This example is from Douglas J. Wilson, *Introductory Logic*, rev. ed. (Moscow, Idaho: Canon, 1992). Technically speaking it is an example of the fallacy of *accent*. For further discussion, see the appendix to this book.

Chapter 11: The Problem with the Pleasure Principle

[1]Jeremy Bentham, *The Principles of Morals and Legislation* (New York: Hafner, 1948), p. 29.

[2]See Jeremy Bentham, *Deontology, Together with A Table of the Springs of Action and The Article on Utilitarianism*, ed. Amnon Goldworth (Oxford: Clarendon, 1983), pp. 268, 276-77.

[3]Modern ethical theorists call this kind of ordering different things *lexical* or *lexicographical* because it resembles the way we order words in a dictionary or lexicon. We begin by considering where a word's first letter falls in the alphabet. Only to break ties between words with the same first letter do we consider where the second letter falls; only to break ties between words with the same second letter do we consider where the third letter falls; and so forth.

[4]Although Judge Grieg's ruling was reaffirmed on appeal, as I write this Michael's mother and sister are continuing to press his cause in yet a higher court. See Wesley J. Smith, "Better Dead than Fed?" *The National Review* 46, no. 12 (June 27, 1994).

[5]I offer more complete discussion on pages 198-202 of *True Tolerance* (New Brunswick,

N.J.: Transaction, 1992).

[6]For complete discussion, with citations, see "The Case Against Kinsey," in E. Michael Jones, *Degenerate Moderns* (San Francisco: Ignatius, 1993), pp. 87-115. My quotations are from pp. 106-7.

[7]Genesis 1:26-28.

[8]The second part of this clause is a quotation from the Creed of St. Athanasius, one of the three great creeds of the universal church.

Intermezzo: The Art of Teaching

[1]Of course I don't mean this term literally; the mind is not a computer. That can be proven: see Stephen M. Barr, "The Atheism of the Gaps," *First Things*, no. 57 (November 1995): 50-53.

[2]C. S. Lewis, "Right and Wrong as a Clue to the Meaning of the Universe," in *Mere Christianity* (New York: Macmillan, 1952), p. 19.

[3]Although, thanks to television, compulsory government-run schooling and other instruments for the infliction of ignorance, the uneducated are catching up.

[4]Example: Six people are on a lifeboat—say, a thief, a minister, a scientist, a nursing mother and her baby, and yourself. The boat stocks food for only five. What should be done? The purpose of the exercise is allegedly to stretch the powers of moral reasoning. Besides inducing moral skepticism, its most common effect is to encourage Nazi-like thinking about who "deserves" to live. For those who insist upon knowing my own "solution," I hope God would grant me the faith and courage to jump off the lifeboat myself. But that is not the point.

Chapter 13: A Christian Appraisal of Natural-Law Theory

[1]I return to such objections later.

[2]Joy Davidman, *Smoke on the Mountain: An Interpretation of the Ten Commandments* (Philadelphia: Westminster Press, 1953-1954), p. 108.

[3]Stanley Hauerwas and William H. Willimon, *Resident Aliens: Life in the Christian Colony* (Nashville: Abingdon, 1989), p. 38. Hauerwas and Willimon differ from Barth, of course, in speaking of competing stories rather than competing systems of thought.

[4]The phrase about general revelation penetrating the mind of man is from Carl F. H. Henry, *God Who Speaks and Shows: Preliminary Considerations*, vol. 1 of *God, Revelation and Authority* (Waco, Tex.: Word, 1976), p. 400; on the point-of-contact controversy generally, see pp. 395-409. Note, however, that for reasons criticized in chapter fifteen, Henry does not connect general revelation with natural law.

Chapter 14: A Reprise of the Older Thinkers

[1]My comments in this paragraph are indebted to Roy A. Clouser, *On the General Relation of Religion, Metaphysics and Science*, Facets of Faith and Science 2, ed. J. van de Meer (Lanham, Md.: University Press of America, 1997); John N. Deck, "St. Thomas Aquinas and the Language of Total Dependence," *Dialogue: Canadian Philosophical Review—Revue Canadienne de Philosophie* 6 (1967): 74-78; and James Ross, "God, Creator of Kinds and Possibilities: *Requiescant universalia ante res*," in *Rationality, Religious Belief and Moral Commitment*, ed. Robert Audi and William J. Wainwright (Ithaca, N.Y.: Cornell University Press, 1986). For a more detailed discussion of the prospects for an ontology which recognizes the total dependence of all things on God, see Clouser, *The Myth of Religious Neutrality* (Notre Dame, Ind.: University of Notre Dame Press, 1991).

[2]The Hebrew word used for creation in the verse (root *qānâh*) is not the same one used for creation in Genesis 1 (root *bārā'*).

[3]E. Michael Jones, *Degenerate Moderns* (San Francisco: Ignatius, 1993), pp. 177, 183, 231.

[4]*First Treatise*, chap. 9, sec. 86: "For the desire, strong desire of Preserving his Life and Being having been planted in him, as a Principle of Action by God himself, Reason, which was the Voice of God in him, could not but teach him and assure, that pursuing that natural Inclination he had to preserve his Being, he followed the Will of his Maker, and therefore had a right to make use of those Creatures, which by his Reason or Senses he could discover would be serviceable thereunto." *Second Treatise*, chap. 2, sec. 11: "And Cain was so fully convinced, that every one had a Right to destroy such a Criminal, that after the Murther of his Brother, he cries out, *Every one that findeth me, shall slay me;* so plain was it writ in the Hearts of all Mankind."

[5]It is in this sense that he repeatedly *denies* that anything is written on the heart in *Essays on the Law of Nature*, chap. 3.

[6]For his criticism of the former, see *An Essay on Human Understanding*, bk. 1, chap. 3.

[7]"It often happens that a thinker takes great trouble controlling, balancing, qualifying, and restricting a certain component of his thought. In spite of all precautions, the restricted component remains active and influential. Since the disciples have neither the skill nor the prudence of the great man, the restricted component of the teacher's thought sometimes quickly proceeds to the foreground of the dialectical scene, where it comes to bear the name of the man who was so eager to keep it balanced and qualified. . . . As it enters history, the deep tendency of a certain thought is no longer protected by the skillful devices of its original interpreter, and it is in this unprotected condition that it plays its dialectical role" (Yves R. Simon, *The Tradition of Natural Law* [New York: Fordham University Press, 1965], p. 13). To see how Simon himself qualifies the idea that the individual is a part of the state, see pp. 86-107, esp. p. 91.

[8]Simon again (*The Tradition of Natural Law*, p. 6): "These things sometimes happen: at a certain time a theoretical philosophy which inclines minds and souls in a certain direction may be held in check by the predominance of an opposite sentiment."

Chapter 15: A Sampling of Recent Thinkers

[1]The literature is voluminous. See Germain G. Grisez, "The First Principle of Practical Reason: A Commentary on *Summa Theologiae*, 1-2, Question 94, Article 2," in *Aquinas: A Collection of Critical Essays*, ed. Anthony Kenney (Notre Dame, Ind.: University of Notre Dame Press, 1969), pp. 340-82; John Finnis, *Natural Law and Natural Rights* (Oxford: Oxford University Press, 1980); Joseph M. Boyle, "Aquinas and Prescriptive Ethics," *Proceedings of the American Catholic Philosophical Association* 49 (1975): 82-95; Germain G. Grisez, John Finnis and Joseph M. Boyle, "Practical Principles, Moral Truth and Ultimate Ends," *American Journal of Jurisprudence* 32 (1987): 99-151; Germain G. Grisez and Russell Shaw, *Fulfillment in Christ: A Summary of Christian Moral Principles* (Notre Dame, Ind.: University of Notre Dame Press, 1991); and references therein.

[2]The ambivalence of Thomas Aquinas over whether concrete moral rules such as those in the Ten Commandments belong to the primary or to the secondary precepts of the natural law suggests that he may have been aware of this problem. He saw the difficulty of deriving them from purely formal principles but hesitated to call them primary themselves.

[3]Earlier we saw that particular moral rules are sometimes taken out of context, distorted and used to beat down other moral rules. The authors are elaborating the idea: particular *human goods* are sometimes taken out of context, distorted and used to beat down other *human goods;* particular *modes of responsibility* are sometimes taken out of context, distorted and used to beat down other *modes of responsibility.* Finnis comments on the device in *Natural Law and Natural Rights*, pp. 102, 127.

[4]Grisez, Finnis and Boyle, "Practical Principles, Moral Truth and Ultimate Ends," pp. 146-47.

[5] *Responsa Rashba,* number 414, 1.150.

[6] The most helpful volumes on Noahide law are David Novak, *The Image of the Non-Jew in Judaism: An Historical and Constructive Study of the Noahide Laws* (New York: Edwin Mellen, 1983), and Aaron Lichtenstein, *The Seven Laws of Noah,* 2nd ed. (New York: Rabbi Jacob Joseph School Press, 1986). For other Jewish treatments of Noahide or natural law, see J. David Bleich, "Jewish Law and the State's Authority to Punish Crime," *Cardozo Law Review* 12 (1991): 829-57; Arnold N. Enker, "Aspects of Interaction Between the Torah Law, the King's Law, and the Noahide Law in Jewish Criminal Law," *Cardozo Law Review* 12 (1991): 1137-56; Everett E. Gendler, "War and the Jewish Tradition," in *Contemporary Jewish Ethics,* ed. Menachem Marc Kellner (New York: Hebrew Publishing, 1978), pp. 189-210; Isaac Husik, "The Law of Nature, Hugo Grotius, and the Bible," *Hebrew Union College Annual* 2 (1925): 381-417; Milton R. Konvitz, "Conscience and Civil Disobedience in the Jewish Tradition," in *Judaism and Human Rights* (New York: Norton/B'nai B'rith Commission on Adult Jewish Education, 1972), pp. 161-178; Aharon Lichtenstein, "Does Jewish Tradition Recognize an Ethic Independent of Halakha?" in *Modern Jewish Ethics: Theory and Practice,* ed. Marvin Fox (Columbus: Ohio State University Press, 1975), pp. 62-88; David Novak, *Jewish Social Ethics* (New York: Oxford University Press, 1992, 1983); David Novak, "Law of Moses, Law of Nature," *First Things,* no. 60 (February 1996); Nahum Rakover, "Jewish Law and the Noahide Obligation to Preserve Social Order," *Cardozo Law Review* 12 (1991): 1073-136; Steven Schwarzschild, "Do Noachites Have to Believe in Revelation?" *Jewish Quarterly Review* 52, no. 4 (1962): 297-308, and 53, no. 1 (1962): 30-65; and Suzanne Last Stone, "Sinaitic and Noahide Law: Legal Pluralism in Jewish Law," *Cardozo Law Review* 12 (1991): 1157-214.

[7] Even those rabbis who denied that Gentiles can marry regarded it as a legitimate question whether they can divorce; the question clearly presupposes that something *like* marriage does exist among them. See for example *p. Qidduŝin* 1.1 (58c).

[8] For discussion, see Novak, *The Image of the Non-Jew in Judaism,* p. 3.

[9] See W. D. Davies, *Paul and Rabbinic Judaism* (London: S.P.C.K., 1948, 1955), pp. 114-19, 325-28, and C. H. Dodd, "Natural Law in the Bible," *Theology,* reprint 17 (May-June 1946): 6-9.

[10] In Paul's view, mere knowledge of God's requirements does not enable either Jew or Gentile to please God by keeping them; rather what the knowledge reveals to us is precisely that we do *not* keep them. In his arguments against the Noahide interpretation of Paul's remark, David Novak (*The Image of the Non-Jew in Judaism,* p. 26) seems to misunderstand this point.

[11] Konvitz, "Conscience and Civil Disobedience in the Jewish Tradition," pp. 173-74.

[12] *Emunot Ve-De'ot* 3.2, quoted in Novak, *The Image of the Non-Jew in Judaism,* p. 224. The wisdom to which Rabbi Gaon refers is the wisdom of God. Proverbs 8:22-31, which speaks of it, was quoted in chapter fourteen.

[13] *Moreh Nebukhim* 3.48: 598-99, quoted in Novak, *Jewish Social Ethics,* p. 248.

[14] *'Abot* 3.2, quoted in Novak, *The Image of the Non-Jew in Judaism,* p. 72.

[15] Novak, *The Image of the Non-Jew in Judaism,* p. 4.

[16] *Kuzari* 3.73, quoted in ibid., pp. 10-11.

[17] The most complete presentation of this kind of argument is found in *Midrash Lequah Tob* 10b-11a. For discussion and references, see Novak, *The Image of the Non-Jew in Judaism,* pp. 32-34.

[18] *B. Yebamot* 24a, quoted in Novak, *The Image of the Non-Jew in Judaism,* p. 398.

[19] This quotation and the next three are taken from Paul Althaus, *The Ethics of Martin Luther,* trans. Robert C. Schultz (Philadelphia: Fortress, 1972), pp. 26-28.

[20] Helmut Thielicke, *Theological Ethics,* Foundations 1, ed. William H. Lazareth (Philadelphia: Fortress, 1966), 1:162-63.

[21]My phrasing for some of these objections has been suggested by passages in Karl Barth, *The Epistle to the Romans*, 6th ed., trans. Edwyn C. Hoskyns (London: Oxford University Press, 1933), pp. 65-70; Werner Elert, *The Christian Ethos*, trans. Carl J. Schindler (Philadelphia: Muhlenberg, 1957), pp. 72-76; Carl F. H. Henry, "Natural Law and a Nihilistic Culture," *First Things*, no. 49 (January 1995): 54-60, with correspondence in *First Things*, no. 52 (April 1995): 2-8; and Thielicke, *Theological Ethics*, pp. 299-301, 393-94, 397-98, and 403-4. Of course not all the objections can be consistently maintained at the same time, nor are the authors equally suspicious of natural-law doctrine. Elert is cautiously sympathetic; Thielicke, at pp. 429-31, is ambivalent.

[22]*Summa Theologica* I-II, Question 109, Article 2, Reply to Objection 2.

[23]Following the usual interpretation of the expression "the righteous of the nations of the world" in *Tosefta* 13.2 and *b. Sanhedrin* 105a. Maimonides, however, maintains in *Mishnah Torah* 8.11 that Gentiles must observe the Noahide laws on grounds of the Sinaitic revelation rather than merely their own rational considerations. For discussion, see Schwarzschild, "Do Noachites Have to Believe in Revelation?"

[24]Genesis 1:26-27; 9:6.

[25]See, for instance, Carl Braaten, *Principles of Lutheran Theology* (Philadelphia: Fortress, 1983), pp. 127-33.

[26]James Q. Wilson, *The Moral Sense* (New York: Free Press, 1993), p. ix.

[27]Ibid., p. 12.

[28]Ibid., p. 238.

[29]Ibid., p. 30.

[30]Ibid., p. 100.

[31]Ibid., p. 79.

[32]Ibid., pp. 60-65.

[33]Ibid., pp. 65-69, 72.

[34]Ibid., pp. 69-70.

[35]Ibid., p. 229. I distinguish between three senses of the term *natural* in my book *The Resurrection of Nature* (Ithaca, N.Y.: Cornell University Press, 1986), pp. 33-43, although if I were to rewrite the explanation now it would be much less Aristotelian.

[36]Wilson, *The Moral Sense*, p. 18.

[37]Ibid., pp. xiii, 10-11, 18, 72, 82, 218, 225-26.

[38]Ibid., p. 12, emphasis added.

[39]Ibid., p. 142, emphasis added.

[40]Ibid., pp. 18-19, 20-23, 226.

[41]Ibid., p. 18.

[42]He calls the incest prohibition a rule both on this page and on p. 226.

[43]The only circumstance in which we do not question our classification is when the conflict results from previous wrongdoing. In the classical example, the biblical judge Jephthah made God the forbidden promise that if he were granted victory over the Ammonites, he would sacrifice the first thing that met his eyes upon his return. He was granted victory, but the first thing that met his eyes upon his return was his beloved daughter. The previous sin of the forbidden promise now produced a catch-22: human sacrifice was forbidden, but so was breaking vows to God. Although there was nothing wrong with either rule, through *his* fault one had to be broken.

[44]Wilson, *The Moral Sense*, pp. 240, 243.

[45]Ibid., pp. 235-36.

[46]See Michael J. Behe, *Darwin's Black Box: The Biochemical Challenge to Evolution* (New York: Free Press, 1996); Phillip E. Johnson, *Darwin on Trial* (Downers Grove, Ill.: InterVarsity Press, 1993); and Michael Denton, *Evolution: A Theory in Crisis* (Bethesda, Md.: Adler & Adler, 1986).

[47]Wilson, *The Moral Sense,* p. 218.

[48]Ibid., p. 238.

[49]Ibid., p. 249.

[50]Ibid., p. 233.

[51]Compare C. S. Lewis, *Mere Christianity* (New York: Macmillan, 1952), chap. 2, response to first objection.

Appendix: Elementary Reasoning

[1]Arguments that pass tests 1 and 2 are sometimes called *valid* whether or not they pass test 3. Bear in mind, however, that a valid argument with false premises may still have a false conclusion.

[2]Douglas J. Wilson, *Introductory Logic,* rev. ed. (Moscow, Idaho: Canon, 1992).

[3]Roy A. Clouser, *The Myth of Religious Neutrality* (Notre Dame, Ind.: University of Notre Dame Press, 1991).

Select Bibliography

Alcorn, Randy. *Pro-life Answers to Pro-choice Arguments.* Sisters, Ore.: Multnomah Press, 1992.

Althaus, Paul. *The Ethics of Martin Luther.* Translated by Robert C. Schultz. Philadelphia: Fortress, 1972.

Aquinas, Thomas. *On Kingship.* In *The Political Ideas of St. Thomas Aquinas.* Edited by Dino Bigongiari. New York: Hafner, 1953.

———. *Summa Theologica.* Translated by Fathers of the English Dominican Province. Westminster, Md.: Christian Classics, 1981. Some scholars give the title of this work as *Summa Theologiae.*

Aristotle. *Nicomachean Ethics.* Translated by Martin Ostwald. Indianapolis: Bobbs-Merrill, 1962.

———. *Politics.* Translated by Ernest Barker. New York: Oxford University Press, 1946.

Arkes, Hadley. *First Things: An Inquiry into the First Principles of Morals and Justice.* Princeton, N.J.: Princeton University Press, 1986.

Armstrong, R. A. *Primary and Secondary Precepts in Thomistic Natural Law Teaching.* The Hague: Martinus Nijhoff, 1966.

Ashton, J. R. "The Psychosocial Outcome of Induced Abortion." *British Journal of Obstetrics and Gynecology* 87 (1980): 1115-22.

Barnard, Catherine. *The Long-Term Psychological Effects of Abortion.* Portsmouth, N.H.: Institute for Pregnancy Loss, 1990.

Barr, Stephen M. "The Atheism of the Gaps." *First Things,* no. 57 (November 1995): 50-53.

Barth, Karl. *The Epistle to the Romans.* 6th ed. Translated by Edwyn C. Hoskyns. London: Oxford University Press, 1933.

Behe, Michael J. *Darwin's Black Box: The Biochemical Challenge to Evolution.* New York: Free Press, 1996.

Bentham, Jeremy. *Deontology, Together with A Table of the Springs of Action and The Article on Utilitarianism.* Edited by Amnon Goldworth. Oxford: Clarendon, 1983.

———. *The Principles of Morals and Legislation.* New York: Hafner, 1948.

Bleich, J. David. "Jewish Law and the State's Authority to Punish Crime." *Cardozo Law Review* 12 (1991): 829-57.

Boyle, Joseph M. "Aquinas and Prescriptive Ethics." *Proceedings of the American Catholic Philosophical Association* 49 (1975): pp. 82-95. See also Grisez, Germain G.

Braaten, Carl. *Principles of Lutheran Theology.* Philadelphia: Fortress, 1983.

Budziszewski, J. "The Balnibarbian Heresies." *First Things,* no. 46 (October 1994).

———. "The Illusion of Moral Neutrality." *First Things,* no. 35 (July/August 1993).

———. *The Nearest Coast of Darkness.* Ithaca, N.Y.: Cornell University Press, 1988.

———. "The Politics of Virtues, the Government of Knaves." *First Things,* no. 44 (June/July 1994)

————. *The Resurrection of Nature.* Ithaca, N.Y.: Cornell University Press, 1986.

————. *True Tolerance.* New Brunswick, N.J.: Transaction, 1992.

————. "What We Can't Not Know." *Human Life Review* 22, no. 4 (1996).

Burke, Edmund. *Reflections on the Revolution in France.* Edited by Thomas H. D. Mahoney. Indianapolis: Bobbs-Merrill, 1955.

Calvin, John. *Institutes of the Christian Religion.* In W. H. Plantinga, maintainer, *Christian Classics Ethereal Library,* November 1996 revision, http://ccel.wheaton.edu/

Chesterton, G. K. *Heretics.* New York: John Lane, 1905.

Clouser, Roy A. *The Myth of Religious Neutrality.* Notre Dame, Ind.: University of Notre Dame Press, 1991.

————. *On the General Relation of Religion, Metaphysics and Science.* Facets of Faith and Science 2, edited by J. van de Meer. Lanham, Md.: University Press of America, 1997.

Colson, Charles W. "Why Women Like Big Government." *Christianity Today* 40, no. 13 (November 11, 1996): 112.

David, H., et al. "Postpartum and Postabortion Psychotic Reactions." *Family Planning Perspectives* 13 (1981): 88-91.

Davies, W. D. *Paul and Rabbinic Judaism.* London: S.P.C.K., 1948, 1955.

Deck, John N. "St. Thomas Aquinas and the Language of Total Dependence." *Dialogue: Canadian Philosophical Review—Revue Canadienne de Philosophie* 6 (1967): 74-78.

Denton, Michael. *Evolution: A Theory in Crisis.* Bethesda, Md.: Adler & Adler, 1986.

D'Entreves, Alexander Passerin. *Natural Law: An Introduction to Legal Philosophy.* New Brunswick, N.J.: Transaction, 1994.

Dobbs, Darrell. "Family Matters: Aristotle's Appreciation of Women and the Plural Structure of Society." *American Political Science Review* 90 (1996): 74-89.

Dodd, C. H. "Natural Law in the Bible." *Theology,* reprint no. 17 (May and June 1946).

Elert, Werner. *The Christian Ethos.* Translated by Carl J. Schindler. Philadelphia: Muhlenberg, 1957.

Enker, Arnold N. "Aspects of Interaction Between the Torah Law, the King's Law, and the Noahide Law in Jewish Criminal Law." *Cardozo Law Review* 12 (1991): 1137-56.

Finnis, John. *Natural Law and Natural Rights.* Oxford: Oxford University Press, 1980. See also Grisez entry below.

Freeman, Derek. *Margaret Mead and Samoa: The Making and Unmaking of an Anthropological Myth.* Cambridge, Mass.: Harvard University Press, 1983.

Fuchs, Josef. *Natural Law: A Theological Investigation.* Translated by Helmut Reckter and John A. Dowling. New York: Sheed & Ward, 1965.

Gendler, Everett E. "War and the Jewish Tradition." In *Contemporary Jewish Ethics.* Edited by Menachem Marc Kellner. New York: Hebrew Publishing, 1978, pp. 189-210.

George, Robert P. *Making Men Moral: Civil Liberties and Public Morality.* New York: Oxford University Press, 1993.

Grisez, Germain G. "The First Principle of Practical Reason: A Commentary on Summa Theologiae, 1-2, Question 94, Article 2." In *Aquinas: A Collection of Critical Essays.* Edited by Anthony Kenney. Notre Dame, Ind.: University of Notre Dame Press, 1969, pp. 340-82.

Grisez, Germain G., John Finnis and Joseph M. Boyle. "Practical Principles, Moral Truth and Ultimate Ends." *American Journal of Jurisprudence* 32 (1987): 99-151.

Grisez, Germain G., and Russell Shaw. *Fulfillment in Christ: A Summary of Christian Moral Principles.* Notre Dame, Ind.: University of Notre Dame Press, 1991.

Grotius, Hugo. *De Jure Belli ac Pacis Libri Tres.* Translated by Francis W. Kelsey. London: Oxford University Press, 1925.

Hauerwas, Stanley, and William H. Willimon. *Resident Aliens: Life in the Christian Colony.* Nashville: Abingdon, 1989.

Henry, Carl F. H. *God Who Speaks and Shows: Preliminary Considerations.* Vol. 1 of *God, Revelation and Authority.* Waco, Tex.: Word, 1976.

———. "Natural Law and a Nihilistic Culture." *First Things,* no. 49 (January 1995): 54-60, with correspondence in *First Things,* no. 52 (April 1995): 2-8.

Herman, Judith Lewis. *Trauma and Recovery.* New York: BasicBooks, 1992.

Hittinger, Russell. *A Critique of the New Natural Law Theory.* Notre Dame, Ind.: University of Notre Dame Press, 1987.

Husik, Isaac. "The Law of Nature, Hugo Grotius and the Bible." *Hebrew Union College Annual 2* (1925): 381-417.

Johnson, Phillip E. *Darwin on Trial.* Downers Grove, Ill.: InterVarsity Press, 1993.

Jones, E. Michael. *Degenerate Moderns.* San Francisco: Ignatius, 1993.

Kilpatrick, William. *Why Johnny Can't Tell Right from Wrong.* New York: Simon & Schuster, 1992.

Konvitz, Milton R. "Conscience and Civil Disobedience in the Jewish Tradition." In *Judaism and Human Rights.* New York: Norton, 1972, pp. 161-78. (Copyright by B'nai B'rith Commission on Adult Jewish Education.)

Kreeft, Peter, and Ronald K. Tacelli. *Handbook of Christian Apologetics.* Downers Grove, Ill.: InterVarsity Press, 1994.

Kusukawa, Sachiko. *The Transformation of Natural Philosophy: The Case of Philip Melanchthon.* Cambridge: Cambridge University Press, 1995.

Lewis, C. S. *The Abolition of Man.* New York: Macmillan, 1947, 1955.

———. *Mere Christianity.* New York: Macmillan, 1952.

———. *The Pilgrim's Regress.* New York: Bantam, 1986.

Lichtenstein, Aharon. "Does Jewish Tradition Recognize an Ethic Independent of Halakha?" In *Modern Jewish Ethics: Theory and Practice.* Edited by Marvin Fox. Columbus: Ohio State University Press, 1975, pp. 62-88.

———. *The Seven Laws of Noah.* 2d ed. New York: Rabbi Jacob Joseph School Press, 1986.

Locke, John. *An Essay on Human Understanding.* Edited by Alexander Campbell Fraser. New York: Dover, 1959.

———. *Essays on the Law of Nature.* Edited by W. von Leyden. Oxford: Clarendon, 1958.

———. *A Letter Concerning Toleration.* Edited by James H. Tully. Indianapolis: Hackett, 1983.

———. *Two Treatises of Government.* Edited by Peter Laslett. Cambridge: Cambridge University Press, 1988.

Maritain, Jacques. *The Rights of Man and Natural Law.* New York: Scribner, 1943.

McInerny, Ralph. *Ethica Thomista.* Washington, D.C.: Catholic University of America Press, 1982.

Mill, John Stuart. *An Examination of Sir William Hamilton's Philosophy, and of the Principal Philosophical Questions Discussed in His Writings.* Vol. 9 of *Collected Works of John Stuart Mill.* Edited by J. M. Robson and Alan Ryan. Toronto: University of Toronto Press, 1979.

———. *Nature.* In *Three Essays on Religion.* New York: Henry Holt, 1874.

———. *On Liberty.* In *John Stuart Mill: Three Essays.* Edited by Richard Wollheim. Oxford: Oxford University Press, 1975.

———. *Utilitarianism.* In *John Stuart Mill: Three Essays.* Edited by Richard Wollheim. Oxford: Oxford University Press, 1975.

National Conference of Catholic Bishops. *The Challenge of Peace: God's Promise and Our Response.* Washington, D.C.: United States Catholic Conference, 1983.

Novak, David. *The Image of the Non-Jew in Judaism: An Historical and Constructive Study of the Noahide Laws.* New York: Edwin Mellen, 1983.

———. *Jewish Social Ethics.* New York: Oxford University Press, 1992.

————. "Law of Moses, Law of Nature." *First Things*, no. 60 (February 1996).

Nozick, Robert. *Anarchy, State and Utopia*. New York: Basic Books, 1974.

Rakover, Nahum. "Jewish Law and the Noahide Obligation to Preserve Social Order." *Cardozo Law Review* 12 (1991): 1073-1136.

Reardon, David C. *Abortion Malpractice*. Lewisville, Tex.: Life Dynamics, 1993.

Ross, James. "God, Creator of Kinds and Possibilities: *Requiescant universalie ante res*." In *Rationality, Religious Belief and Moral Commitment*. Edited by Robert Audi and William J. Wainwright. Ithaca, N.Y.: Cornell University Press, 1986.

Schwarzschild, Steven. "Do Noachites Have to Believe in Revelation?" *Jewish Quarterly Review* 52, no. 4 (1962): 297-308, and 53, no. 1 (1962): 30-65.

Simon, Yves R. *The Tradition of Natural Law: A Philosopher's Reflections*. New York: Fordham University Press, 1965.

Stone, Suzanne Last. "Sinaitic and Noahide Law: Legal Pluralism in Jewish Law." *Cardozo Law Review* 12 (1991): 1157-1214.

Thielecke, Helmut. *Theological Ethics*. Foundations 1, edited by William H. Lazareth. Philadelphia: Fortress, 1966.

Veatch, Henry B. *Human Rights: Fact or Fancy?* Baton Rouge: Louisiana State University Press, 1985.

Wilson, Douglas J. *Introductory Logic*. Rev. ed. Moscow, Idaho: Canon, 1992.

Wilson, James Q. *The Moral Sense*. New York: Free Press, 1993.

————. *On Character*. Washington, D.C.: American Enterprise Institute, 1991.

Woodhouse, A. S. P., ed. *Puritanism and Liberty: Being the Army Debates (1647-9) from the Clarke Manuscripts with Supplementary Documents*. London: Dent, 1992.

Wooten, David, ed. *An Anthology of Political Writing in Stuart England*. New York: Viking Penguin, 1986.

Index